RESEARCH GUIDE
TO AMERICAN LITERATURE

Colonial Literature
1607–1776

RESEARCH GUIDE
TO AMERICAN LITERATURE

RESEARCH GUIDE
TO AMERICAN LITERATURE

Colonial Literature
1607–1776

Benjamin Franklin V
University of South Carolina

A BRUCCOLI CLARK LAYMAN BOOK

Facts On File
An imprint of Infobase Publishing

Research Guide to American Literature: Colonial Literature, 1607–1776
Copyright © 2010 by Benjamin Franklin V

Facts On File, Inc.
An imprint of Infobase Publishing
132 West 31st Street
New York NY 10001

Library of Congress Cataloging-in-Publication Data
Research guide to American literature. -- New ed.
  p. cm.
"A Bruccoli Clark Layman book."
Includes bibliographical references and index.
ISBN 978-0-8160-7861-5 (v. 1 : acid-free paper)—ISBN 978-0-8160-7862-2 (v. 2 : acid-free paper)—ISBN 978-0-8160-7863-9 (v. 3 : acid-free paper)—ISBN 978-0-8160-7864-6 (v. 4 : acid-free paper)—ISBN 978-0-8160-7865-3 (v. 5 : acid-free paper)—ISBN 978-0-8160-7866-0 (v. 6 : acid-free paper)—ISBN 978-0-8160-7867-7 (v. 7 : acid-free paper) 1. American literature—Research—Methodology—Handbooks, manuals, etc. 2. American literature—History and criticism. 3. Canon (Literature) I. Franklin, Benjamin, 1939– II. Vietto, Angela III. Habich, Robert D., 1951– IV. Quirk, Tom, 1946– V. Scharnhorst, Gary. VI. Anderson, George Parker, 1957– VII. Cusatis, John. VIII. Moser, Linda Trinh, 1964– IX. West, Kathryn, 1962– X. Facts on File, Inc.
PS51.R47 2010
810.7'2—dc22
                                    2009047815

Text design by Erika K. Arroyo
Composition by Bruccoli Clark Layman
Cover printed by Art Print, Taylor, PA
Book printed and bound by Maple Press, York, PA
Date printed: February 2010
Printed in the United States of America
10 9 8 7 6 5 4 3 2 1
This book is printed on acid-free paper.

As always, for Jo, Abigail, Rebecca, Elizabeth, and Louisa

Contents

Acknowledgments

I could not have met the deadline for this book without the support of the inter-library loan and reference departments at the Thomas Cooper Library, University of South Carolina. The librarians who helped me, always with good humor, are Robert Amerson, Brian Barr, Marilee Birchfield, William Boland, Karen Brown, Mary Bull, Gerri Corson, Joshua Garris, Beki Gettys, Amber Gibbs, Marna Hostetler, Laura Ladwig, Tom Marcil, Francess Murray, Timothy Simmons, Bob Skinder, William Suddeth, Sharon Verba, Virginia Weathers, Andrea Wright, and Deborah Yerkes. I am grateful to Thomas F. McNally, William E. Rivers, and Tucker Taylor for supporting my work. Margaret Bendroth clarified Congregational polity. Sarah Hartwell provided information about Samson Occom's manuscripts. Ellen and Don Greiner nourished me on a weekly basis.

Series Introduction

Research Guide to American Literature is a series of handbooks for students and teachers that recommends strategies for studying literary topics and frequently taught literary works and authors. The rationale for the series is that successful study is predicated on asking the right questions and then devising a logical strategy for addressing them. The process of responsible literary investigation begins with facts and usually ends with opinions. The value of those opinions depends on the ability of the reader to gather useful information, to consider it in context, to interpret it logically, and finally to decide what the interpretation means outside the confines of the literary work. Often the answers to questions a sophisticated reader asks about a literary topic are subjective, involving a reader's perception of an author's or a character's motive; always the search for the answer to a meaningful question involves a process of self-education and, in the best of circumstances, self-awareness.

    RGAL is intended as a resource to assist readers in identifying questions to ask about literature. The seven volumes in this series are organized chronologically, corresponding to generally accepted literary periods. Each volume follows this general pattern:

    Part I provides the social and historical context for a literary period, explaining its historical boundaries, describing the nature of the literary output of the time, placing the literature in its social and historical contexts, identifying literary influences, and tracing the evolution of critical approaches.

    Part II comprises ten study guides on general themes or topics related to the period, organized alphabetically. Each guide first provides necessary background information, then suggests questions or research topics that might be fruitfully considered, and with suggestions of specific primary and secondary works that students will find useful. Each guide also includes an annotated checklist of recommended secondary works and capsule identifications of people mentioned.

    Part III comprises some thirty study guides for particular literary works or authors, organized alphabetically by the author's name. Each guide begins with a brief overview of the author's career to provide context, and then suggests some half-a-dozen topics for discussion and research, with advice about how to begin investigating the topic. These topics are meant to facilitate classroom discussion as well as to suggest interesting ideas for research papers. Each guide includes an annotated checklist of recommended secondary works.

Part IV is an annotated general bibliography recommending the most useful general works of literary history, literary criticism, and literary reference pertinent to the period.

Part V is a glossary of terms used in the volume.

A keyword index is included in each volume.

The purpose of *RGAL* is not to tell students what literature means but to help them determine the meaning for themselves by asking significant questions and seeking answers diligently and thoughtfully. That is how learning that matters takes place. The method is as old as Socrates.

—*Richard Layman*

Part I
Overview

Boundaries of the Period

This book of study guides covers the years 1607–1776, the almost century-and-three-quarters period during which English-speaking people sailed to, settled in, and flourished in America. Although by 1607 there had been numerous accounts of North America—by explorers from Spain (Cabeza de Vaca and others), France (the Italian Giovanni da Verrazano, the Frenchman Jean Ribault, and others, including Jacques Cartier), Holland (Adriaen van der Donck and others), Sweden (David Pieterszoon De Vries and others), and England (Richard Hakluyt and others)—none of them originated in or reported on a permanent English-speaking settlement, because there was none before Jamestown. The earliest date for this study guide, 1607, is when Captain Christopher Newport and approximately a hundred colonists founded Jamestown as the first permanent English-speaking settlement in North America, though had it not been for the efforts of John Smith, another English explorer and the man who named New England, the community might not have survived. (The *Mayflower*, carrying the Pilgrims, landed at Plymouth thirteen years later, in 1620.) The latest date, 1776, is when the Declaration of Independence was adopted by the Second Continental Congress. This document, written mainly by Thomas Jefferson, begins as follows: "When in the Course of human events it becomes necessary for one people to dissolve the political bands which have connected them with another and to assume among the powers of the earth, the separate and equal station to which the Laws of Nature and of Nature's God entitle them, a decent respect to the opinions of mankind requires that they should declare the causes which impel them to the separation." And declare the causes the document does. It levels charges against George III; then, it separates America from Britain, and, on the grounds that Americans' unalienable rights had been violated, justifies the Revolutionary War, which had begun in 1775. The satisfactory completion of this conflict led to the establishment of the United States of America.

WHY STUDY THIS PERIOD AND THESE WRITERS

This period is of supreme importance because it came first: it is when English settlement began in North America; when the initially small but slowly increasing English population was confronted with, but ultimately overcame, often-difficult conditions, including harsh weather, lack of necessities, and conflict with the Indians, whose land the English had usurped and continued usurping; when the majority of New Englanders believed that their presence and success in America were ordained by God and that their experiment in New England would appear, in the words of John Winthrop, as "a City upon a Hill," a place observed by many as a beacon unto the world, a symbol of American exceptionalism; when the dominant culture in the North, the Puritans, faced what it considered threats from within, threats that it quashed confidently and often severely; when people holding religious views at odds with the prevailing faith were persecuted, though they persevered and even flourished, as is the case with the Quakers, who, under William Penn, established Pennsylvania; when New England lost a benign charter and saw it replaced with one that imposed royal governors; when, around the year 1700, a swelling of the population, with its attendant diversity of views and values, caused the culture in Massachusetts in particular to become significantly less religious and more secular than previously, though the culture, including the Congregational church, adapted to this change; when Enlightenment ideas from England—especially those formulated by Sir Isaac Newton and John Locke—influenced the American intelligentsia and further weakened the influence of religion; when these same new ideas influenced many of the most advanced American thinkers essentially to abandon theology for deism, which offered a rational way of considering the universe; when religious lassitude led to a revival of old-time belief augmented by emotionalism in a movement known as the Great Awakening; and when the population at large but especially in Massachusetts objected so strenuously to onerous laws imposed by George III that the colonies declared their independence and became a new country, with a government answerable not to a monarch of another country but solely to the citizens of this new one. Imperfect by definition (slavery was an obvious blight and many people, including women, did not have the franchise), democracy in America had begun.

During its growth from a handful of English-speaking people in 1607 and another handful in 1620 to millions of inhabitants in 1776, America produced an impressive body of writing, from Smith and William Bradford early in the period to John Trumbull and Mercy Otis Warren at the time of the Revolution. Despite the abundance of works published during this time, almost all still available, these creations are not widely known. Yet, the era, which constitutes the beginning and early development of American literature in English, produced some writing of lasting aesthetic value as well as an abundance of historically significant works. Not only is this literature important as documentation of early American life, values, accomplishments, and taste, but some of it inspired such later and now canonical nineteenth-century authors as Washington Irving, James Fenimore Cooper, Nathaniel Hawthorne (especially Hawthorne), and Herman Melville, as well as such twentieth-century writers as William Carlos Williams, Stephen Vincent Benét, and Robert Lowell—and even such an English writer as D. H. Lawrence.

MOVEMENTS AND SCHOOLS ACTIVE DURING PERIOD

Puritanism was the dominant force in seventeenth-century New England, as is reflected in the writing of this time and place. The early Puritans in particular shared several beliefs and attitudes. While they followed the teachings of John Calvin, Martin Luther, and others, they also had an aversion to the Church of England because they considered it impure; and because they did, they would not be forced to attend church and be Anglicans. As a result, they were persecuted in their homeland, England, and needed a residence where they could worship as they wished. This place was New England.

Yet, Puritanism was not monolithic; even at the beginning of Puritan life in America there were distinctions to be made. This was especially the case with the initial two groups of Puritans. The first, known as the Pilgrims, settled at

Plymouth in 1620. These people are also known as Separatists because they separated not only physically but also theologically from the Church of England, which they thought irredeemably corrupt. The next group of Puritans landed at Salem in 1630 and soon established Boston. While these people separated physically from the Church of England, they remained, technically, members of it, believing that it could possibly be reformed from within. This belief was more an abstraction than a call for action, though, because these people, living an ocean away from their homeland, were in no position to reform the Church. In 1691, the Boston group absorbed the one from Plymouth.

After these groups became established, they had to adapt to changing conditions. The Half-Way Covenant of 1662 is an important example of Puritans confronting a problem and altering positions and beliefs in order to resolve it. The issue was inspired by declining church membership, which the Puritans attempted to reverse by offering partial membership to some people, though these semimembers were not permitted to receive the Lord's Supper.

Though most American publications of the seventeenth century were written by Puritans and frequently concerned religious topics, the new century brought a new worldview. In general, it was more secular and urbane than that of the seventeenth century, and these qualities became more pronounced as the eighteenth century progressed; still, Congregationalism—the church of the Puritans—continued as the dominant faith of New Englanders, even though other faiths were represented, including the Puritans' nemeses, Anglicans and Catholics.

Despite the importance of New England and Puritanism during the colonial period, all America was not located in New England, and not all influence was Puritan. Quakers gravitated to Pennsylvania, which also welcomed other faiths. Anglicanism was a major force in such areas as Virginia, Maryland (which also had a large Catholic presence), and the Carolinas; Lutherans settled in and influenced New York, New Jersey, and Pennsylvania; Presbyterians resided in Delaware and elsewhere. Of the colonies, New York was especially pluralistic.

Dominant Genres and Literary Forms

With the exception of the novel, colonial America produced literature in all the genres that were then popular in England. The first book published in English in the New World of which a copy is known to exist is *The Whole Booke of Psalmes Faithfully Translated into English Metre* (1640), better known as the *Bay Psalm Book*. It initiated the publication of religious texts that predominated in the seventeenth century, though most of them were sermons, not psalters, which is understandable. The original English settlers in New England were religiously devout and believed that the way to understand God was through the Bible, which ministers helped them interpret. Therefore, ministers not only delivered sermons but disseminated them widely by having them published. People read them, as may be documented not only by the number of them but also by numerous references to them in such a work as Samuel Sewall's diary.

Beginning with John Smith, colonists wrote histories. Puritans were inspired to compose them because they viewed their experiences in America as reflecting God's will: a careful recording and examining of historical events, therefore, informed them about what they considered the most important of all topics. Eighteenth-century historians did not generally hold to this interpretation of history, and those in the South definitely did not.

Perhaps surprisingly to readers unfamiliar with colonial American letters, colonists wrote verse prolifically. In the early years in New England a predictable amount of poetry was religious in nature, though not all of it was. Some focuses on nature, some deals with domestic issues, some is elegiac, some is historical. Some poets wrote about the Indians, others about classical themes; some addressed love, while others addressed warfare; some composed acrostics, others composed satires. In time, the example of Alexander Pope not only influenced American poets, but dominated them to the degree that most eighteenth-century American verse is neoclassical in nature. As the century progressed and as revolutionary fervor grew, Americans wrote political poems.

Biographical and autobiographical writing, including journals and diaries, was popular for much the same reason that histories were valued. In the eighteenth century, such writing was modified to create a new genre, the Indian captivity narrative, often, but not exclusively, written by women.

Drama came haltingly to the colonies. Dramatic performances were first presented in the South and were popular there; a few were given in New England, but were banned there in the middle of the eighteenth century. The first professional production of a play composed by an American did not occur until 1767. Several closet plays with a political theme were published in the 1770s, as the Revolution approached.

Belletristic essays came into prominence in the 1720s. As most eighteenth-century verse was influenced by the poetry of one person above all others, Pope, so were the urbane essays composed early in the century similarly influenced, by the sophisticated creations of Joseph Addison, as published in England in *The Tatler* and *The Spectator*. As tensions developed between the colonies and the Crown, some Americans wrote polemical essays.

DOMINANT WRITERS

Although seemingly most seventeenth-century and many eighteenth-century ministers published sermons, some sermons are more important than others, and some of these are of paramount significance. One of the most essential and famous sermons of the colonial era was composed and delivered by John Winthrop, who was primarily a political leader. Sometime before landing in America in 1630 (before departing England or at sea aboard the *Arbella*) he delivered *A Modell of Christian Charity*, a sermon in which he presciently depicts America as "a Citty upon a Hill," a phrase that has resonated ever since as a statement of American exceptionalism. John Cotton was one of the crucial first-generation Puritans in America. Among his numerous published sermons is *God's Promise to His Plantation* (1630), which he delivered to the passengers of the *Arbella* before it departed England. In this sermon, he emphasizes the emigrants' ability to worship in America as they desire, while justifying the taking of land belonging to the Indians. Cotton's contemporary Thomas Hooker—they arrived in America together in 1633—is generally considered one of the most effective American ministers of the seventeenth century; his sermons, written in a plain style, were so admired that many were published. Among his notable sermons are seven from the 1630s, collected in *The Saints Dignitie, and Dutie* (1651), that deal with the Antinomian Controversy. As the century progressed, Solomon Stoddard's sermons proved important, even though published later, because in some of them he expresses views that challenged the Congregational status quo. One such is *Sermon on Paul's Epistle to the Galatians* (delivered in 1690), which details his view that the Lord's Supper is a converting ordinance. Perhaps no sermon of the colonial era by a resident of America was more influential than *Sinners in the Hands of an Angry God* (1741), composed by Stoddard's grandson, Jonathan Edwards. It helped inspire the Great Awakening. Even before the Great Awakening, many ministers evolved away from the religious certainties of the Puritan fathers, a tendency that became more pronounced after midcentury when such a minister as the liberal Jonathan Mayhew overtly attacked the conservative beliefs of colleagues and reflected, in keeping with the times, a rational approach to religion.

Histories, poetry, biographies, drama, and essays are treated in detail in the study guides, so here I give them abbreviated notice. The two most important histories of the colonial era are William Bradford's *Of Plymouth Plantation* (written in the seventeenth century but published in 1856) and Cotton Mather's *Magnalia Christi Americana* (1702). The first tells the story of the Pilgrims in Europe, at sea, and in the New World; the second relates the main religious events of and details the main people in seventeenth-century America. The dominant poets of the era were Anne Bradstreet, Michael Wigglesworth, and Edward Taylor. Bradstreet is mostly valued now for her personal poems, including love poems to her husband, that were published only posthumously, in *Several Poems* (1678). In the threatening, harsh "The Day of Doom" (published in *The Day of Doom*, 1662), his major creation, Wigglesworth depicts his interpretation of the realities of Judgment Day in an attempt to halt the backsliding nature of the times. Like Bradstreet, Taylor was a private poet, one who did not intend for his verses to be published. Over four decades, he composed more than two hundred poems that constitute his major work, *Preparatory Meditations;* he wrote them to prepare himself for administering the Lord's Supper.

The major biographers of colonial America were Increase Mather, Cotton Mather, and Ebenezer Turell. The first wrote a biography of his father, *The Life and Death of That Reverend Man of God, Mr. Richard Mather* (1670); Cotton Mather wrote one of his father, Increase Mather, in *Parentator* (1724), as well as biographies of many others in his mammoth *Magnalia Christi Americana* (1702); Turell details the life of his late wife in *Memoirs of the Life and Death of the Pious and Ingenious Mrs. Jane Turell* (1735) and of her father in *The Life and Character of the Reverend Benjamin Colman, D.D.* (1749).

Because playwriting came late to America, few Americans wrote plays during the colonial period. Of them, Thomas Godfrey and Mercy Otis Warren are most important. He composed *The Prince of Parthia* (published 1765), the first play by an American to be performed professionally (in 1767); in the 1770s she wrote closet plays dealing with political issues of the day.

Beginning in the 1720s, some Americans wrote belletristic essays in the manner of Addison. They were published in the relatively new medium of newspapers. The major essayists were sixteen-year-old Benjamin Franklin (the Dogood papers) and three men who collaborated under the pseudonym Proteus Echo: John Adams (died 1740), Matthew Adams, and Mather Byles. Other writers composed essays of a political nature. These grew in number as revolutionary fervor increased. The major political essayists writing before the Declaration of Independence were John Dickinson and, at the beginning of his career, Thomas Paine. Dickinson's *Letters from a Farmer in Pennsylvania, to the Inhabitants of the British Colonies* (1768) encourages vigilant monitoring of British rule; Paine's *Common Sense* (1776) calls for a declaration of independence, which was forthcoming.

Historical and Social Context

KEY HISTORICAL EVENTS OF THE PERIOD

Because of the long, formative nature of the colonial era, many historical events are important, from the establishment of Jamestown in 1607 to the Declaration of Independence in 1776. An event with enormous repercussions occurred in Jamestown in 1619. This was the arrival of slaves from Africa. Although no contemporaneous written comment about it is known to exist, later in the century organizations and individuals began protesting the institution of slavery, not only in Virginia but throughout the colonies. The first such expression was by a group of Germantown Friends in 1688; Samuel Sewall wrote against slavery in *The Selling of Joseph, a Memorial* (1700). In time, an abolitionist movement formed (the initial abolitionist society was established in Philadelphia in 1775), the Civil War was fought, and slavery was ended in the United States.

The first major event after the establishment of Jamestown and the introduction of slavery was the landing at, establishment of, and development of Plymouth by the Pilgrims in 1620. Not only did their leader, William Bradford, write the history of the group in *Of Plymouth Plantation* (1856), but some of its details form the basis for aspects of American mythology, such as the landing of the Pilgrims at Plymouth and the celebration of the first Thanksgiving, though Bradford barely alludes to the latter. In *New English Canaan* (1637), Thomas Morton responds not to Bradford's history but rather to the actions of the Pilgrims, who destroyed his Merry Mount community and forced him to return to England. Nathaniel Hawthorne used this conflict as the basis for the tale "The May-Pole of Merry Mount" (1836); it also figures in Robert Lowell's *Endecott and the Red Cross,* a 1965 play revised in 1968, as well as in other artistic works.

The beginning of the great migration of Puritans to America in 1630 is important because in settling Massachusetts Bay these people established a society based on religious principles, ones that not only governed people's lives but that also generated discussion and debate among the most imposing American intellects of the century. Because these intellects—mostly ministers—wrote about the issues they confronted, an impressive record of their thoughts and positions exists. John Cotton and Roger Williams disagreed on the issue of freedom of conscience, for example. Williams embraced it, but Cotton did not. They debated this issue openly in a series of publications during the 1640s and 1650s. Winthrop explained Puritan political theory in his 1645 speech to the General Court. When numerous people wanted the Congregational church to assume a Presbyterian nature, ministers met to discuss the issue and rejected it in *A Platform of Church Discipline Gathered out of the Word of God* (1649), better known as the Cambridge Platform, written mainly by Richard Mather. No American fiction writer addressed Puritanism more effectively than Hawthorne. Not only did he compose one of the most important of all American novels, *The Scarlet Letter* (1850), but he set it in Puritan times, with Puritan characters, including some actual ones. He also wrote several stories dealing with Puritan issues, such as "Young Goodman Brown" (1835).

Trials of supposed witches were held in Salem in 1692. Although such trials were not unique to Salem—many had been held in Europe—those in Salem, which resulted in the execution of twenty people, left a permanent mark on what might be called the American psyche. Some of the most important people of the time supported the trials, including Cotton Mather. His *Memorable Providences, Relating to Witchcrafts and Possessions* (1689) helped establish a climate in which the witchcraft frenzy could develop. When the trials began, he urged the judges' caution but recommended, in *The Return of Several Ministers* (1692), that the judges prosecute witches fully. That same year, he published a narrative of the trials in *The Wonders of the Invisible World*, which was ridiculed in 1700 by Robert Calef in *More Wonders of the Invisible World*. Cotton Mather's father, Increase, believed that the Salem trials should be held, but thought that reliance on spectral evidence alone was inadequate for convicting someone, an opinion expressed in *Cases of Conscience Concerning Evil Spirits* (1692). One of the trial judges was John Hathorne, whose participation in the proceedings apparently so affected a great-great-grandson that guilt became a major theme in his fiction, such as *The House of the Seven Gables* (1851). This writer was Hawthorne, who changed the spelling of his surname. Arthur Miller's play *The Crucible* (1953) is probably the most famous literary work dealing directly with the trials.

In the decade or so before the middle of the eighteenth century, religion underwent a transformational change, initially in Massachusetts but ultimately almost everywhere in America. This phenomenon was based on the serious, philosophical writings of Jonathan Edwards, including the terrifying sermon *Sinners in the Hands of an Angry God* (1741), writings that promoted an emotional approach to religion. Encouraging such an approach in compositions is one thing; disseminating it is another. Popularizing his ideas fell not to Edwards but primarily to George Whitefield, an English evangelist who, upon arriving in America in 1739, propagated them. His magnetism and oratorical skills, combined with his message of opening oneself to religious affections, resulted in a great awakening of religious awareness and conversion. This ecstatic response concerned Edwards, who pondered the genuineness of some people's religious affections. He expressed his thoughts about this and other issues, including the revivals themselves, in *A Treatise Concerning Religious Affections* (1746). Major figure though Edwards was as a religious thinker, his ideas—and their popularization—did not go unchallenged. His most formidable opponent was Charles Chauncy, who, as a result of believing in a reasoned, rational approach to religion, thought that people stirred by Whitefield were largely delusional. He presented his positions in such works as *An Unbridled Tongue a Sure Evidence, That Our Religion is Hypocritical and Vain* (1741), *The New Creature Describ'd, and Consider'd as the Sure Characteristick of a Man's Being in Christ* (1741), *Enthusiasm Described and Caution'd Against* (1742), and *Seasonable Thoughts on the State of Religion in New-England* (1743), his most significant work. In the mid 1740s, the intensity of the Great Awakening began to diminish.

Soon after the lessening of religious fervor, religious concerns continued but became secondary to many people as political realities intruded on their lives. Specifically, in the mid 1760s, Parliament began passing a series of acts intended to generate revenue. These included the Sugar Act (1764), the Currency Act (1764), the Quartering Act (1765), the Stamp Act (1765), the Declaratory Act (1766), the Townshend Acts (1767), the Tea Act (1773), the Coercive Acts (1774), and the New England Restraining Act (1775). Many Americans objected to these acts ("no taxation without representation"), increasingly so as time passed. Event led to event, and in 1675 the Revolution began; the Declaration of Independence was written the next year, thereby concluding the colonial era in American history. The politics of the time generated an outpouring of writing, which helped drive events. One of the earliest protesters against England was James Otis, who, though he did not actually call for revolution, presented his views on natural rights in four publications, including *A Vindication of the House of Representatives* (1762) and *The Rights of the British Colonies Asserted and Proved* (1764). Stephen Hopkins wrote in favor of the American cause in *The Rights of Colonies Examined* (1765), a pamphlet answered by the Tory Martin Howard in *A Letter from a Gentleman in Halifax, to His Friend in Rhode Island* (1765). In *A Dissertation on the Canon and Feudal Law* (1765), future president John Adams places the dispute between America and England in the context of realities of classical Greece and Rome. Mercy Otis Warren, sister of James Otis, wrote several anti-British plays beginning in 1773. Benjamin Franklin satirized the English attitude toward America in "An Edict by the King of Prussia" and "Rules by Which a Great Empire May Be Reduced to a Small One" (both 1773), as did Francis Hopkinson in *A Pretty Story* (1774). At the beginning of his literary career, Philip Freneau satirized the English in several poems, including "General Gage's Soliloquy," "General Gage's Confession," and "A Political Litany" (all 1775). Few works were as effective in influencing opinion against the British as John Dickinson's *Letters from a Farmer in Pennsylvania, to the Inhabitants of the British Colonies* (1768), though one did exceed its impact: Thomas Paine's *Common Sense* (1776), which, in its call for political independence, helped generate broad support for the American Revolution, already in progress.

MAJOR SOCIAL ISSUES

Social issues also generated literary responses. Once the Puritan experiment in New England was on solid footing, education became an issue. This was so because the Puritans required a ministry to preach and help people interpret God's word as expressed in the Bible. In order to produce young men who could do these things, in 1636 they established in Newe Towne (Cambridge) the first American college; in 1639 it was named Harvard College in honor of John Harvard, who endowed the enterprise and left the college his impressive collection of books. The college fulfilled its purpose, as seemingly most seventeenth-century New England ministers reared in America studied there. The college inspired writing almost immediately. In 1643, the year after the first class was graduated, a tract promoting settlement in America was published in England. Among the inducements presented in *New Englands First Fruits* is Harvard College; the publication describes the building, identifies the president (Henry Dunster), details the curriculum, and explains the rules. Yet, in time Harvard became the object of ridicule in some quarters. In 1722, sixteen-year-old Benjamin Franklin derided it and its graduates in the fourth Dogood paper, published in *The New-England Courant,* the newspaper of his brother James. In this essay, the widow Silence Dogood tries to decide whether to send her son to college. In a dream she observes that most young men who attend this school are dunces, that a majority of them are incapable of learning, and that many are plagiarists. When she relates this dream to her boarder, Clericus, he says that she has accurately described Harvard. Although she does not indicate whether she will send her son there, surely she will not. Phillis Wheatley treats the school more respectfully in "To the University of Cambridge, in New-England" (1773). Numerous fictions—novels and stories—have been written about or involve Harvard, beginning with Justin Jones's *The Belle of Boston: or, the Rival Students of Cambridge* (1844). Others include Louisa May Alcott's *Kitty's Class Day* (1868), Owen Wister's "Philosophy 4" (1901), and George Santayana's *The Last Puritan* (1935).

As the seventeenth century neared the two-thirds point, Congregationalists confronted the serious issue of declining church membership: children of the church founders often lacked the religious fervor of their parents and could not evidence saving grace. The Congregationalists decided that such children could be admitted to church membership by virtue of having been born to church members. But what of the third generation, children born to church members (second generation) who were unable to demonstrate evidence of saving grace? A synod met in 1662 to resolve this issue, which it did in what is known as the Half-Way Covenant. This document permitted children of the unregenerate second generation to be baptized and subjected to church discipline, as long as these people knew the Bible, but did not permit them to receive the Lord's Supper or vote. That is, they became half-way members. In time, largely because of the thinking and efforts of Solomon Stoddard, who considered communion a converting ordinance, children of unregenerate parents were permitted full membership. Yet this liberal position was reversed in the mid eighteenth century by Stoddard's grandson, Jonathan Edwards, who required evidence of saving grace for church membership. Much was written about the issue of church membership. Richard Mather addressed it in *A Disputation Concerning Church-Members and Their Children, in Answer to XXI. Questions* (1659) and, with Jonathan Mitchell, in *A Defence of the Answer and Arguments of the Synod Met at Boston in the Year 1662. Concerning the Subject of Baptism, and Consociation of Churches* (1664). Charles Chauncy favored the recommendations of the synod, as may be observed in *Anti-Synodalia Scripta Americana* (1662). Thomas Shepard detailed his support of such membership in *The Church-Membership of Children, and Their Right to Baptisme* (1663). A leading opponent of the recommendation was John Davenport, who expressed his opinion in *Another Essay for Investigation of the Truth* (1663), which includes a lengthy preface by Increase Mather, who also opposed it. Stoddard wrote about church membership in *The Doctrine of Instituted Churches Explained and Proved from the Word of God* (1700) and *An Appeal to the Learned* (1709). Edwards published his views in *An Humble Inquiry into the Rules of the Word of God Concerning the Qualifications Requisite to a Compleat Standing and Full Communion in the Visible Christian Church* (1749).

At the same time that Benjamin Franklin was writing the Dogood papers, Boston was being devastated by a smallpox epidemic that began the previous year, 1721. It was not the first such epidemic there, but it was the most severe. Long after the fact, the issue of inoculation seems unarguable; then, it was a new concept and caused controversy. A debate raged between people favoring inoculation against the disease and those opposing it. Those endorsing the procedure included the doctor Zabdiel Boylston, the minister Benjamin Colman, and, perhaps ironically, two men who had endorsed the witchcraft trials of 1692, Increase Mather and Cotton Mather. All the other doctors and some other ministers opposed it, as did James Franklin, publisher of *The New-England Courant*. Several publications resulted from this dispute. In 1721 Colman wrote about the issue in *Some Observations on the New Method of Receiving the Small-Pox by Ingrafting or Inoculation,* as did Increase Mather in *Several Reasons Proving That Inoculating or Transplanting the Small Pox, Is a Lawful Practice, and That It Has Been Blessed by God for the Saving of Many a Life* and *Sentiments on the Small Pox Inoculated;* Cotton Mather expressed his views in *The Angel of Bethesda* (1722); Boylston addressed inoculation in *An Historical Account of the Small-pox Inoculated in New England* (1726). William Douglass was the doctor probably most adamantly opposed to inoculation; he expresses his views in *Inoculation of the Small Pox as Practised in Boston* (1722). This controversy indicates, among other things, that ministers steeped in seventeenth-century Puritanism, such as the two Mathers, could adapt to changing times and embrace science, even when its findings might not yet have been widely accepted.

DEVELOPMENTS WITHIN PUBLISHING THAT AFFECTED LITERARY PRODUCTION

One measure of the value American Puritans placed on reading and books is that in 1638—less than two decades after the landing of the *Mayflower*—a printing press was imported from England and was put to use probably that year in Cambridge. Neither of the first two publications of this press exists—*The Freeman's Oath* and an almanac—though the third publication does: *The Whole Booke of Psalmes Faithfully Translated into English Metre* (1640), better known as the *Bay Psalm Book*. From this point forward, Americans were able, at least theoretically, to produce their own reading material, which in the early years was mostly religious in nature, though because printing of the Bible was the prerogative of the Crown's printers in England, Americans were forbidden to publish a Bible during colonial times. Printing spread slowly throughout the colonies. Pennsylvania had a functioning press by the 1680s, as did Maryland; New York had one in the next decade. Connecticut did not have a press until the first decade of the eighteenth century; the first one in Rhode Island dates from the 1720s. Presses were established in South Carolina and Virginia in the 1730s, though there was an earlier effort to establish one in Virginia in the 1680s. Printing in New Hampshire, New Jersey, and North Carolina began in the middle of the eighteenth century, while that in Delaware, Georgia, and Louisiana was initiated in the 1760s. One effect of the availability of presses was that America could accommodate new forms of publication when necessary, as was the case with newspapers and magazines in the eighteenth century. Although there was no American copyright law during the colonial era (the first was enacted in 1790), Americans could not then publish books copyrighted in England.

Literary Influences

FOREIGN INFLUENCES

For the entirety of the colonial period in America, all literary influence was foreign. This is true not only because the early writers had no American antecedents, but also because a native literary culture did not emerge until after the era concluded.

The sermons of early American Puritans were influenced by sermons present in the Bible (such as by Christ and Paul), by sermons they recalled by fellow but nonemigrating English Puritans (such as Richard Sibbes and John Dod), and manuals about preaching and sermons (such as *The Arte of Prophesying* [1592] by William Perkins and *The Faithfull Shepheard* [1607] by Richard Bernard). For example, Perkins, who believed that the proper subject of sermons is Christ, proposes a logical development in sermons, a development that moves from presenting a biblical text to clarifying it to providing examples illustrating its meaning to applying doctrine plainly and clearly to worshippers. John Cotton, who heard Perkins preach in England, is one minister who adopted Perkins's recommendations. Another English divine, William Ames, introduced Puritan ministers to the logic of Petrus Ramus, a French martyr who recommended structuring arguments or positions by categories that can be divided and subdivided, which is what many Puritan ministers did. As a result, worshippers could easily follow and, if they wished, outline the sermons as ministers delivered them.

Early American biographers followed the example of seventeenth-century English Puritan biographies such as those collected by Samuel Clarke in *A General Martyrologie* (1651) and *The Lives of Sundry Eminent Persons in This Later Age* (1683). They were also inspired by such English Puritans as John Bunyan—who depicts trials overcome in *Grace Abounding to the Chief of Sinner* (1666), an autobiography, and *Pilgrim's Progress* (1678, 1684), an allegory—and Richard Baxter with his autobiographical *Reliquiæ Baxterianæ* (1696). Seventeenth-century American biographies are largely hagiographic in nature. They describe lives lived well—which is to say, piously—in order to provide examples for readers to emulate. They are utilitarian, instructional, and didactic, as were many English biographies. Not only were American biographers influenced by their English predecessors, but a subject's departure from England was a frequent topic in the stories of American lives, as, for example, in John Norton's *The Life and Death of the Deservedly Famous Mr. John Cotton* (1657) and Increase Mather's *The Life and Death of That Reverend Man of God, Mr. Richard Mather* (1670). American biographies of people who led exemplary lives continued being written in the eighteenth century, especially in the first half of the century by Ebenezer Turell in *Memoirs of the Life and Death of the Pious and Ingenious Mrs. Jane Turell* (1735), about his wife, and *The Life and Character of the Reverend Benjamin Colman, D.D.* (1749), about his former father-in-law.

The major early American poets were influenced by authors and books from abroad. The first of them, Anne Bradstreet, was most indebted to the French poet

Guillaume Du Bartas's *La Semaine; ou, Création du Monde* (1578), which Bradstreet knew in a translation by Joshua Sylvester. She learned from Du Bartas how to unify various areas of knowledge in poems, areas that include science, religion, and history; she accomplished this in her quaternions. Someone familiar with the works of both poets cannot help but notice her indebtedness to him. Nathaniel Ward is one person who did, calling her, in a poem prefatory to Bradstreet's *The Tenth Muse Lately Sprung up in America,* "a right Du Bartas Girle." Further, Bradstreet acknowledges Du Bartas's greatness, and her inferiority to him, in what is probably her most famous poem, "The Prologue"; additionally, she composed a poem titled "In Honour of Du Bartas." Both these Bradstreet poems appear in *The Tenth Muse.* Bradstreet was also influenced by Helkiah Crooke's medical book *Microcosmographia, or a Description of the Body of Man* (1615) and, as was the case with all the major seventeenth-century American poets, the Bible; she was also familiar with works by Edmund Spenser, Sir Philip Sidney, and numerous other authors, though the degree to which they influenced her is open to question.

Michael Wigglesworth's main foreign influence was the Bible. Although it was the most important book for all Puritans, it was foreign in the sense that the King James Version was translated by Englishmen and published in England; the Crown did not permit its publication in America during Wigglesworth's era. In depicting Judgment Day, "The Day of Doom," Wigglesworth's major poem, draws on apocalyptic books of the Bible, such as Daniel in the Old Testament and especially Revelation in the New. The Puritans also used the sixteenth-century Geneva Bible, translated in Switzerland, which includes a great number of annotations, or marginal glosses. Wigglesworth uses glosses in "The Day of Doom" and *Meat out of the Eater,* the latter of which is Wigglesworth's longest work, a series of meditations. When Christ rejects infants' claim of innocence in stanza 181 of "The Day of Doom," for example, Wigglesworth cites three Bible verses to support Christ's position, Romans 3:19 paramount among them. Throughout his poems, Wigglesworth uses biblical language.

Edward Taylor's major poems are in two series, titled *Preparatory Meditations.* He composed every one of these poems (over two hundred of them) to prepare himself for administering the Lord's Supper. Each begins with a Bible verse, which serves as the subject of the poem. In addition to being inspired by the Bible, Taylor was influenced by other foreign texts. These include verses by some of the English metaphysical poets, including John Donne (metaphysical conceits, as evidenced in Taylor's "Huswifery") and George Herbert (metrical experimentation, noticeable in many of Taylor's poems). In writing meditative poems, Taylor was probably influenced by English divine Richard Baxter's *The Saints Everlasting Rest* (1650), which reflects on meditation, as well as on life temporal and eternal; in what has become known as *The Metrical History of Christianity,* Taylor drew inspiration from *Ecclesiastica Historia* (known in English as the *Magdeburg Centuries*), by Matthias Flacius and others.

When, in the eighteenth century, American life became more cosmopolitan, poets—some of them ministers—were influenced by sophisticated English poets, especially Alexander Pope. American poets began writing in heroic couplets, for example, though never with the skill of the master. This form of versifying predominated until the Revolution. Also, following Pope's example, the colonialists began writing about worldly issues, occasionally with a satirical edge, and sometimes addressed aesthetic issues. At least one American poet, Mather Byles, went so far as to initiate a correspondence with Pope, one that was only moderately successful. As a result of emulating the most accomplished English poets of the day, Byles and others, including John Adams (died 1740), introduced neoclassical verse to America in the 1720s. In "An Address to the Supreme Being," Adams expresses the literary values of the time:

Thro' all my Works, let Order clearly shine,
And let me know the Reason of each Line.
Give me to trace out Nature in each Thought,
And let each Piece be to Perfection brought;
A Subject for my Genius fit to chuse,
Not vainly light, nor yet prophanely loose,
But innocent, at least, if not sublime,
And let my Numbers smoothly flow in Rhyme.
May each Production, writ with Strength and Ease,
The Ear, the Judgment, and the Fancy please.

Clearly, this statement reflects a new aesthetic in American verse.

Byles, Adams, and others, including Jane Colman Turell, were also influenced by *The Creation*, a philosophical epic by English poet and physician Sir Richard Blackmore. In it, he establishes an aesthetic, the religious sublime, in which poetic descriptions of supernatural events and objects cause readers to comprehend God's design and thereby feel awe. The major American poem in this mode is Adams's "On Society."

As the eighteenth century progressed, American poets, inspired by Jonathan Swift but also Pope, wrote satirical poems. Perhaps the most important of these poets is John Trumbull, whose *The Progress of Dulness* (1772, 1773) satirizes education and the clergy and whose *M'Fingal* (1776, 1782) satirizes primarily the British. *M'Fingal* shows the direct influence of Samuel Butler's *Hudibras*. Poems by others published in 1774 and 1775 satirize the royal governor of Massachusetts, General Thomas Gage, and some published in 1776 satirize his successor, General William Howe.

The earliest plays performed in English-speaking America were all foreign because no American is known to have written a play by then. Among the plays performed around the middle of the eighteenth century were Shakespeare's *Romeo and Juliet, Othello, Richard III, Hamlet,* and *The Merchant of Venice;* Joseph Addison's *Cato;* George Farquhar's *The Beaux Stratagem;* John Gay's *The Beggar's Opera;* Richard Steele's *The Conscious Lovers;* Nicholas Rowe's *Tamerlane;* and Colley Cibber's *The Careless Husband.* In the early years of drama in America, touring troupes of English actors performed plays. The initial groups were led by Lewis Hallam and David Douglass. Few Americans wrote plays during the colonial era. This is probably so because they lacked an incentive to write them—even had they wished to compose some—because of the availability of a large number of sophisticated British plays, plays that had often been performed professionally in England. The first real play composed by an American and produced professionally is Thomas Godfrey's *The Prince of Parthia* (published 1765, produced 1767), a five-act tragedy indebted primarily to the plays of Shakespeare. The most important American dramatist of the colonial era is Mercy Otis Warren, who wrote closet plays in the 1770s. The title page of her *The Adulateur* (1773) includes a quotation from Addison's *Cato;* especially in the naming of characters, she is indebted to such a British playwright as Richard Brinsley Sheridan.

Early in the eighteenth century, such a minister as John Wise wrote essays on religious topics. In the 1720s, though, some Americans began writing belletristic essays patterned after those of Addison, in particular, as published in *The Tatler* and *The Spectator* in London. The colonists' creations coincided with the appearance of newspapers that published literature, in addition to news. The first American to create them was sixteen-year-old Benjamin Franklin in his witty Dogood papers, published in 1722 in *The New-England Courant*. During 1727–1728, Matthew Adams, John Adams (died 1740), and Byles wrote a series of fifty-two such essays in Samuel Kneeland's *The New-England Weekly Journal*. Similar essays were published elsewhere, including Philadelphia, where in 1729 Franklin and Joseph Breintnall published the Busy-Body series in thirty-two issues of the *American Weekly Mercury*. Essays appeared in Southern newspapers. They are featured in *The Maryland Gazette* (Annapolis), *The Virginia Gazette* (Williamsburg), and *The South-Carolina Gazette* (Charleston). All these essays were inspired by Addison's creations.

Beginning around the time of the 1765 Stamp Act, as the Revolution approached, many writers wrote political essays, some published in newspapers and others as pamphlets. In *Letters from a Farmer in Pennsylvania, to the Inhabitants of the British Colonies* (1768), John Dickinson's speaker, a farmer who wants the best for mankind, has antecedents as far back as Horace, while the author's political ideas are derived from several Europeans, including the Frenchman Montesquieu, the Englishman John Locke, and the Scotsman David Hume. These dozen letters, which are as much essays as letters, were first published in a newspaper, *The Boston Chronicle,* before being published as a pamphlet. Franklin's satirical essays, such as "An Edict by the King of Prussia," are indebted to the writing of Swift. Many of the ideas in Paine's *Common Sense* (1776), a pamphlet, are derived from Locke's political theories.

THE AUDIENCE

Because the early settlers came to New England primarily for religious reasons, they welcomed religious publications, which started appearing in Cambridge in 1640 with the *Bay Psalm Book*. The community's desire for something akin to religious purity led the translators of this book to render the Psalms as literally as possible. When, in time, this translation proved too artless, Henry Dunster and Richard Lyon attempted a new, more euphonic, more artful translation, one more congenial to the community's needs. This revision is titled *The Psalms Hymns and Spiritual Songs of the Old and New Testament, Faithfully Translated into English Metre* (1651).

The issue of literacy bears on the nature of the audience for writing during the colonial period. Literacy was important to the Puritans because it permitted people to read the word of God, as revealed in the Bible. To prepare young men for the ministry, they established the Boston Latin School in 1635 and Harvard College the next year. In 1642 the Massachusetts Bay General Court made parents responsible for teaching their children to read; the 1647 General School Law forced communities to create schools and assume responsibility for teaching their residents to read and write. (Alone among the New England colonies in the seventeenth century, Rhode Island did not enact laws pertaining to reading instruction.) Also in the 1640s, dame schools were established; while not particularly focused on education, they nonetheless helped children learn to read, which was especially important for girls, who did not have access to more formal schools. Around age seven, boys began grammar school, which had a classical curriculum. Many children learned to read by studying catechisms, such as John Cotton's *Milk for Babes* (1646). *The New-England Primer* (probably first published in the early 1680s), which went through many editions that produced millions of copies, helped generations of children learn to read by offering easily memorized two-line rhymes, beginning, for the letter A, with "In *Adam's* Fall/We Sinned all." Because of the religious beliefs of the early settlers of Massachusetts Bay and the importance they placed on reading, it was, by far, the most literate colony during the colonial era. Another reason for this is that newspapers originated in Massachusetts during the early years of the eighteenth century; they encouraged literacy, if only for practical reasons because people wanted to know the news. Further, a sizable, educated mercantile class aspired to cultivation, so these people welcomed and possibly influenced the creation of polite letters—primarily Addisonian essays—in colonial newspapers. By 1754, ninety percent of the colony's men and forty percent of its women were literate. Also in the eighteenth century, literacy in other areas, especially New York and Philadelphia, increased markedly, primarily among men, to a lesser degree among women. Although this resulted in large part from the proliferation of schools, it was also aided in cities by a growing number of libraries, the increasing amount of printed material, and discussions in taverns, clubs, and coffeehouses. Because of this high rate of literacy, especially in Boston, New York, and Philadelphia, but increasingly in smaller communities and in the hinterlands, a large number of literate people lived in the various colonies. As a result, authors could arrange to have their creations published by colonial printers, who knew that at least the potential for adequate sales existed.

Evolution of Critical Opinion

CRITICAL APPROACHES TO COLONIAL LITERATURE

Criticism of early American literature began in the nineteenth century. For the half-century after 1829, various scholars interpreted the literature and published books of selections from it. In general, approaches to colonial literature matured to the degree that by 1878 sophisticated criticism had begun, setting a high standard for later scholars. Nineteenth-century—and early twentieth-century—criticism was ad hoc in nature, in the sense of scholars working largely unsupported on what amounted to labors of love. Beginning around the middle of the twentieth century, universities not only encouraged but demanded literary criticism of its professors, while supporting scholarly enterprises with presses, journals, research assistants, reduced teaching assignments, funds for traveling to conferences, and so forth. Criticism became professional.

Samuel L. Knapp wrote what is probably the first study of colonial American literature. After addressing the subject in a series of fifteen talks, he published them in 1829 as *Lectures on American Literature,* with the goal of validating American literature and providing details about the American "mind." That same year, Samuel Kettell published *Specimens of American Poetry.* In the first of three volumes, he devotes approximately two hundred pages to colonial American verse. He provides information—often substantial—about each author's life and literary productions, followed by selections from the author's poetry. Most subsequent nineteenth-century anthologies of early American literature follow this format, though typically with less impressive introductions than Kettell's. In *The Poets and Poetry of America* (1842), Rufus W. Griswold presents what he considers the development of American verse. He treats colonial poetry in the introduction, subtitled "From the Landing of the Pilgrims to the Revolution." Here, Griswold includes selections from such colonial poets as Anne Bradstreet, Urian Oakes, Benjamin Tompson, and Michael Wigglesworth, though he is dismissive of all the verse of the period. He begins the main part of the book—where he presents what he believes is the major American poetry—with selections from Philip Freneau and John Trumbull. Griswold is only slightly more generous with colonial authors in *The Prose Writers of America* (1847), in which he provides information about Jonathan Edwards and includes several light compositions of Benjamin Franklin. In both of these books, Griswold's commentary is often brief and superficial. The Duyckinck brothers—Evert and George—are far more accepting of the early writers than is Griswold. In *The Cyclopædia of American Literature* (1856), which was enlarged in editions after the first, they attempt to document American literature from the beginning, dividing their work into three sections, one dealing with the colonial period, to which they devote approximately 350 pages of commentary about the authors and selections from the authors' works. Their approach, though, is similar to Kettell's and Griswold's: information about the authors, followed by selections from their writings. Serious study of early American literature began with two, two-volume books by Moses Coit Tyler, initially of the University of Michigan and then of Cornell University. The first, *A History of American Literature, 1607–1765,* was published in 1878. In this book of literary and cultural history, Tyler includes excerpts from colonial works only to augment the points he makes. His book is not an anthology or a casual survey of the literature of the period. Comprehensive, elegantly written, opinionated, mature, and supremely intellectual, it alone of the nineteenth-century studies of the early period warrants serious consideration today, despite opinions that have long been challenged and dismissed. He succeeds in his goal of providing an understanding of colonial Americans through a study of their literature. Approximately half of Tyler's next book, *The Literary History of the American Revolution, 1763–1783* (1897), treats the colonial period. It shares the qualities of the earlier study. The antithesis of Tyler's studies is *Library of American Literature* (1887–1890), by Edmund Clarence Stedman and Ellen Mackay Hutchinson. The editors devote the first two-and-a-half volumes of their eleven-volume series of books to writers of colonial America. In order to permit readers to make their own literary judgments, however, the editors include, in addition to literary selections, only the authors' birth and death dates; they include no commentary. Most of the studies mentioned in this paragraph value colonial American literature for its "firstness"—for initiating the American literary tradition—while generally dismissing its value as art.

Twentieth-century criticism of colonial American literature began much as in the nineteenth century, with a serious study that would seem dated half a century later. In *American Verse, 1625–1807* (1909), William Bradley Otis surveys the poetry of the period, focusing on how it informs its culture and how it elucidates history; reflecting some earlier critical opinion, he does not argue for the aesthetic quality of the verse because he believes it is largely artless. Published in four volumes from 1917 to 1921, *The Cambridge History of American Literature,* edited by William Peterfield Trent, et al., was a major accomplishment in that notable scholars contributed significant, intelligent essays on various aspects of colonial American letters. Similar in concept to the fourteen-volume *Cambridge History of English Literature,* these books helped establish American literature as an area of study independent of English literature. In the 1920s, two creative writers made idiosyncratic studies of American literature, focusing at least to a degree on the colonial period. In *Studies in Classic American Literature* (1923), Englishman D. H. Lawrence addresses Benjamin Franklin. He is most often perceived as a beloved wit, ingenious inventor, successful diplomat, and amiable autobiographer, among other things. Yet, Lawrence's Franklin sees life simplistically; he does not honor, because he does not comprehend, humans' multiple selves, individuals' depth, people's souls. Lawrence admires, but does not like, Franklin, whom he considers too limiting in his various pronouncements. In *In the American Grain* (1925), the poet William Carlos Williams tries to determine literary and historical realities that are concealed because they are misnamed, mislabeled. His technique usually is to print original documents and comment on them. He compares the accounts of the Merry Mount community by William Bradford and Thomas Morton, for example, and sides with Morton, because of the Pilgrim community's overreaction to Morton's sexual activities—

activities that should not have concerned the Pilgrims. During the early twentieth century, numerous works from the colonial period were retrieved. These included creations by Benjamin Tompson (and other Tompsons), John Wilson, and Samuel Danforth in Kenneth B. Murdock's *Handkerchiefs from Paul* (1927) and especially the poems, previously unknown, of Edward Taylor in Thomas H. Johnson's *The Poetical Works of Edward Taylor* (1939). The beginning of the change in the general approach to literature from mostly historical to mainly literary began with the publication of two books by I. A. Richards: *Principles of Literary Criticism* (1924) and *Practical Criticism* (1929). In time, they were augmented by Cleanth Brooks and Robert Penn Warren's *Understanding Poetry* (1938) and John Crowe Ransom's *The New Criticism* (1941). The scholar who provided the most comprehensive understanding of the intellectual history of the colonial period was Perry Miller. In several intellectual histories that reflect enormous reading, assimilation, and study, he debunked many previous notions about the Puritans in particular and influenced every serious scholar of the period who came after him, even though, in time, some of his own approaches and interpretations were challenged. His books include *Orthodoxy in Massachusetts* (1933), *The New England Mind: The Seventeenth Century* (1939), *The New England Mind: From Colony to Province* (1953), and *Errand into the Wilderness* (1956), as well as a biography, *Jonathan Edwards* (1949). *The Literary History of the United States,* edited by Robert Spiller, et al. (1948), replaced *The Cambridge History of American Literature* as the comprehensive study of the entirety of American literature, including the colonial period. New approaches to early American literature did not end with Miller; they continued, and continue, unabated. Among the many major post-Miller scholars of the period are Sacvan Bercovitch, Robert Daly, Richard Beale Davis, Emory Elliott, Philip F. Gura, David D. Hall, J. A. Leo Lemay, Jill Lepore (a historian), David S. Shields, and Kenneth Silverman. Established in 1966, the journal *Early American Literature Newsletter* (which continues as *Early American Literature*) provided a dependable outlet for scholars' work, including studies that offered new approaches to the field. Expansion of the early American canon evolved over time, with Davis's mammoth *Intellectual Life in the Colonial South* (1978) standing as perhaps the major contribution to this trend. *The Heath Anthology of American Literature* (1990), edited by Paul Lauter, was a new kind of anthology in that it focused on expanding the canon by including selections by writers previously ignored, such as women and blacks, as well as by presenting translations of works by early French and Spanish authors, among others. As the twentieth century drew to a close, two new histories of the literature of the colonial period were published, with different approaches from earlier histories: *Columbia Literary History of the United States* (1988), edited by Elliott, and *The Cambridge History of American Literature, volume 1, 1590–1820* (1994), edited by Bercovitch. The first of these books acknowledges no consensus about the history of American literature and therefore presents only the opinions of the various contributors; the second focuses on American literatures (plural), which include writings similar to those represented in the Heath anthology. The authors of the various essays in these volumes incorporate into their studies the most current critical thoughts of the time, as do the scholars who contribute to *The Oxford Handbook of Early American Literature* (2008), edited by Kevin J. Hayes, a book that reflects the expanding canon of early American literature.

DOMINANT SCHOOLS OF CRITICISM TREATING COLONIAL LITERATURE

Many twentieth-century schools of criticism have examined early American literature and culture. One of the earliest, a socioeconomic approach, is perhaps best exemplified by Vernon Louis Parrington's three-volume *Main Currents of American Thought* (1927-1930). The author considers the uneasy mingling of liberal politics and conservative theology in colonial America by examining various early American authors, including John Cotton, Roger Williams, Nathaniel Ward, Samuel Sewall, and the Mathers, among others. In discussing the effect of later immigration on colonies outside New England, he addresses such authors as Sarah Kemble Knight, William Byrd, Jonathan Edwards, and Benjamin Franklin.

When Parrington wrote *Main Currents of American Thought,* the poems of Taylor were unknown. After Johnson discovered them and, in the late 1930s, published Taylor's poetical works, the poet attracted immediate attention from scholars approaching him from various critical perspectives. Not only did they have substantial (in quality and quantity) poems to examine, but an excitement attended such study because of the seemingly miraculous appearance of a previously unknown major Puritan writer from the late seventeenth and early eighteenth centuries.

The timing of the discovery of Taylor's poems was propitious: they appeared when American literature was emerging as a serious area of study and the so-called new criticism was becoming perhaps the dominant critical approach to literature, one that retained primacy through the 1950s and into the 1960s. The new critics considered a poem an organic creation that should be read primarily in order to understand how it works, as by examining its unifying elements and ironies. Because they were previously unknown and so seemingly important, Taylor's verses attracted this kind of analysis. While such close readings provided valuable insights, the new critical approach served Taylor less well than some other early poets, such as Anne Bradstreet, because Taylor's poems are probably best considered not as individual entities but rather as part of the context in which he wrote them, as in preparing to administer the Lord's Supper, for example.

Inspired by the ideas of Sigmund Freud and the practice of psychoanalysis, some critics take a psychological approach to literature, one that seeks and finds in a text insight about its author. Taylor attracts such critics. Some find in his work evidence of schizophrenia, despair (in the context of salvation), anality, homoeroticism, and sexual confusion.

Taylor has drawn the attention of critics interested in sources of writers' ideas and techniques. They have found him most obviously indebted to the Bible but also to the metaphysical poets, the baroque style, medieval traditions, classical authors, the Cambridge Platonists, biblical typology, emblem books, science, and so forth.

Taylor's work, like that of many colonial artists, has also been approached from the perspective of reader-response, archetypes, semiology, anthropology, structuralism, post-structuralism, deconstruction, and more—from seemingly all significant twentieth-century critical approaches to literature. This reality—that various critical schools have found value in him and other colonial authors—indicates the seemingly endless fecundity of the body of American literature created before the establishment of the United States of America.

Part II
Study Guides
on General Topics

Biography

When discussing colonial American biographies, definition becomes an issue. Biographical information appears in histories (by such as William Bradford), as well as in journals (John Winthrop), diaries (Samuel Sewall), eulogies (Benjamin Colman), letters (Roger Williams), and autobiographies (Thomas Shepard); so all these genres are biographical to a degree. For the purposes of this study guide, however, I discuss only narratives that focus on the life and accomplishments of a person other than the author.

By the middle of the seventeenth century, New Englanders had published sermons, promotional tracts, poems, journals, histories, almanacs, and other forms of writing. Biographies came late, having then, in the few years around 1650, just begun. This tardy appearance can probably be attributed to the fact that few of the Puritan fathers died before midcentury, and these men who had established a religious society to which others were heirs were those whose lives, though imperfect because all lives are imperfect, were considered exemplary and instructive, and therefore worthy of documentation, study, and emulation. Because the much respected John Cotton was one of the first of these men to die, it is not surprising that the earliest known biography by an American focuses on him: Samuel Whiting's "Concerning the Life of the Famous Mr. Cotton" (1653), composed the year following Cotton's death but not published until over a century later. Although Whiting's brief biography—fewer than one thousand words—remained unpublished until 1769, the manuscript was known and consulted, not least of all by John Norton, who incorporated much of Whiting's information into *The Life and Death of the Deservedly Famous Mr. John Cotton* (1657), published the next year in London as *Abel Being Dead yet Speaketh*, by which title it is better known. Norton's biography is a much fuller account than Whiting's of Cotton's life. In this first biography published in America, Norton explains why Cotton came to the New World and tells about his life in Boston. In showing similarities between Cotton's experiences and events in the Bible, Emory Elliott has observed, Norton established a model for later biographers.

In depicting his father in a manner similar to that of Norton's treatment of Cotton, Increase Mather, in *The Life and Death of That Reverend Man of God, Mr. Richard Mather* (1670), helps prove Elliott's point. Both biographies illustrate what William J. Scheick identifies as the main theme of Puritan biographies: "the progressive unfolding of divine will through the spiritual fathers of the Puritan community." Neither of these early biographies, though, reveals much about the physical being or personal lives of the subjects, especially in the "tell-all" manner that modern readers have come to expect; Norton and Increase Mather provide, rather, respectful and instructive spiritual biographies, ones focusing on religion and morality and tending toward the hagiographic. Despite the seriousness of these biographies, Increase Mather, for one, was not averse to lightening the mood when making a serious point about his father, as may be observed in an anecdote involving Mr. Gillebrand, who, upon hearing Richard Mather preach for the first time, asked the minister's name. When told that it is Mather, he responded, "Nay (said Mr. *Gillebrand*) call him *Matter*, for believe it this man hath Substance in him." (This biography of Richard Mather includes the first engraving published in America, John Foster's woodcut likeness of the subject.)

As Increase Mather wrote a biography of his father, so did Richard Mather's grandson, Cotton Mather, write one of his father, Increase. Titled *Parentator*, it was published in 1724, the year following Increase Mather's death and four years before Cotton Mather's. Like the biographies of John Cotton and Richard Mather, *Parentator* depicts a life well worth emulating; unlike the previous biographies, Cotton Mather's book provides glimpses into the subject's personality, perhaps because readers in 1724 had different expectations from readers of half-a-century earlier, but also possibly because of Cotton Mather's own psychological quirks. Another significant difference between the two Mather biographies is that, as Scheick observes, Increase Mather does not intrude in the biography of Richard Mather, while Cotton Mather does when relating his father's life.

Parentator is the last of Cotton Mather's biographies; the first is one of John Eliot titled *The Triumphs of the Reformed Religion, in America* (1691). Between these two, he wrote many others and published them in his major work, *Magnalia Christi Americana* (1702). They constitute the most significant biographical studies of the colonial era. Some brief, others quite long, they depict numerous Puritan divines and other figures important to colonial America, among whom are such men as William Bradford, John Winthrop, Simon Bradstreet, and Sir William Phips. Although Mather intended the biographies to inspire readers at the beginning of a new century, when New England was becoming increasingly secular, they serve as a rich source of biographical and historical information, as is especially the case with the life of Phips.

The numerous biographies in *Magnalia Christi Americana* might be read as a collective biography because Mather intended them all "to be studied, admired, and imitated . . . ," as Christopher R. Reaske suggests. Reaske also notes that as the eighteenth century progressed, "biography was trying to move toward longer sketches of particular individuals, toward a fuller examination of a single life, and away from the collective biographies such as . . . Mather's *Magnalia*."

Ebenezer Turell composed two longer sketches. In the first, *Memoirs of the Life and Death of the Pious and Ingenious Mrs. Jane Turell* (1735), he records, in sixty-one pages, the life of his late wife and includes her poems, as well as letters to her from her father, Benjamin Colman. Parts of the text indicate that societal secularization continued after Cotton Mather's *Magnalia Christi Americana*. In recounting meeting Jane Colman for the first time when she was approximately nineteen, for example, Turell states that "I was supriz'd and charm'd to find her so accomplished. I found her in a good measure Mistress of the politest *Writers* and their Works; could point out the Beauties in them, and had made many of their best Tho'ts her own: And as she went into more free Conversation, she discours'd how admirably on many Subjects!" Primarily, he was smitten by her intellectual sophistication, an impression reinforced by the word "ingenious" in the title of this biography. Not long before this time, a widower—especially a minister, like Turell—probably would have recorded, possibly accurately, that he was first attracted to his late wife because of her devotion to religion.

Turell's other biography, of his late father-in-law in *The Life and Character of the Reverend Benjamin Colman, D.D.* (1749), helps support Reaske's point about the emergence of extended biographies in eighteenth-century America. At 238 pages, it is a real book, not a biographical sketch, as was occasionally the case with some previous biographies, including several in *Magnalia Christi Americana.* Like earlier biographers, Turell presents his subject as worthy of emulation, and he supports many of his claims by providing documentary evidence in the form of letters and such.

Another substantial eighteenth-century biography is Samuel Hopkins's *The Life and Character of the Late Reverend Mr. Jonathan Edwards* (1765). Of the 279 pages, 98 constitute the biography, while Edwards's sermons fill the other pages. Longer than seventeenth-century biographies, Hopkins's life of Edwards is similar to earlier ones in arguing for something like his subject's perfection. Hopkins states his intention: "to inform in what way, and by what means [Edwards] attained to such an uncommon stock of knowledge and holiness; and how, in the improvement of this, he did so much good to mankind; that others may hereby be directed and excited to go and do likewise." In other words, this biography is intentionally hagiographic.

TOPICS FOR DISCUSSION AND RESEARCH

1. Emory Elliott posits that the Puritans trusted accounts of past events only as depicted in the Bible; yet, they wrote numerous accounts of the past, including histories and biographies. Why was this so? Were the Puritans hypocrites on this issue? Did they reflect a compelling human need to know about the past, even if renderings of it are imperfect? Or did they have other reasons for attempting to understand and learn from possibly unreliable history? Elliott addresses these questions in *The Cambridge Introduction to Early American Literature.*

2. Perry Miller and Thomas H. Johnson state that "the art of formal biography" in America began with Increase Mather's biography of his father and Cotton Mather's of his. What constitutes a formal biography? What are its characteristics? How does it differ from an informal biography? To answer these questions, students should familiarize themselves with some Puritan biographies, trying to discern differences on their own. For assistance, though, consult Miller and Johnson's *The Puritans.*

3. "Less concerned with factual detail and more toward presentation and image," notes Steven R. Serafin, "the majority of [American Puritan] biographical writing was either commemorative or hagiographic." Why are many early biographies hagiographic? Puritans believed that as descendants of Adam, all mortals are imperfect. Because even the most serious and moral people are human (as evidenced, for example, by the diary of Michael Wigglesworth), no one would actually believe that a human could live life flawlessly. Does this human reality undercut the hagiographical impulse, as realized in the biographies mentioned above? Did authors anticipate readers' willing suspension of disbelief? Does the adjective in the term "spiritual biography" assume importance within this context? Any study of the Puritan biography will

address aspects of this issue. See, for example, Serafin's "Biography" and Mason I. Lowance Jr.'s "Biography and Autobiography."
4. The three generations of Mather ministers—Richard, Increase, and Cotton —constitute something of an early American religious dynasty. Often, the Mathers agreed on issues (Increase and Cotton on smallpox inoculation); occasionally, they did not (Richard and Increase on the Half-Way Covenant). While there are obvious similarities between Increase Mather's biography of Richard and Cotton Mather's of Increase, there are also significant differences, other than those about the details of the subjects' lives. One reason is that they were written in different eras, the first in the seventeenth century; the second, in the eighteenth. A student of these two biographies, William J. Scheick, argues that the two works are "as much about their authors as about their subject, and within this mutual concern lies their fundamental difference." What does Scheick mean by this and what evidence does he present to support his claim? Is his statement convincing?
5. In the introduction to his life of Benjamin Colman, Ebenezer Turell comments on the nature of biography, hoping that his study differs from the typical one. In particular, he wants to avoid depicting his subject as perfect in every regard; he desires rather to humanize Colman, to show "those particular excelling Qualities which distinguish him from others." Did Turell succeed in doing this? Reading a few of his chapters and comparing them with some biographies in Cotton Mather's *Magnalia Christi Americana* will lead to an answer. If Turell's treatment of Colman is significantly different from the handling of subjects in previous biographies, how is it so? For guidance, consult Christopher R. Reaske's introduction to *The Life and Character of the Reverend Benjamin Colman, D.D.*

RESOURCES

Criticism

Emory Elliott, *The Cambridge Introduction to Early American Literature* (Cambridge, England: Cambridge University Press, 2002).
In telling "the story of the literature of the New England Puritans," Elliott discusses personal narratives.

Mason I. Lowance Jr., "Biography and Autobiography," in *Columbia Literary History of the United States*, edited by Elliott, et al. (New York: Columbia University Press, 1988), pp. 67–82.
In discussing colonial American biographies and autobiographies, Lowance notes that most of them were written by New Englanders and observes that they have "cohesive, didactic, and spiritual purpose[s]."

Perry Miller and Thomas H. Johnson, Introductions, *The Puritans*, edited by Miller and Johnson (New York: American Book Company, 1938).
Comments authoritatively on various types and subjects of Puritan writing, including biographies, and provides generous selections from Puritan authors.

Kenneth B. Murdock, Introduction, *Magnalia Christi Americana, Books I and II*, by Cotton Mather, edited by Murdock (Cambridge, Mass.: Belknap Press of Harvard University Press, 1977).
Surveys the life of Cotton Mather and discusses issues relating to *Magnalia Christi Americana*.

Christopher R. Reaske, Introduction, *The Life and Character of the Reverend Benjamin Colman, D.D.* (1749), by Ebenezer Turell (Delmar, N.Y.: Scholars' Facsimiles and Reprints, 1972).
Identifies problems Turell confronted when writing his biography of Colman and discusses biography as genre.

Steven R. Serafin, "Biography," in *Encyclopedia of American Literature*, edited by Serafin (New York: Continuum, 1999), pp. 98–100.
Discusses the nature of American biographies published from the seventeenth century through the twentieth.

William J. Scheick, Introduction, *Two Mather Biographies:* Life and Death *and* Parentator, edited by Scheick (Bethlehem, Pa.: Lehigh University Press, 1989).
Discusses issues relating to biographies by Increase Mather (of Richard Mather) and Cotton Mather (of Increase Mather).

PEOPLE OF INTEREST

Simon Bradstreet (1603–1697)
Was active in the political life of Massachusetts Bay, including serving as governor. His first wife was Anne Bradstreet, who wrote him moving love poems.

John Eliot (1604–1690)
The Apostle to the Indians, was dedicated to converting Indians to Christianity, going so far as to translate the Bible into Algonquian (1663).

Samuel Hopkins (1721–1803)
Was a minister who was heavily influenced by the ideas of Jonathan Edwards, whose biography he wrote.

John Norton (1606–1663)
Helped draft the Cambridge Platform and was an ardent opponent of Quakerism; at the suggestion of John Cotton, he succeeded Cotton at the First Church in Boston.

Sir William Phips (1651–1695)
Was a military man who became the first royal governor of Massachusetts, as which he established the court that oversaw the Salem witchcraft trials. He was the first American to be knighted.

Thomas Shepard (1605–1649)
Minister and a founder of Harvard College, is best known as the author of *The Sincere Convert* (1641).

Ebenezer Turell (1702–1778)

Harvard College class of 1721, was minister of the church at Medford, Massachusetts, for over half a century; he was married to Jane Colman Turell, now valued as a poet.

Samuel Whiting (1597–1679)

Minister of the church at Saugus (soon named Lynn), Massachusetts Bay, composed what is believed to be the first biography by an American, one of John Cotton, though it was not published until 1769.

Dissent

Permanent English-speaking presence in New England began as a result of dissent —protest against religious requirements in England. In 1608, religious persecution caused a group of English men and women to flee to Holland, where they lived before returning briefly to England, in 1620, to sail to America on the *Mayflower*. One of the men, William Bradford, details these experiences and attendant events in a manuscript written in America and ultimately published as *Of Plymouth Plantation*. From the establishment of the Pilgrim community in 1620 and the Massachusetts Bay Colony a decade later, dissent was a feature of American colonial life, often, for a century, against the practices of the original dissenters and their progeny, but also, as time passed, against British rule and the institution of slavery.

Two of the earliest important examples of dissent within the Puritan community occurred in the 1630s. Roger Williams, a Puritan minister, protested against the belief that Englishmen had a right to the American land they inhabited; in so doing, he questioned the charter that governed the colony. Further, his belief that church and state should be separate entities struck at the heart of the colony's government, which was theocratic. To keep Williams from causing civil unrest, the General Court ordered him to return to England. Instead, he fled the colony and founded Providence, Rhode Island, as a place of religious toleration where church and state were separate institutions. Williams defended his positions in a published debate with John Cotton in the 1640s and 1650s.

Cotton was also involved in the other great dissension of the 1630s, that known as the Antinomian Controversy. It involved Anne Hutchinson, a parishioner of Cotton's in England and Boston. She propounded the belief, which she thought she learned from Cotton, that good works (sanctification) do not constitute evidence of saving grace (justification). Her views found an audience and threatened established society. In emphasizing the indwelling of the Holy Spirit, which implies that people possessing it need not obey the Ten Commandments because they are already assured of salvation, she jeopardized the smooth functioning of Boston society by eliminating sacred instructions for moral living. Part of her situation implied an issue central to Williams's case: the separation of church and state. Even if her religious views are incorrect, should a civil court have jurisdiction over religious beliefs? After defending herself at a trial during which Cotton essentially betrayed her, she was exiled to Rhode Island.

Seemingly all religions have internal doctrinal disputes, and such was the case with the Congregationalists. A major development occurred in 1677, for example, when Solomon Stoddard, in Northampton, Massachusetts Bay, dissented against the practice of limiting Holy Communion to people who could demonstrate evidence of saving grace. Because he believed that the sacrament is a converting ordinance, one that causes salvation, he began offering it to all adults who wished to partake of it, as long as they subscribed to the articles of faith and behaved well. In doing so, he incurred the wrath of the Congregational establishment, including Increase Mather and Cotton Mather, as well as the disapproval of Edward Taylor. In this instance, one individual's dissent changed the establishment, for in time all Congregational churches viewed the Lord's Supper as a converting ordinance. An irony attends Stoddard's interpretation of the sacrament, however, because Jonathan Edwards, Stoddard's grandson and successor in the Northampton pulpit, dissented against Stoddard's practice by limiting the Lord's Supper to those who could provide evidence of saving grace, as had been the case in Congregational churches before Stoddard objected to the practice. Edwards also dissented against the established Congregational rational approach to religion by emphasizing the importance of emotion in the conversion experience, a concept that, when disseminated primarily by George Whitefield, led to the Great Awakening of the 1740s.

Although colonial governments were relatively stable until the mid eighteenth century, rebellions occurred. As Williams was dissatisfied with the government of Massachusetts Bay, for example, so was Nathaniel Bacon with that of Virginia in 1676. He and other settlers feared the Indians, who lived on land protected by treaty. Hoping to avert war, Governor William Berkeley forbade the attacking of Indians. Disregarding the governor's wishes, Bacon and his men attacked them. This defiance of authority forced Berkeley to call a special election, one effect of which was the limiting of the governor's power. Bacon's Rebellion was the first settlers' uprising against governmental authority in colonial North America.

It was not the last. Other rebellions followed. These include a farmers' revolt against customs duties in South Carolina (1677), Leisler's Rebellion in New York City (1689), and the Protestant Association's taking over the Catholic government of Maryland (1689). In all cases, the colonists' dissent resulted primarily from dissatisfaction with local representatives of the Crown, not from disagreement with the concept of English rule itself. For many people, this acceptance of rule from abroad began changing no later than 1764, when England imposed the Sugar Act on the colonies. Attempting to reduce its debt following the French and Indian War, Britain enforced taxation on the trading of sugar, without the colonists' consent. Numerous colonial assemblies protested the Sugar Act, but before they could dissent officially, England imposed the more onerous Stamp Act (1765), which affected all colonists and led to the ultimate colonial dissent.

The Stamp Act taxed various printed documents. Before the act became effective late in the year, colonists reacted to it quickly and sometimes violently, going so far as to attack the homes of officials charged with enforcing the act. Representatives of the colonies met in the Stamp Act Congress to formulate a response to it. Their dissent against it was one factor in its repeal the next year. Still needing money, Parliament passed the Quartering Act in 1765 and the Townshend Acts in 1766, both requiring financial outlay by the colonies. Again the colonists dissented, this time to the degree that animosity between them and the Crown intensified, culminating in the Boston Massacre (1670). Continued colonial dissent against other Parliamentary actions inspired events, such as the Boston Tea Party (1773), that led to the outbreak of hostilities between the colonists and British at Lexington and Concord in 1775 and to the full-blown American Revolution. Sustained dissent resulted, ultimately, in independence from the Crown and the establishment of the United States of America.

Religious doctrine and matters of state were not the only issues to generate serious dissent in colonial America. So did the institution of slavery, even though a significant number of dissenters did not develop until the nineteenth century.

The earliest American document known to oppose the institution is Germantown Friends Protest against Slavery (1688, though published much later); the first published manumissionist tract is probably Samuel Sewall's *The Selling of Joseph, a Memorial* (1700). The beginning of what became the abolitionist movement possibly dates from the Quakers' forbidding members from owning slaves (1750s) and Quaker John Woolman's dissenting against the institution in *Some Considerations on the Keeping of Negroes. Recommended to the Professors of Christianity of Every Denomination* (1754). Slowly, in the 1760s and 1770s, antislavery sentiments began being published. James Otis calls the institution into question in his *Rights of the British Colonies Asserted and Proved* (1764), for example, while Benjamin Rush identifies it as "a national crime" in *An Address to the Inhabitants of the British Settlements in North America* (1773). The Quakers established the first abolitionist society in the 1770s. In time, the dissenters against slavery, initially few in number, proved successful when the Thirteenth Amendment to the United States Constitution (1865) forbade it.

Of the dissenting positions mentioned here, all except Edwards's views about Holy Communion have been vindicated by history. The United States separates the state and religion (Williams, Hutchinson), Protestant faiths typically view the Lord's Supper as a converting ordinance (Stoddard), colonial rule was overthrown (Bacon and many other colonists), and slavery is not permitted (Quakers).

TOPICS FOR DISCUSSION AND RESEARCH

1. Although the issue continues generating debate, the separation of church and state is a bedrock principle of the United States. In the context of being persecuted by a Puritan theocracy, Roger Williams and Anne Hutchinson were the first residents of American to argue or at least imply that one should have religious freedom, that church and state are separate entities, and that religious beliefs should not be controlled by the state. Over time, this position gained adherents to the degree that such a separation is guaranteed in the First Amendment to the Constitution (1791). Students might beneficially chart the development of Williams's and Hutchinson's thought from the dissent of two individuals to its becoming a hallmark of American life. Many books discuss the separation of church and state. A reliable one dealing with Williams is Edwin S. Gaustad's *Liberty of Conscience;* for information about Hutchinson as dissenter, see Amy Schrager Lang's *Prophetic Woman.*

2. Students wishing to investigate aspects of events surrounding the American Revolution will be faced with an enormous amount of material, mostly historical or political in nature. Numerous books have been written about the Stamp Act, for example. Students would benefit from reading reliable summaries of issues relating to the Revolution but also from investigating how serious literary figures of the following century deal with the issue of dissent as it occurred around the time of the Revolution. Two readily available nineteenth-century stories treat it—Washington Irving's "Rip Van Winkle" (1819) and Nathaniel Hawthorne's "My Kinsman, Major Molineux" (1832)—as do novels, including James Fenimore Cooper's *The Spy* (1825) and Herman Melville's *Israel Potter* (1855).

3. Students might reasonably ask why the Quakers were the first American organization to oppose slavery. Their position was moral. What aspects of the Quaker faith might have caused them to adopt their position? Are these aspects also present in other faiths, all of which sanctioned slavery at least into the 1770s? If so, why did these other religions not dissent against slavery as early and vocally as the Quakers? Does geography come into play? Self-interest? Satisfaction with the status quo? Further, by what logic could Americans argue against their political enslavement by England—going so far as to fight a war to liberate themselves—while permitting slavery to flourish in America? Any reputable history of slavery will discuss these issues. See, for example, Ira Berlin, *Many Thousands Gone,* and Gary B. Nash, *Race and Revolution.* For an early statement of the Quaker position, consult John Woolman's *Some Considerations on the Keeping of Negroes* and *Considerations on Keeping Negroes,* as well as an examination of his position in Thomas P. Slaughter, *The Beautiful Soul of John Woolman, Apostle of Abolition.*

RESOURCES

Biography

Thomas P. Slaughter, *The Beautiful Soul of John Woolman, Apostle of Abolition* (New York: Hill & Wang, 2008).

The most detailed, comprehensive, and convincing study of Woolman's life and thought.

Criticism

Ira Berlin, *Many Thousands Gone: The First Two Centuries of Slavery in North America* (Cambridge, Mass.: Belknap Press of Harvard University Press, 1998).

Considers the complexities of American slavery, arguing that slavery meant different things at different times.

Edwin S. Gaustad, *Liberty of Conscience: Roger Williams in America* (Grand Rapids, Mich.: Eerdmans, 1991).

Discusses the issues with which Williams was involved and places them in historical context.

Amy Schrager Lang, *Prophetic Woman: Anne Hutchinson and the Problem of Dissent in the Literature of New England* (Berkeley: University of California Press, 1987).

A full discussion of Hutchinson as dissenter that considers the symbolic value of her story.

Gary B. Nash, *Race and Revolution* (Madison, Wis.: Madison House, 1990).

In a series of three essays, discusses slavery during the Revolutionary era.

James Otis, *The Rights of the British Colonies Asserted and Proved* (Boston: Edes & Gill, 1764).

Strongly defends colonial rights.

Benjamin Rush, *An Address to the Inhabitants of the British Settlements in North America on the Slavery of the Negroes in America* (Philadelphia: J. Dunlap, 1773).
Attacks the institution of slavery.

John Woolman, *Some Considerations on the Keeping of Negroes. Recommended to the Professors of Christianity of Every Denomination* (Philadelphia: James Chattin, 1754).
Woolman, *Considerations on Keeping Negroes; Recommended to the Professors of Christianity, of Every Denomination, Part Second* (Philadelphia: B. Franklin & D. Hall, 1762).
Argues for the abolition of slavery.

PEOPLE OF INTEREST

James Otis (1725–1783)
Lawyer, pamphleteer, and brother of the author Mercy Otis Warren, was a prominent proponent of colonial liberty.

Benjamin Rush (1745–1813)
Was a Pennsylvania physician who signed the Declaration of Independence.

Drama

One of the glories of classical Greece and the English Renaissance, drama was slow becoming established in New England. The primary reason was moral. Following the lead of the English Puritans, who closed the London theaters in 1642 at the beginning of the English Civil War, the Puritans who settled in America viewed plays as, among other things, untrue and therefore sinful and dangerous to society. For the entirety of the colonial era, they and their progeny—and their attitudes—dominated Boston and environs, the cultural center of the English-speaking New World. Their antidrama bias resulted in the banning of plays (1750) and became especially pronounced during the Revolutionary era when the occupying British forces staged plays: not only were plays corrupting, but they were admired by the colonists' arch enemies. Although plays met resistance elsewhere, including Philadelphia and New York, these other cities were more accepting of drama than Boston and therefore have an early history of theatrical productions. The Boston ban was not rescinded until 1793.

The history of American drama probably begins in 1665 with the performance of William Darby's *Ye Bare and Ye Cubbe* at a tavern in Accomac County, Virginia, though no copy of the play is known to exist. There is little information about American plays performed during the next quarter century. In 1690, *Gustavus Vasa* by Benjamin Colman, later an important Congregational minister, was performed by Harvard students. It was possibly the first play written by an American to be performed. Theatrical activity increased early in the new century when students at William and Mary College recited a colloquy for the Virginia governor (1702) and the British actor Anthony Aston performed in Charleston, South Carolina (1703). The first play written and published in America is *Androboros* (1715), by Robert Hunter, the governor of New York. The next year, the first known American playhouse was constructed in Williamsburg, Virginia. Performed in New York in 1730, *Romeo and Juliet* is the first Shakespearean play produced in America. The Dock Street Theatre in Charleston opened in 1736, the same year students at William and Mary presented several plays, including Joseph Addison's *Cato,* one of the plays most frequently performed throughout the colonies.

In the same year that Massachusetts banned theatrical performances, 1750, the English professional actors Walter Murray and Thomas Kean performed *Richard III* and other plays at the Nassau Street Playhouse in New York; the next year, these players opened their own playhouse in Williamsburg, where, in 1752, the company of Lewis Hallam performed *The Merchant of Venice,* which young George Washington is said to have attended. As societal unrest began and intensified in response to acts imposed on the colonies by England (such as the Stamp Act of 1765), theatrical activity increased. In 1766, Robert Rogers's *Ponteach; or the Savages of America* became the first play written by an American and with an American subject to be published. The Douglass company's 1767 production of Thomas Godfrey's *The Prince of Parthia* at the Southwark Theatre, Philadelphia, was the first professional performance of a play by an

American. This same year, the John Street Theatre opened as the first permanent playhouse in New York. In the early 1770s, as political tensions increased, Mercy Otis Warren wrote several closet plays with a political theme, all critical of the Tories. Acknowledging the importance of political strife, in 1774 the First Continental Congress encouraged seriousness among the citizenry and discouraged such an extravagance as the theater. During the siege of Boston, British general John Burgoyne established a theater in Faneuil Hall (1775) and had his play *The Blockade of Boston* performed the next year. The year 1776 was also the date of publication of plays by Hugh Henry Brackenridge *(The Battle of Bunkers-Hill)* and John Leacock *(The Fall of British Tyranny, or American Liberty Triumphant);* the title of the latter proved prophetic.

TOPICS FOR DISCUSSION AND RESEARCH

1. Some of the earliest American theatrical performances occurred in Virginia (William and Mary College) and South Carolina, southern colonies. Even though Charleston was an important port city, these were not major population centers, as were Boston, New York, and Philadelphia. Ordinarily, one might expect the theater to have originated and flourished in large urban areas because of the number of people living there and the probable sophistication of a sizable educated class. What was the audience for plays in the South? Students might ponder why areas of the southern colonies were receptive to plays. Were the performances professionally acted? Or were the players amateurs? How might southern societal, including cultural, attitudes have differed from those in Boston, for example, which banned this form of entertainment in the eighteenth century? For help in answering these questions, consult Richard Beale Davis's *Intellectual Life in the Colonial South.*

2. Truly professional American drama is generally considered to have begun with the arrival of Lewis Hallam and his company from England in 1752. Why are they and not the team of Walter Murray and Thomas Kean—who antedated Hallam and established their own theater—so credited? Why is the company of David Douglass—who produced plays at the same time as Hallam, who led Hallam's actors following Hallam's death, and who, in 1761, introduced professional theater to New England—not considered the father of the professional American theater? In other words, what differentiates Murray-Kean, Hallam, and Douglass? For assistance in answering this question, consult, among other sources, Glenn Hughes's *A History of the American Theatre* and Howard Taubman's *The Making of the American Theatre.*

3. When Douglass introduced professional theater to New England in 1761, he did so in Newport, Rhode Island. Because of New England antipathy toward the theater, he needed to present himself and his company as upstanding and engage in subterfuge to produce *Othello* without having it appear to be a play. Understanding the specifics of his ordeal will help students comprehend some of the serious cultural problems companies confronted. What did Douglass do to ease his acceptance in Newport? How did he advertise *Othello*? How did he guarantee that playgoers interpreted Shakespeare's play as moral in nature? He

succeeded to the degree that he soon erected, in Newport, a theater at which he gave some performances "for the benefit of the poor" in order to appear respectable if not altruistic. Details about his activities in Newport may be found in Barnard Hewitt's *Theatre U. S. A.* and Glenn Hughes's *A History of the American Theatre.*

4. *The Prince of Parthia*, the first play by an American to be professionally produced, includes few American elements. Its author, Thomas Godfrey, was obviously influenced by English plays, especially those of Shakespeare. Why might he have shunned local color in favor of established dramatic conventions, themes, and techniques, such as the murder of a king, revenge, and so forth? For information about Godfrey's dramatic borrowings, consult William E. McCarron's *Bicentennial Edition of Thomas Godfrey's "The Prince of Parthia."*

RESOURCES

Criticism

Jared Brown, *The Theatre in America during the Revolution* (Cambridge, England: Cambridge University Press, 1995).
Thoroughly surveys and analyzes American theater of the Revolutionary era.

The Cambridge History of American Theatre, Volume One: Beginnings to 1870, edited by Don B. Wilmeth and Christopher Bigsby (Cambridge, England: Cambridge University Press, 1998).
Details the development of the American theater to 1870.

Richard Beale Davis, *Intellectual Life in the Colonial South, 1585–1763,* volume 3 (Knoxville: University of Tennessee Press, 1978), pp. 1280–1306.
Describes the history of the drama in the colonial South.

Joel D. Eis, *A Full Investigation of the Historic Performance of the First Play in English in the New World—the Case of* Ye Bare & Ye Cubbe, *1665* (Lewiston, New York: Edwin Mellen Press, 2004).
Scrutinizes seemingly every detail relating to the first play known to have been performed in British North America.

Michael T. Gilmore, "The Drama," in *The Cambridge History of American Literature, Volume I: 1590–1820,* edited by Sacvan Bercovitch (Cambridge, England: Cambridge University Press, 1994), pp. 573–590.
Examines American drama of the Revolutionary and Early National periods.

Barnard Hewitt, *Theatre U. S. A., 1668 to 1957* (New York: McGraw-Hill, 1959).
A history of the American theater from the beginning to the mid twentieth century.

Arthur Hornblow, *A History of the Theatre in America: From Its Beginnings to the Present Time,* volume 1 (1919; New York: Benjamin Blom, 1965).
A history of the first two centuries of the American theater.

Glenn Hughes, *A History of the American Theatre, 1700–1950* (New York: S. French, 1951).
A history of the American theater from the beginning to the mid twentieth century.

William E. McCarron, *Bicentennial Edition of Thomas Godfrey's* The Prince of Parthia, A Tragedy *(1765)*, edited by McCarron (Colorado Springs, Colo.: United States Air Force Academy, 1976).
Provides an authoritative text of Godfrey's play and discusses the author's use of dramatic conventions.

Howard Taubman, *The Making of the American Theatre* (New York: Coward McCann, 1965).
Surveys the history of the American theater.

William C. Young, *Documents of American Theater History, Volume 1: Famous American Playhouses, 1716–1899* (Chicago: American Library Association, 1973).
Discusses American playhouses established through the nineteenth century and reproduces documents relating to them; for the colonial period, treats twelve theaters, from the first one in Williamsburg, Virginia (1716), to the Church-Street Theatre in Charleston, South Carolina (1773).

PEOPLE OF INTEREST

Joseph Addison (1672–1719)
Was a British politician, poet, playwright, and essayist whose contributions to *The Tatler* and *The Spectator* influenced eighteenth-century American essayists.

Hugh Henry Brackenridge (1748–1816)
A Princeton graduate and Pennsylvania jurist, wrote plays and political discourses, though he is best known for his novel *Modern Chivalry*.

John Burgoyne (1722–1792)
A British army officer, was a general in Boston during the siege of 1775–1776.

William Darby (dates unknown)
Was an Englishman who in 1659 apparently sailed from Bristol for Barbados, though he disembarked on the Eastern Shore of Virginia; he wrote *Ye Bare and Ye Cubbe*, the first dramatic production known to have been performed in British North America.

Thomas Godfrey (1736–1763)
A Philadelphian, was mentored by Benjamin Franklin, Benjamin West, and William Smith; he wrote *The Prince of Parthia* while a factor in North Carolina; he also wrote poems in the neoclassical mode.

Robert Hunter (1666–1734)
Respected governor of New York and New Jersey (1710–1719) and later of Jamaica, was, in addition to his military and political activities, an author whose work appeared in *The Tatler*.

John Leacock (1729–1802)

A Philadelphia silversmith and goldsmith,was the probable author of *The Fall of British Tyranny, or American Liberty Triumphant* (1776), a play by "Dick Rifle" that encourages Americans to support the Patriot cause.

Robert Rogers (circa 1731–1795)

Was a Massachusetts native who sympathized with the Indians.

Essays and Newspapers

Some early settlers in America wrote poems, and the number and quality of them increased as the seventeenth century progressed. American drama probably dates from the 1665 performance of William Darby's *Ye Bare and Ye Cubbe* at a tavern in Virginia, though the first professional performance of a play written by an American did not occur until the production of Thomas Godfrey's *The Prince of Parthia* in 1767. The first American novel, written by William Hill Brown, was not published until after the colonial period. Another major genre of belles-lettres, the urbane essay, initially was published in America in the 1720s.

The primary reason the essay was not published before then is that an appropriate vehicle for it was not available. By definition, an essay is relatively short, which means that one would not likely be published in book form. Conceivably, one could appear as a broadside. The best medium for an essay is a periodical. The first American magazines were published in 1741 (Andrew Bradford's *American Magazine* and Benjamin Franklin's *General Magazine, and Historical Chronicle*); newspapers were published earlier, though essays did not immediately appear in them. The initial American newspaper to have more than one number, *The Boston News-Letter,* began publication in 1704; the second, *The Boston Gazette,* first appeared in 1719. These were *news* papers, ones that provided information to their readerships: local, regional, and international (much delayed) news; social items; shipping facts; current prices of goods; and other such reports, including many advertisements. They were the mass media of the time. With the next newspaper, James Franklin's *The New-England Courant* (initially published in 1721) and especially with the one following his, Samuel Kneeland's *The New-England Weekly Journal* (which began publication in 1727), newspapers featured essays. These were generally not just dry, formal compositions with a thesis, body, and conclusion. Instead, the most engaging of them were either witty or satirical or both, and they were intended both to entertain and delight. That is, the authors of these essays emulated the sophisticated English essays of the early eighteenth century, especially those composed for *The Tatler* and *The Spectator* by Joseph Addison.

Some authors wrote not just an occasional essay but a series of essays in the manner of some in English periodicals. The first, most witty, and most accomplished of these series was written in 1722 by a sixteen-year-old, who composed fourteen essays for publication in his brother's newspaper. This person was Franklin, whose creations are known as the Dogood papers because they consist of compositions supposedly written by the widow Silence Dogood. She criticizes drunkenness and fashion and poetry, the last as represented by funeral elegies; institutions receiving the widow's barb include government, religion, and education—especially education, and particularly the education offered, she implies, by Harvard College. The sophistication and wit of adolescent Benjamin Franklin prefigure such of his later essays as "The Witch Trial at Mount Holly" (1730), "The Speech of Polly Baker" (1747), and "An Edict by the King of Prussia" (1773).

The Dogood papers were not the only essays published by *The New-England Courant*. It also published some by the Couranteers, a group of writers that included Benjamin Franklin, Matthew Adams, and others. Adams also contributed to the second series of American essays. Proteus Echo, which appeared on the front page in fifty-two consecutive issues of *The New-England Weekly Journal* in 1727 and 1728, was the enterprise of him, his nephew John Adams, and Mather Byles. Similar to *The Spectator* in consisting of a club of members, in using epigraphs, and in addressing such topics as pride, society, religion, and literary theory, Proteus Echo was more ambitious and far ranging than the Dogood papers. It also has societal importance. John Adams and Byles were young ministers when they and Matthew Adams wrote these essays. This assumes significance in the context of characterizing the decade of the 1720s. By then, the religious zeal of the original American Puritans had diminished to the degree that such ministers as Adams and Byles could write the occasional light, even whimsical essay and in their more serious essays deal not with religion so much as with ethics and morals. This reality may be understood in the context of the essay Byles composed for his master's degree at Harvard in 1727, the year Proteus Echo began: in it, he argues that "polite literature is an ornament to a theologian" (Shipton), a sentiment he and John Adams obviously believed. Ministers were becoming more worldly, more accommodating of the secular arts than their predecessors.

Boston was not the only colonial American city with newspapers featuring essays. In Philadelphia in 1729, Benjamin Franklin and Joseph Breintnall published the Busy-Body series in thirty-two issues of the *American Weekly Mercury*. It addresses topics similar to those treated by Proteus Echo, though it also engaged in a feud with Samuel Keimer, for whom Franklin once worked and who in 1728 started *The Universal Instructor in All Arts and Sciences* in order to hinder Franklin's effort to begin a newspaper. Franklin and Breintnall's attacks were so effective that within a year Keimer sold his newspaper to Franklin and his partner Hugh Meredith; the new owners changed its title to *The Pennsylvania Gazette*.

Essays appeared in Southern newspapers. They are featured in *The Maryland Gazette* and *The Virginia Gazette*, both begun by William Parks; the former in Annapolis in 1727, the latter in Williamsburg in 1736. *The Maryland Gazette* published an essay series, the Plain-Dealer. Of the ten essays, only the first two are original; the others are from the English newspaper *The Free-Thinker*, operated by poet Ambrose Phillips and a partner. Like the Busy-Body series, the Plain-Dealer treats topics similar to those in Proteus Echo, as does the Monitor series published in *The Virginia Gazette*. The Monitor essays were probably composed by officials at the College of William and Mary. Essays also appeared *The South-Carolina Gazette*, begun in Charleston in 1732.

The essays mentioned here share certain features because they all derive from the same source: the cultivated English essay as published in *The Tatler* and *The Spectator*, especially as composed by Addison.

TOPICS FOR DISCUSSION AND RESEARCH

1. In the fullest examination of American essay series, Bruce Granger states that "early southern serials . . . remind us that eighteenth-century Annapolis, Williamsburg, and Charleston were culturally closer to London than to Boston and Philadelphia. Essay writing seems to have come naturally and easily to the southerner whose mood is sunnier and less partisan than the northerner." What does he mean by this? What evidence does he present? Essayists from both parts of the country were inspired by the same source, so how, specifically, do essays composed in the North and South differ? Granger quotes generously from essays. Students would benefit from reading representative excerpts and consulting Granger's commentary in *American Essay Serials from Franklin to Irving*.

2. In the Dogood papers, Benjamin Franklin speaks through the character of Silence Dogood. Why did this sixteen-year-old not speak in his own voice? What were the immediate circumstances that might have forced him to conceal his identity? From a literary point of view, what did he gain from having a woman as his speaker? Does it matter that she is a widow? Might recent events in and around Boston have inspired him to create a widow as his speaker? Did the subjects of the papers influence his decision to create the widow Dogood? For help in answering these questions, consult Richard E. Amacher's *Benjamin Franklin*.

3. Some essayists of the colonial period address the issue of literary criticism, or literary theory. Franklin treats it in the seventh Dogood paper; so do Mather Byles and John Adams address it in several Proteus Echo essays, notably in the third (by Byles) and the tenth (by Adams). Both Proteus Echo essayists want to foster good writing, and they do so by focusing on the prose of characters they create. Byles distinguishes between grubstreet and bombastic writing (by George Brimstone); Adams creates Dick Grubstreet, who personifies and writes grubstreet prose. What do Byles and Adams mean by bombastic and grubstreet? (In his 1755 *Dictionary*, Samuel Johnson defines grubstreet: "originally the name of a street in Moorfields in London, much inhabited by writers of small histories, dictionaries, and temporary poems; whence any mean production is called grubstreet.") What are their impressions of it? How do these styles help the authors encourage good writing? Assistance in answering these questions may be found in *The Other John Adams*, by Benjamin Franklin V.

4. In writing about the Plain-Dealer essays, Elizabeth Christine Cook notes that the prevalence of "allegory, vision, dream literature of all sorts" is almost as common in eighteenth-century American periodicals as in homilies of the fourteenth century. She believes that this reality calls into question the belief that the eighteenth century is purely an age of reason. What examples does she use when supporting her claim? Is her finding convincing? Consult her *Literary Influences in Colonial Newspapers*.

5. Cook also notes that the Addisonian essay is easily imitated, which is an important reason why such essays proliferated in colonial American newspapers. Other than their being easily composed, why else might newspaper editors have been interested in publishing such essays? Frequently, newspapers

carried essays—and poems, too—on the front page. What does this indicate about the newspaper readership, or the editors' impressions of it? For help in answering these and related questions, consult Cook's *Literary Influences in Colonial Newspapers*.

RESOURCES

Biography

Clifford K. Shipton, "Mather Byles," in *Biographical Sketches of Those Who Attended Harvard College in the Classes 1722–1725*, volume 7 of *Sibley's Harvard Graduates* (Boston: Massachusetts Historical Society, 1945), pp. 464–493.
A detailed, wittily written survey of Byles's life based in part on archival material.

Criticism

Richard E. Amacher, *Benjamin Franklin* (New York: Twayne, 1962).
Examines Franklin's life and career, including the composition of the Dogood papers.

Charles E. Clark, *The Public Prints: The Newspaper in Anglo-American Culture, 1665–1740* (New York: Oxford University Press, 1994).
Examines newspapers as a means of understanding the larger culture.

Elizabeth Christine Cook, *Literary Influences in Colonial Newspapers, 1704–1750* (1912; Port Washington, N. Y.: Kennikat Press, 1966).
Surveys literature published in American newspapers during the first half of the eighteenth century.

Benjamin Franklin V, *The Other John Adams, 1705–1740* (Madison, N.J.: Fairleigh Dickinson University Press, 2003).
Examines the career of Adams and analyzes his essays, as well as those by Matthew Adams and Mather Byles.

Norman S. Grabo, "The Journalist as Man of Letters," in *Reappraising Benjamin Franklin: A Bicentennial Perspective*, edited by J. A. Leo Lemay (Newark: University of Delaware Press, 1992), pp. 31–39.
Indicates that Franklin attempted "to elevate his role as journalist to that of man of letters, citizen of an international republic of enlightened reason devoted to universal benevolence and perfection."

Bruce Granger, *American Essay Serials from Franklin to Irving* (Knoxville: University of Tennessee Press, 1978).
A thorough survey of essay series, including those published in colonial American newspapers.

Christine A. Modey, "Newspapers and Magazines," in *The Oxford Handbook of Early American Literature*, edited by Kevin J. Hayes (New York: Oxford University Press, 2008), pp. 301–320.

Discusses American newspapers and magazines published through the American Revolution; topics include "the business of newspapers," "freedom of the press," and "the Stamp Act crisis."

PEOPLE OF INTEREST

John Adams (1705–1740)
Harvard class of 1721, was a poet and essayist who failed in his Newport ministry.

Matthew Adams (circa 1694–1753)
Was the uncle of John Adams and an essayist for *The New-England Courant* and *The New-England Weekly Journal;* he lent books to his friend Benjamin Franklin, as Franklin acknowledges in his *Autobiography.*

Joseph Addison (1672–1719)
Was a British politician, poet, playwright, and essayist whose contributions to *The Tatler* and *The Spectator* influenced eighteenth-century American essayists.

Joseph Breintnall (died 1746)
A Quaker, was a member of Benjamin Franklin's Junto Club; he was also a scrivener, merchant, engraver, and sometime poet.

William Hill Brown (1765–1793)
Was a poet, essayist, playwright, and novelist. His *The Power of Sympathy* (1789) is the first American novel.

William Darby (dates unknown)
Was an Englishman who in 1659 apparently sailed from Bristol for Barbados, though he disembarked on the Eastern Shore of Virginia; he wrote *Ye Bare and Ye Cubbe,* the first dramatic production known to have been performed in British North America.

Thomas Godfrey (1736–1763)
A Philadelphian, was mentored by Benjamin Franklin, Benjamin West, and William Smith; he wrote *The Prince of Parthia* (1765) while living in North Carolina; he also wrote poems in the neoclassical mode.

Ambrose Phillips (1674–1749)
Was an English poet who published essays in *The Free-Thinker,* a newspaper he and Hugh Boulter began in 1718 and that lasted until 1721.

Histories

Historical writing about the English experience in America dates from near the beginning of English presence in the New World. John Smith was the first Englishman to write about North America, including New England, an area he named. Over time, he wrote several books about his experiences in America, which began with his arrival in Virginia in 1607. The titles of his works indicate their contents: *A True Relation of Such Occurrences and Accidents of Noate as Hath Hapned in Virginia since the First Planting of That Collony* (1608), *A Map of Virginia. With a Description of the Countrey, the Commodities, People, Government and Religion* (1612), *A Description of New England; or, the Observations and Discoveries of Captain John Smith* (1616), *The Generall Historie of Virginia, New-England, and the Summer Isles* (1624), and *The True Travels, Adventures, and Observations of Captaine John Smith* (1630). While these books are historical and documentary, significant parts of them are dramatic because of the outsized nature of Smith's personality and ego and because of his numerous exploits. One captivating and now mythic episode, for example, concerns his being saved from possible death by Pocahontas, an event he recounts in *New Englands Trials* (1622). In addition to describing what he saw, relating his experiences, and presenting himself as heroic, Smith's histories serve as promotional tracts, ones that, he hoped, would inspire the English to settle in America, especially in Virginia.

Puritans in New England composed histories primarily to record their experiences, which they viewed as reflecting God's will, so, if their works were published, succeeding generations could learn from the experiences and adjust their behavior as necessary to avoid problems similar to those about which they read. Although their histories sometimes include dramatic events, they lack the flamboyance of Smith's histories, at least partly because the authors, while present in the text, do not focus on themselves. Further, unlike Smith, they typically wrote in a plain style that did not attract attention to itself, that gave the impression that the author is writing transparently, and that led readers to think, therefore, that the events depicted are represented faithfully. In other words, such writing gives the impression of truth plainly told.

The glory of American Puritan histories is William Bradford's *Of Plymouth Plantation*, arguably the most important, most impressive book of any kind written during the entire colonial period, though it was not published until 1856. Before beginning his narrative, Bradford announces that he will write in a plain style, as is indeed the case. The tone of the book is consistently measured. An air of modesty pervades the text: when Bradford refers to himself, for example, he uses the third person. He acknowledges but does not belabor difficulties within the Plymouth Plantation that he long served as governor; his characterization of Thomas Granger's bestiality is a case in point. He cites numerous positive experiences but does not gloat, as when telling of overcoming severe adversity—the voyage to America on the *Mayflower* and surviving a hostile winter during which half the Puritans died—and having the Plymouth colony survive. Unlike some other Puritan historians, he seldom claims that events occur because of God's involvement in or judgment on human affairs. The most detailed account of the

Pilgrim experience in Europe and America, *Of Plymouth Plantation* is a humane book: balanced, understanding, contemplative, humble, moving.

Although John Winthrop did not write an actual history, in the sense of a book-length historical narrative, his journal records information he expected to transform into a history. He details life primarily in Boston for the two decades before the middle of the seventeenth century, from the landing of the *Arbella* at Salem in 1630 until his death in 1649. He writes about things large and small, important and seemingly insignificant. As chief prosecutor of Anne Hutchinson, he writes from a privileged position about her trial during the Antinomian Controversy, for example, a crisis that he believed threatened the very nature of Puritan society. In keeping with the Puritan belief that God causes everything and therefore a historian must record as much as possible, he notes seemingly innocuous events that assume great importance. An example of this occurs when Winthrop tells about a mouse eating a snake, which the minister John Wilson interpreted as God's people devouring the devil.

A measure of the importance of Bradford's and Winthrop's manuscripts is that several historians writing subsequent to them consulted their work and used many of their episodes and facts. A measure of Bradford's and Winthrop's skill may be observed by comparing their work with that of some historians who consulted their manuscripts, such as Bradford's nephew Nathaniel Morton, author of *New-Englands Memoriall* (1669), and William Hubbard, who borrowed from Winthrop when writing *A General History of New England* (composed in the seventeenth century but published in 1815). In discussing Morton's borrowings from Bradford and Hubbard's from Winthrop, Perry Miller and Thomas H. Johnson state that the work of neither later author "contributed anything worth much in itself; the chief value of both books came from the fact that the authors had access to unpublished manuscripts by the two great governors of the colonies at the time of the respective settlements. Morton and Hubbard did little more than plagiarize . . ." (Miller and Johnson, *The Puritans*). Observation, skill, artistry, and accomplishment resided with the originators, not with later users of this material. (Bradford was governor of the Plymouth Colony; Winthrop, of the Massachusetts Bay Colony.)

As Bradford and Winthrop are major historians of the Puritan experience in New England, so is Cotton Mather, who, in *Magnalia Christi Americana* (1702), takes as his subject the church's history in America to the time of his writing, the 1690s. In his effort to record as much as possible, he is similar to Winthrop. His voluminous work consists of seven parts: the founding of New England, lives of governors, lives of ministers, a history of Harvard College, a discussion of church polity, a recording of events that reveal God's pleasure or displeasure (in this, he is again like Winthrop), and a survey of the difficulties the church confronted and overcame. Praised (for its scope and detail) and derided (for lacking unity and objectivity), it is an indispensible book, a judgment acknowledged when, as Babette M. Levy reminds us, in 1963 scholars selected it as one of approximately 1,800 books from the entirety of American writing for inclusion in the White House library, the only colonial American book so honored.

Other histories of New England were published as the eighteenth century progressed. Yet, there are two notable historians of the colonial era who do not focus on religion or write from a religious perspective. Their histories are also less expansive than those by Bradford and especially Mather. These men are Thomas Morton and William Byrd II.

Morton was not a Puritan; he was an Anglican, which is important to consider when reading *New English Canaan* (1637) because the Puritans were in New England partly to escape persecution by Anglicans in England. His book is divided into three sections: one focuses on Indians (he depicts them generally positively), another details the area's natural resources (he wants to encourage English settlement of the area), and the last concerns his interactions with the Puritans. The third of these is by far the best known because it presents an outsider's view of the Puritans as they and Morton come into conflict over his actions and the existence of his small community, Merry Mount. His rendering of events contrasts with Bradford's treatment of the same proceedings in *Of Plymouth Plantation*. Of the historians discussed here, Morton is most like Smith, primarily in the nature of the narrator: in telling his own history, each author is engaging and occasionally preposterous. Neither is stuffy; there is a life to both of them.

Like Smith, Byrd writes about the South, Virginia in particular. Like Smith and Thomas Morton, he is extroverted. Like Morton, he details nature as he finds it. He comments on the Indians he encounters and concludes that the best way to avoid hostilities between them and the settlers is for the two groups to intermarry. He has a point of view; he has prejudices. For example, in his best-known work, *The History of the Dividing Line Betwixt Virginia and North Carolina*, he ridicules and caricatures the North Carolinians with whom he worked, in 1728, in establishing the line that divides Virginia and North Carolina. An interesting aspect of Byrd's dividing line experience is that he wrote about it twice, once in *The History of the Dividing Line* and again in *The Secret History of the Line*. Because Byrd wrote the latter version for his friends, it is occasionally more candid than the other text, as when discussing sexual activity. Although Byrd wrote other histories—*A Progress to the Mines* and *A Journey to the Land of Eden A.D. 1733*—his reputation as a historian rests primarily on *The History of the Dividing Line*. None of these works was published during his lifetime.

TOPICS FOR DISCUSSION AND RESEARCH

1. In commenting about early American histories, Benjamin W. Labaree states that Cotton Mather's *Magnalia Christi Americana* is "by far the best work of history written up to that time in the colonies." "Best" is an elusive term, devoid of meaning unless there is an objective standard of measure; otherwise, it is just a statement of preference. Some informed readers might claim that William Bradford's *Of Plymouth Plantation* is the "best" colonial history. On what basis does Labaree declare Mather's work superior? How does the phrase "work of history" come into play when comparing the histories of Mather and Bradford? The two histories are clearly different, perhaps most obviously because the author of one experienced the described events (Bradford) while the other

did not in most instances (Mather). Does this involvement in or distance from events become an issue when considering "work of history"? For help in answering these questions, consult Labaree's *Colonial Massachusetts*.

2. In analyzing early American promotion literature, Karen Schramm discusses the writings of John Smith and Thomas Morton. What aspects of their works make them promotional? Why do the histories of Bradford, John Winthrop, and William Byrd not qualify as promotion literature? In "Promotion Literature," Schramm provides useful information.

3. Naoki Onishi investigates the characteristics of Puritan historiography and demonstrates how Puritans employed them in their various histories. What are these characteristics? Where and to what degree are they present in works by Bradford, Winthrop, and Cotton Mather? Onishi provides guidance for answering these questions in "Puritan Historians and Historiography."

4. Bradford and Morton are often considered together because they treat the same issue: the conflict between the Puritans and Morton, which the Puritans won. In observing that Bradford is given more space than Morton in anthologies of American literature and is the subject of more critical attention, Michael J. Colacurcio asks a provocative question: "Granted that history is written by the winners, can we yet discover any apolitical reason why Bradford's annals of certain weather-beaten Pilgrims have proved more largely repeatable than Morton's racier account of love and sport in the New World Canaan?" In other words, why is Bradford more highly valued than Morton? Read Colacurcio's answer and ask if it is convincing.

RESOURCES

Biography

Benjamin W. Labaree, *Colonial Massachusetts, A History* (Millwood, N.Y.: KTO Press, 1979).
Introduces each of fifteen chapters by focusing on a person representative of the topic of each chapter, such as Jonathan Edwards for provincial culture.

Criticism

Michael J. Colacurcio, *Godly Letters: The Literature of the American Puritans* (Notre Dame, Ind.: University of Notre Dame Press, 2006).
Demonstrates that Puritan culture valued words highly and produced a significant number of excellent books and that some of the writers were "men of rare genius as surely as they were old-time dogmatists."

Babette M. Levy, *Cotton Mather* (Boston: Twayne, 1979).
A reliable consideration of Mather's works.

Perry Miller and Thomas H. Johnson, Introductions, *The Puritans*, edited by Miller and Johnson (New York: American Book Company, 1938).
Comments authoritatively on various types and subjects of Puritan writing, including histories, and provides generous selections from Puritan authors.

Naoki Onishi, "Puritan Historians and Historiography," in *The Oxford Handbook of Early American Literature*, edited by Kevin J. Hayes (New York: Oxford University Press, 2008), pp. 93–113.
From reading the histories of various Puritans—including Bradford, Winthrop, and Cotton Mather—Onishi identifies aspects of Puritan historiography.

Karen Schramm, "Promotion Literature," in *The Oxford Handbook of Early American Literature*, edited by Kevin J. Hayes (New York: Oxford University Press, 2008), pp. 69–89.
Discusses various features of promotion literature, including its language, attitude toward the environment, and what is omitted from it.

PEOPLE OF INTEREST

William Hubbard (circa 1621–1704)
Member of the first graduating class of Harvard College (1642), was a minister who wrote the derivative *A General History of New England* (1815).

Nathaniel Morton (1613–1686)
Was active in the political affairs of Plymouth colony and wrote *New-Englands Memoriall* (1669), based on the manuscript of his uncle, William Bradford.

John Wilson (circa 1591–1667)
Was a Congregational minister who wrote anagrams and poems, including *A Song, or, Story, for Lasting Remembrance of Divers Famous Works* (1626).

Indians and Captivity Narratives

Whether Pocahontas actually saved John Smith when her father, Powhatan, was preparing to have him killed in 1607 is open to question. Real or not, this event became the earliest mythic image to emerge from the English presence in North America. For the remainder of the colonial period, the relationship between settlers, mostly English, and Indians was uncertain, with periods of peace and others of warfare. Warfare came soon to Jamestown, where Powhatan attacked in 1622, killing over 300 settlers. This conflict would last for almost a decade. Smith writes about the Pocahontas episode and Indian-Jamestown relations in *New Englands Trials* (1622).

When the Pilgrims (Separatists) arrived at Plymouth in 1620, Wampanoags helped them survive by teaching them how to plant corn, showing them where to fish, and so forth. The second mythic image in America's history is probably that of the landing of the Pilgrims at Plymouth Rock, along with what is a called the first Thanksgiving, a 1621 feast involving Wampanoags and Pilgrims, an event that symbolizes a harmonious relationship between dissimilar people and cultures. After this first Thanksgiving, relative Indian-settler harmony lasted in New England for fifteen years, until the Pequot War of 1636–1638, in which the Pequots were slaughtered. This conflict constitutes the beginning of significant hostility between Indians and settlers in New England. The best source for information about the Pilgrims' interactions with Indians is William Bradford's *Of Plymouth Plantation*.

As midcentury approached, serious Indian-settler hostilities occurred in New Netherlands (New York), Connecticut, and Virginia. The conflict that dwarfed all others, though, was King Philip's War (1675–1676). This was and remains the deadliest war in American history, when considered as the percentage of the population killed. The results were so devastating that the war effectively broke the Indians' resistance to the colonists' continued settlement of Indian land. In the most compelling book about the war, *The Name of War*, Jill Lepore argues that the manner in which it was written about hardened perceptions of the Indians and the settlers and made distinct and permanent the boundaries between them.

The longest conflict between Indians and settlers began in 1689. Known as the French and Indian War (actually a series of wars), it lasted until 1763. In the eighteenth century, other hostilities occurred in North Carolina (the Tuscarora War), South Carolina (the Yemasee War), Maine (Abenaki Indians against the settlers), Pennyslvania (the Paxton Riots), and elsewhere. Helpful books dealing with the relations between Indians and settlers include James Axtell's *The European and the Indian* and Daniel K. Richter's *Facing East from Indian Country*.

Not all relations between Indians and settlers were hostile. Pocahontas married the Englishman John Rolfe, for example, and other intermarriage occurred. Roger Williams is one who sympathized with Indians to the degree that he argued against the settlers' practice of taking land belonging to Indians, published a history of them, and wrote understanding poems about them. One of the Puritans' goals in America was converting Indians—often perceived as the devil's representatives—to Christianity, though few ministers made much of an effort to do so. One who did, John Eliot, was so dedicated to this calling that he composed the first book in an Indian language to be published in America—*A Primer or Catechism in the Massachusetts Indian Language* (1654?)—and, in a major undertaking, translated the Bible into Algonquian. He became and still is known as the Apostle to the Indians. Grindall Rawson translated Thomas Shepard's *The Sincere Convert* and John Cotton's catechism *Milk for Babes* into Massachusett, the first in 1689 and the second in 1691.

An important American literary genre resulted from settlers' interactions with Indians. This is the Indian captivity narrative, which tells of English-speaking settlers' (usually women's) experiences while involuntarily held by Indians. (Non-English examples of this genre date from no later than the sixteenth century.) The earliest American example is probably Smith's account of being captured by Powhatan in Virginia in 1607; he was, according to him, saved from death by Powhatan's daughter, Pocahontas. The first American book devoted entirely to captivity is that of Mary White Rowlandson published in 1682, six years after experiencing the events she details. Subsequent colonial American Indian captivity narratives include Hannah Dustan's, in Cotton Mather's *Magnalia Christi Americana* (1702); the Quaker Elizabeth Hanson's *God's Mercy Surmounting Man's Cruelty* (1728); and *A Journal of the Captivity of Jean Lowry and Her Children* (1760).

These narratives by women were instructional in that they related generally unknown details about Indians and evidenced the hand of God in saving the captive. Further, Kathryn Zabelle Derounian-Stodola notes that some such accounts—including Rowlandson's and Dustan's—serve as anti-Indian propaganda *(Women's Indian Captivity Narratives)*. She also identifies common elements in women's narratives: the absence of male family members, a pregnant woman or one who recently gave birth, a child who is killed, and children who survived an Indian attack but who are separated from the family. In other words, the narratives are dramatic, riveting. These women depict themselves differently: Rowlandon and Hanson are largely passive in their narratives; Dustan is active in hers (she scalped ten of her captors); Lowry is pitiable.

TOPICS FOR DISCUSSION AND RESEARCH

1. Writings about Indians by colonists who knew them or who recorded experiences of others who knew them depict them generally but not exclusively negatively. Students would benefit from examining settlers' characterizations of the Indians and comparing the characterizations with the historical record. Are the accounts generally accurate, as best as can be determined? If not, which ones are not, and why? Do the authors or recounters of inaccurate or questionable depictions have reasons for shading or avoiding the truth? Any reliable recent history of Indian-settler relations will provide information for answering these questions. See, for example, Jill Lepore's *The Name of War,* including chapter 4 and the answering of the question "Why was John Sassamon killed?" Also consult Neal Salisbury's introduction to Mary Rowlandson's captivity narrative.

2. Indian-colonist relations have inspired serious writers, one of the foremost being James Fenimore Cooper in several novels including *The Last of the Mohicans*

(1826) and *The Deerslayer* (1841), both set during the French and Indian War. How does he depict Indians from the colonial period? Are they noble? Ignoble? Both, according to the individual or group? Cooper's most important Indian is Chingachgook. What is his role in *The Last of the Mohicans* and *The Deerslayer*? Is he a believable character? Are Cooper's Indians generally believable characters? What other post-eighteenth-century authors treat, in their creative work, Indians of the colonial period? How do these authors depict the Indians?

3. Indian captivity narratives raise numerous questions that students would benefit from pondering. Why, for example, did the Indians take captives when doing so would have been troublesome to some degree? In narratives by women, the question of their possible sexual relations with Indians is sometimes raised. Mary Rowlandson, for example, states that her captors did not violate her sexually. Although no one now can know for certain what happened in this regard, why might women such as Rowlandson have made a point of denying sexual contact with their captors? Why did women captives write about their experiences? In order to provide catharsis? To provide a historical record? To achieve fame? Why were such narratives popular? To answer these and collateral questions, consult James Axtell's *The European and the Indian*, Kathryn Zabelle Derounian-Stodola's *Women's Indian Captivity Narratives*, Neal Salisbury's introduction to Rowlandson's narrative, Alden T. Vaughan and Edward W. Clark's *Puritans among the Indians*, and similar sources.

RESOURCES

Criticism

James Axtell, *The European and the Indian: Essays in the Ethnohistory of Colonial North America* (New York: Oxford University Press, 1981).
Offers an ethnohistorical approach to "the social and cultural interactions of the various peoples in the greater northeastern quadrant of colonial North America."

William Bradford, *Of Plymouth Plantation*, edited by Samuel Eliot Morison (1952; New York: Knopf, 1966).
A detailed, first-hand account of the Pilgrim experience in Europe and America by the most important Pilgrim in America.

Mitchell Robert Breitwieser, *American Puritanism and the Defense of Mourning: Religion, Grief, and Ethnology in Mary White Rowlandson's Captivity Narrative* (Madison: University of Wisconsin Press, 1990).
Argues that Mary Rowlandson sublimates her real emotions in deference to seventeenth-century Puritan values while attempting to retain grief at the death of her daughter and refusing to characterize her captors as totally evil.

Kathryn Zabelle Derounian-Stodola, Introduction, *Women's Indian Captivity Narratives*, edited by Derounian-Stodola (New York: Penguin, 1998).
Examines the narratives of women captured by the Indians and reproduces ten of their texts, beginning with Rowlandson's (1682) and concluding with one published in 1892.

Derounian-Stodola and James Arthur Levernier, *The Indian Captivity Narrative,
1550–1900* (New York: Twayne, 1993).
Analyzes captivity narratives published over a large time span, including that of
Rowlandson, while acknowledging narratives by and about captives other than
European Americans and while attempting to debunk stereotypes.

Rebecca Blevins Faery, *Cartographies of Desire: Captivity, Race, and Sex in the
Shaping of an American Nation* (Norman: University of Oklahoma Press,
1999).
Treats "American accounts of white women's captivity and of self-sacrificing
Indian women as 'liminal narratives' . . . where cultures meet and are mutually
transformed."

David D. Hall, Introduction, *Puritans in the New World: A Critical Anthology*,
edited by Hall (Princeton: Princeton University Press, 2004).
Argues against viewing Puritans as a monolith and insists that they must be
considered "on their own terms," which Hall facilitates by reproducing numerous
Puritan texts.

Karen Ordahl Kupperman, *Indians and English: Facing Off in Early America*
(Ithaca, N.Y.: Cornell University Press, 2000).
Examines relationships between Indians and settlers along the Atlantic coast,
detailing each group's uncertainties and fears.

Jill Lepore, *The Name of War: King Philip's War and the Origins of American Identity*
(New York: Knopf, 1998).
Argues that writings about King Philip's War clarified the previously blurred
distinctions between Indians and settlers and, as a result, hardened the feelings
each group had toward the other.

Daniel K. Richter, *Facing East from Indian Country: A Native History of Early
America* (Cambridge, Mass.: Harvard University Press, 2001).
Discusses the development of early America from the Indian point of view, look-
ing eastward.

Neal Salisbury, Introduction, *The Soveraignty and Goodness of God, Together with
the Faithfulness of His Promises Displayed, Being a Narrative of the Captivity
and Restoration of Mrs. Mary Rowlandson*, by Rowlandson, edited by Salisbury (Boston: Bedford Books 1997).
Places Rowlandson's narrative in historical, social, and literary context.

Gordon M. Sayre, Introduction, *Olaudah Equiano, Mary Rowlandson, and Others:
American Captivity Narratives*, edited by Sayre (Boston: Houghton Mifflin,
2000).
Discusses captivity narratives published from 1557 to 1906, including Rowlandson's and two related by Cotton Mather.

John Smith, *New Englands Trials. Declaring the Successe of 26. Ships Employed
Thither within These Six Years* (London: W. Jones, 1622).

This revised edition of the book initially published in 1620 contains John Smith's first account of his rescue by Pocahontas.

Teresa A. Toulouse, *The Captive's Position: Female Narrative, Male Identity, and Royal Authority in Colonial New England* (Philadelphia: University of Pennsylvania Press, 2007).
Examines "how and why religious narratives of *women's* captivity came so powerfully to represent a distinctive identity position for powerful second- and third-generation colonial *men.*"

Alden T. Vaughan and Edward W. Clark, Introductions, *Puritans among the Indians: Accounts of Captivity and Redemption, 1676–1724,* edited by Vaughan and Clark (Cambridge, Mass.: Belknap Press of Harvard University Press, 1981).
Analyzes New England captivity narratives and reproduces four of them, in addition to accounts of captivity reported by Increase Mather and Cotton Mather.

Phillip M. White, *American Indian Chronology: Chronologies of the American Mosaic* (Westport, Conn.: Greenwood Press, 2006).
Provides a chronology of important events involving Indians from prehistoric times to the twenty-first century.

PEOPLE OF INTEREST

Hannah Dustan (Duston, Dustin) (1657–1736)
Was captured by Abenaki Indians in 1697; her account of captivity was delivered from the pulpit by Cotton Mather, who also recorded it in his *Magnalia Christi Americana* (1702).

John Eliot (1604–1690)
The Apostle to the Indians, was dedicated to converting Indians to Christianity, going so far as to translate the Bible into Algonquian (1663).

Elizabeth Hanson (1684–1737)
Was a Quaker whose diary of her five-month captivity by Indians in 1724 was published, four years later, as *God's Mercy Surmounting Man's Cruelty.*

Jean Lowry (flourished 1756)
Taken captive with two children while she was pregnant and wrote about her experiences in a tone of self-pity.

Grindall Rawson (1659–1715)
Was a member of the Harvard class of 1678 and a minister who preached to the Indians in their own language.

Thomas Shepard (1605–1649)
Minister and a founder of Harvard College, is best known as the author of *The Sincere Convert* (1641).

Poetry

Published in Cambridge, Massachusetts Bay, in 1640, only twenty years after the landing of the *Mayflower* at Plymouth, *The Whole Booke of Psalmes Faithfully Translated into English Metre* (1640), better known as *The Bay Psalm Book*, is both the earliest book published in America of which a copy is known to exist and the first published volume of verse by Americans, ministers who were transplanted Englishmen. As a result, it initiated the American poetic tradition. Although the quality of colonial American verse is, with notable exceptions, not great, the quantity is significant, perhaps surprisingly so given the stereotyped, incorrect view of the earliest generations of Americans, especially the Puritans, as being indifferent to, if not antagonistic toward, beauty and art.

The case of Anne Bradstreet corrects this misconception. Because her father, Thomas Dudley, and husband, Simon Bradstreet, were important men in Massachusetts Bay, she was a woman of relative privilege. She was also educated. Despite the many onerous demands placed on women in mid-seventeenth-century America, including Bradstreet, she was inclined to write verse and found time to do it. Her family knew of her activity and so approved of it that her brother-in-law, John Woodbridge, took her poems to England, possibly surreptitiously, and had them published in 1650 as *The Tenth Muse Lately Sprung up in America*, the first book of original poetry by a resident of America. For the next century and a quarter, many colonists, mainly men, courted the poetic muse.

By almost any measure, the most significant seventeenth-century American poets were the Puritans Bradstreet, Michael Wigglesworth, and Edward Taylor, the last of whom wrote into the next century. Although Bradstreet's poems include religious elements, she was not primarily a religious poet, as were Wigglesworth and Taylor. In the long "The Day of Doom," Wigglesworth attempts to frighten readers into embracing Christ by depicting Him meting out justice on Judgment Day. The book of which this poem is the major part, *The Day of Doom* (1662), became the first American best seller. Like Bradstreet but unlike Wigglesworth, Taylor did not intend his poems to be published. He composed his major poems, *Preparatory Meditations*—two series of poems; over two hundred poems, total—to prepare himself for administering the Lord's Supper in his role as minister in the small community of Westfield, Massachusetts.

Poems by Bradstreet and Taylor are probably included in every anthology including colonial American literature, though Wigglesworth is generally ignored because his major work is lengthy and is considered by some as more versified doctrine than art. Yet, Wigglesworth is far from the only seventeenth-century poet to be generally ignored; almost all the others are, too, except in specialized studies by scholars of early American literature. Many of these relatively unknown poets wrote verse of some interest and accomplishment. In *The Simple Cobler of Aggawam in America* (1647), for example, Nathaniel Ward is both serious and lighthearted as the narrator argues against religious extremism because he favors a unified society; he depicts women's fashion as silly. Most readers of this work consider it a satire.

Other poets of merit are even less known than Ward. These include Benjamin Tompson, Ward's approximate poetic equal. Tompson's *New Englands Crisis* (1676) presents King Philip's War—then being fought—as a crucial event in the history of Massachusetts Bay. John Saffin wrote, in his notebook, poems that express his genuine emotion as he writes about the death of his children. Some writers present verse in their prose works. Edward Johnson, for example, includes some engaging poems in *A History of New England* (1654), a work better known as *Wonder-Working Providence*. So, too, do notable verses appear in Roger Williams's *A Key into the Language of America* (1643); these poems are significant especially because they present the Puritans as no better than the Indians.

The non-Puritan seventeenth-century South produced some ballads and occasional poems. One reason for the paucity of southern poetry and writing generally is that the area had no printer until the 1680s, in Maryland. Some of the people writing verse were notables, including John Smith, William Strachey, and George Sandys.

In New England, religious verse continued being written well into the eighteenth century, though secular poetry became increasingly frequent. Among the first poems of the new century, for example, are secular ones by Sarah Kemble Knight, who wrote six in a journal (not published until 1825) that details her trip by horseback from Boston to New Haven, and on to New York, in 1704–1705. As time passed, American poets were inspired by and wrote in imitation of the verse of Alexander Pope, particularly his use of heroic couplets. Among the earliest of these American neoclassical poets are the ministers John Adams and Mather Byles, writing in the 1720s when they were in their early twenties. Pope's influence continued for most of the century.

The most important southern poem of eighteenth-century colonial America was published early: Ebenezer Cook's *The Sot-Weed Factor* (1708), which satirizes the naive expectations of Englishmen who immigrate to Maryland; this poem arguably initiates the rich tradition of southern humor. It inspired John Barth's novel *The Sot-Weed Factor* (1960), whose protagonist is Ebenezer Cook. Another Maryland resident, Richard Lewis, over thirty years Cook's junior, wrote nature poems, one of which is, according to Richard Beale Davis, "the most effective neoclassical poem of colonial America," "A Journey from Patapsco to Annapolis, April 4, 1730." Maryland, Virginia, and South Carolina newspapers published satirical poems around midcentury. Southerners wrote pastorals, religious poems, verse about gallantry and patriotism, and occasional poems, among other kinds of verse.

Almost no poetry was published in New York and Pennsylvania before 1776.

The American Revolution inspired verse by such poets as John Trumbull (parts of *M'Fingal,* 1776), Philip Freneau ("A Political Litany," 1775), and the Loyalist Joseph Stansbury (the song "When Good Queen Elizabeth Governed the Realm," 1774), as well as the song "Yankee Doodle," originally a British composition that derided Americans' provincialism but that the colonists made into a statement of emerging national pride.

TOPICS FOR DISCUSSION AND RESEARCH

1. Anne Bradstreet wrote primarily for herself, though family and friends knew of and admired her verse. Edward Taylor wrote entirely for himself, to prepare for administering the Lord's Supper. The other major seventeenth-century American poet, Michael Wigglesworth, wrote his most significant poem, "The Day of Doom," for an audience that he perceived as losing—or having lost—the religious commitment of earlier generations. Students would benefit from pondering the effect of the intended audience on the creation of these Puritan poets' works. Within this context, how do the private poems of Bradstreet and Taylor differ from the public verse of Wigglesworth? Further, how do some of Bradstreet's most ambitious poems, such as "The Foure Monarchies" and the quaternions, differ from Taylor's most important effort, the two series of poems titled *Preparatory Meditations*? Reading selected verses by these poets will help answer these questions. For assistance, consult such works as Charlotte Gordon's *Mistress Bradstreet*, Ronald A. Bosco's introduction to *The Poems of Michael Wigglesworth*, and Karl Keller's *The Example of Edward Taylor*.

2. Well into the 1960s and beyond, scholars of American verse generally derided Puritan poetry as artless. Among the later critics to object to this characterization is Robert Daly. In *God's Altar*, the first serious study of American Puritan poetry, he posits, among other things, that Puritan poets "knew that part of their work in this world was to wean their affections from the unmixed love of it. But they also knew that this world was God's metaphor for His communicable glories and that another part of their duty was to see and utter that metaphor, to use the figural value of this world to turn their attention and affections to the next." Students would benefit from examining metaphors in selected Puritan poems and considering them within the context of Daly's statement. The poems of Taylor are especially fruitful in this regard.

3. Kenneth Silverman has determined that six volumes of verse were published in the South during the entirety of the colonial era, a number so modest partly because of the dearth of publishers in this area of the country. He observes that because of this lack of publishing opportunities, "Southern poets never formed a habit of allusion to the local past, a memory of earlier writers, in short no literary tradition such as the long succession of New England elegies provided." As a result, "poetry in the South remained the leisure-hour dabbling of unambitious amateurs, some of whom gathered into literary clubs." Yet, Richard Beale Davis observes that "there are scores of examples of eighteenth-century mourning poems in the South," while acknowledging that these elegies were written after the New England tradition of such poems had ended. Students would benefit from asking if these southern elegies constitute a "literary tradition," as Silverman implies they do not. Students should also examine the arguments of Silverman and Davis and the evidence they use in their claims about elegies in the North and South. Is one scholar more convincing than the other? If so, why? How do these writers characterize the elegies of the two areas? How are northern and southern elegies similar? Different?

4. Silverman observes that poetic expression in the colonial North and South
is most different in its depiction of America: the northern poets idealize the
country but the southern ones do not. What examples does he give to support
this claim? How convincing is his argument?

RESOURCES

Biography
Charlotte Gordon, *Mistress Bradstreet: The Untold Life of America's First Poet* (New
York: Little, Brown, 2005).
The most modern and complete biography of Anne Bradstreet.

Criticism
Ronald A. Bosco, Introduction, *The Poems of Michael Wigglesworth* (Lanham,
Md.: University Press of America, 1989).
Surveys criticism of Michael Wigglesworth's poetry and offers new interpreta-
tions of it.

Robert Daly, *God's Altar: The World and the Flesh in Puritan Poetry* (Berkeley:
University of California Press, 1978).
Argues, against received wisdom, that the Puritans were not hostile toward art
and that their beliefs led to the creation of it.

Richard Beale Davis, *Intellectual Life in the Colonial South, 1585–1763*, volume 3
(Knoxville: University of Tennessee Press, 1978), pp. 1330–1506.
Thoroughly discusses southern literature to 1763.

Jane Donahue Eberwein, Introductions, *Early American Poetry: Selections from
Bradstreet, Taylor, Dwight, Freneau, and Bryant*, edited by Eberwein (Madi-
son: University of Wisconsin Press, 1978).
Comments in detail about five major American poets from Bradstreet to
Bryant.

Karl Keller, *The Example of Edward Taylor* (Amherst: University of Massachusetts
Press, 1975).
Examines Edward Taylor's life and work.

Harrison T. Meserole, *Seventeenth-Century American Poetry* (Garden City, N.Y.:
Doubleday, 1968); republished as *American Poetry of the Seventeenth Century*
(University Park: Pennsylvania State University Press, 1985).
This major anthology of seventeenth-century verse establishes a hierarchy of early
American poets, identifying Wigglesworth, Bradstreet, and Taylor as the major
writers, others as minor writers, and yet others as representative writers.

Kenneth Silverman, Introductions, *Colonial American Poetry*, edited by Silverman
(New York: Hafner, 1968).
Examines various aspects of colonial American verse, from promotional poetry
to the rising empire.

PEOPLE OF INTEREST

John Adams (1705–1740)
Minister, poet, and essayist, was among the first Americans to write verse in the neoclassical mode.

Simon Bradstreet (1603–1697)
Was active in the political life of Massachusetts Bay, including serving as governor. His first wife was Anne Bradstreet, who wrote him moving love poems.

Thomas Dudley (1576–1653)
Was the father of Anne Dudley Bradstreet and longtime governor of Massachusetts Bay; he composed at least one poem, which was discovered in his pocket following his death.

Philip Freneau (1752–1832)
Was the major American poet of the years immediately following the American Revolution.

Edward Johnson (1598–1672)
Was an English soldier who helped found Woburn, Massachusetts Bay.

Sarah Kemble Knight (1666–1727)
Is noted for her diary of an arduous trip by horseback in 1704–1705. It depicts her as a strong, no-nonsense woman.

Richard Lewis (circa 1700–1734)
A Maryland teacher, was one of the major eighteenth-century American nature poets.

Alexander Pope (1688–1744)
Was the major and the most influential eighteenth-century English poet.

John Saffin (1626–1710)
Was a successful Boston lawyer and businessman.

George Sandys (1578–1644)
Served on the Virginia governor's council and translated Ovid's *Metamorphoses*.

William Strachey (1572–1621)
Member of the Virginia Company of London, wrote about his brief residence in the colony of Jamestown, which he served as secretary.

John Woodbridge (1613–1695)
Took the poems of Anne Bradstreet, his sister-in-law, to England, where they were published as *The Tenth Muse* (1650), for which he wrote a prefatory poem.

Politics (Massachusetts)

Until the American Revolution, English-speaking colonies operated under charters granted by the Crown. James I awarded the first of them in 1606 to the London Company, which the next year established Jamestown, the initial permanent American English colony. Colonial governance, though, had the greatest ramifications in Massachusetts Bay because its dealings with the Crown led, ultimately, to the Revolution.

Before Massachusetts Bay, an English colony existed in what is now the state of Massachusetts. This was the Plymouth Colony, settled by a group that arrived on the *Mayflower* in 1620. Because these Puritans, known as Pilgrims, failed to inhabit land controlled by the London Company, to which they were entitled, they needed authorization to occupy the area where they lived. This was granted the next year and again in 1630 by the Council for New England. Even though these colonists swore allegiance to the Crown, they were governed by the Mayflower Compact, which bound them to create laws for the common good and allowed for majority rule, for example. In 1643, the colony joined the colonies of Massachusetts Bay, Connecticut, and New Haven in establishing the New England Confederation, largely for reasons of defense. The Plymouth Colony lasted until 1691, when it was absorbed, by charter, into the Massachusetts Bay Colony. The Plymouth Colony is of great importance. One reason is that it endured for seventy years as a religious society, the effects of which are still evident in America, as indicated by the continued concern about the proper balance between church and state. Another is that the most important person of the colony, William Bradford, wrote the history of the Pilgrims' experiences in Europe and America in a manuscript ultimately published as *Of Plymouth Plantation,* probably the most important book written in the entirety of the colonial period in America.

The people who settled Massachusetts Bay were different from the Pilgrims, though both groups were Puritans who wanted to worship as they pleased, which was impossible in England, where they were persecuted for their nonconformist ways. The difference is technical: although both groups separated physically from their native land, the Pilgrims also rejected the Church of England because its numerous impurities, from their perspective, caused them to consider it no church at all; the later group was non-Separatist in the sense that its people remained members of the Anglican church, hoping to reform it from within. The later group also operated under different authority from that of the Pilgrims. The New England Company held the patent to land that included what is now Salem, Massachusetts. Here, Puritans under the leadership of John Endecott settled in 1628. The following year, the Company's successor, the Massachusetts Bay Company, received a charter for this land. Because the charter failed to stipulate the place of the Company's annual meeting, the Company located the government in New England and made the colony self-governing. The great migration of Puritans from England to America began in 1630. Led by John Winthrop on the *Arbella,* this group settled first in Salem but soon populated other areas, including Boston. The government consisted of the governor (Winthrop), his assistants, and the General Court.

The 1629 charter figured in two of the early crises in Massachusetts Bay, both in the 1630s. One involved Roger Williams, who believed, among other things, that the charter could not usurp the natural ownership of Indian land by granting it to settlers. He was exiled from the colony. Another concerned Thomas Morton, who threatened the Puritans by, among other actions, selling guns to Indians and consorting with Indian women. After being forced to return to England, he protested his treatment at the hands of the Puritans by working to have the charter revoked. Although he succeeded in convincing authorities, events kept the Crown from pursuing the matter.

An important development in the governance of Massachusetts Bay occurred in 1641 when the General Court adopted *The Body of Liberties*. Written mainly by Nathaniel Ward, it was the first code of laws in New England, one that protected commoners from the power of magistrates. *The Body of Liberties* remained in effect until expanded upon by the *The Book of General Lavves and Libertyes* in 1648. These two documents permitted several freedoms, some of which are incorporated in the Bill of Rights of the United States Constitution.

In 1684, Englishman Edward Randolph, after spending time in Massachusetts Bay, reported to the Crown that the colonists were not obeying certain British laws. As a result, the 1629 charter was annulled. Smarting from the unpopular actions of the Massachusetts governor, Sir Edmund Andros, in 1688 Increase Mather sailed for England to consult with James II, hoping to have the original charter restored. Though he failed in this regard, he secured a new charter, that of 1691, which brought Plymouth and Maine into Massachusetts and allowed for the Crown to appoint colonial governors, but permitted an elected legislature. With this charter, Puritan governance in Massachusetts ended, and secular rule was established. For half a century, though, the colonists attempted to reduce or neutralize the influence of the Crown and the royal governors. The charter remained in effect until annulled by the Massachusetts Government Act of 1774.

Although dating the beginning of American revolutionary sentiment precisely is impossible, one could argue that it dates from 1761 when James Otis challenged the constitutionality of the Writs of Assistance, which gave search warrants to customs officials. Because of debts incurred during the French and Indian War, England needed revenue, which it attempted to raise by taxing colonists. Passed by Parliament in 1764, the Sugar Act constituted the first attempt to reduce English debt by taxing the colonists. The colonists objected, and the phrase "no taxation without representation" helped rally support against the Sugar Act and English heavy-handedness. Subsequent acts further angered the colonists. These include the Currency Act (1764), the Quartering Act (1765), the Stamp Act (1765), the Declaratory Act (1766), the Townshend Acts (1767), the Tea Act (1773), the Coercive Acts (1774), and the New England Restraining Act (1775). These acts and other events created a revolutionary fervor. Fighting between colonists and English troops occurred at Lexington and Concord in 1775, and two months later the Battle of Bunker Hill was fought. The next year, on 4 July, the American colonies declared their freedom from England with the Declaration of Independence.

TOPICS FOR DISCUSSION AND RESEARCH

1. Two significant early American authors caused major problems for the Puritans in the 1630s. In different ways, Roger Williams (now venerated) and Thomas Morton (less known but important in his own right) challenged the legitimacy of the 1629 charter, Morton going so far as to urge its revocation, and almost succeeding. Williams thought the charter invalid on the issue of land ownership; Morton believed that the Puritans had acquired land illegitimately. What were the details of these men's complaints? Were their objections legitimate? Did one or the other have ulterior motives? Did the Puritan establishment have ulterior motives in its dealings with Williams in particular? Help in answering these questions may be found in Donald F. Connors's *Thomas Morton* and Edwin S. Gaustad's *Roger Williams*.

2. Students would benefit from understanding the importance of seventeenth-century ministers in society at large, especially in political matters, and comprehending the nature of charters and their effect on American colonies. Increase Mather and the 1691 charter constitute an example. Not only was Mather possibly the major American minister of his time, but he also served as president of Harvard College and was one of the earliest American diplomats. When the charter of 1629 was annulled, he sailed to England to seek its renewal directly from the Catholic James II. Although he ultimately failed because James abdicated the throne, he succeeded in influencing William III in the drafting of a new charter, one less onerous than might reasonably have been expected. Mather even influenced the appointment of the person who succeeded the unpalatable Sir Edmund Andros as governor of Massachusetts, Sir William Phips. Aside from enlarging the territory of Massachusetts, dictating the appointment of colonial governors by the Crown, and permitting the election of legislatures, how does the 1691 charter that Mather influenced differ from the one of 1629? Importantly, how did the new charter differ from the old one on the issue of the franchise? What were the practical effects of some of these changes? What is the significance of Mather's representing the colony in England? What does this indicate about his reputation among his fellow Massachusetts colonists? What does it imply about the role of religion in colonial politics? For assistance in answering these and collateral questions, consult Michael G. Hall's *The Last American Puritan* and Benjamin W. Labaree's *Colonial Massachusetts*.

3. In *Letters from a Farmer in Pennsylvania* (1768), John Dickinson wrote against the 1767 Townshend Acts. In particular, he encouraged colonists to petition against the acts. On what basis did he and others object to them? How successful were his efforts? For assistance in answering these questions, consult Milton E. Flower's *John Dickinson, Conservative Revolutionary*.

4. Why did the colonists object to paying taxes imposed by England? The colonists benefited from England's fighting and winning the French and Indian War, which depleted English resources. Did the colonists have a responsibility to provide some degree of recompense? Were they ingrates? Under what authority could they challenge England on this or any other issue? What, really, were the colonists' complaints? For help in answering these questions, consult Fred Anderson's *The War That Made America*.

RESOURCES

Biography

Michael G. Hall, *The Last American Puritan: The Life of Increase Mather, 1639–1723* (Middletown, Conn.: Wesleyan University Press, 1988).
A thorough biography of Increase Mather.

Samuel Eliot Morison, *Builders of the Bay Colony* (1930; revised, Boston: Houghton Mifflin, 1962).
Biographies of some of the major figures of the first generation in the Massachusetts Bay Colony.

Criticism

Fred Anderson, *The War That Made America: A Short History of the French and Indian War* (New York: Viking, 2005).
Discusses the French and Indian War, including, in the aftermath, English taxation of American colonies.

Bernard Bailyn, *The Ordeal of Thomas Hutchinson* (Cambridge, Mass.: Belknap Press of Harvard University Press, 1974).
Examines the American Loyalists by focusing on the most important of them, Thomas Hutchinson.

Richard D. Brown and Jack Tager, *Massachusetts: A Concise History* (Amherst: University of Massachusetts Press, 2000).
Provides a succinct, helpful history of Massachusetts, from the beginning to the 1970s.

Richard L. Bushman, *King and People in Provincial Massachusetts* (Chapel Hill: University of North Carolina Press, 1985).
Examines the Massachusetts political culture from the time of the second charter (1691) to the American Revolution.

Donald F. Connors, *Thomas Morton* (New York: Twayne, 1969).
Analyzes Thomas Morton's career and analyzes his efforts to have the 1629 charter revoked.

Encyclopedia of American History, edited by Richard B. Morris and Jeffrey B. Morris, sixth edition (New York: Harper & Row, 1982).
A reliable source of information about most of the important events of the colonial period and beyond.

Milton E. Flower, *John Dickinson, Conservative Revolutionary* (Charlottesville: University Press of Virginia, 1983).
Focuses on John Dickinson's political career and writings, emphasizing the subject's political moderation within a radical context.

Edwin S. Gaustad, *Roger Williams* (New York: Oxford University Press, 2005).
Discusses the career and ideas of Roger Williams, including his thoughts about land ownership.

Benjamin W. Labaree, *Colonial Massachusetts, A History* (Millwood, N.Y.: KTO
    Press, 1979).
A history of colonial Massachusetts that treats "social, economic, and cultural as
well as political developments."

PERSON OF INTEREST

James Otis (1725–1783)
Lawyer, pamphleteer, and brother of the author Mercy Otis Warren, was a prominent proponent of colonial liberty.

Religion

Personae non gratae in England because they refused to obey the Acts of Uniformity of the mid sixteenth century, the group known as the Pilgrims fled to Holland where, in time, they feared losing their individuality and religious focus because they were becoming assimilated into Dutch culture. To avoid this fate and to worship as they pleased, they sailed for North America aboard the *Mayflower*, landing at Plymouth in late 1620. Thus was established the first sustained English religious community in North America. The Pilgrims were Separatists, people who removed themselves physically and also theologically from the Church of England, which they thought impure because it permitted and even mandated the membership of people obviously not of the elect, because of its similarity to Roman Catholicism, because of its hierarchical form of church government, and because of other reasons. The most important Pilgrim was William Bradford, who frequently served as their governor and wrote their history, *Of Plymouth Plantation*. A decade after the Pilgrims settled in Plymouth, another group, under the leadership of John Winthrop, arrived in nearby Salem, then Boston, establishing the Massachusetts Bay Colony. The newcomers are known as non-Separatists because, while distancing themselves physically from England, they remained, technically speaking, members of the Anglican Church, which they viewed as a true church, as the Separatists did not. These non-Separatists were also Congregationalists. The great migration of these people, Puritans, lasted the decade of the 1630s; as a result, they quickly outnumbered the Pilgrims. With the charter of 1691, the groups became one, as the smaller one was incorporated into the larger. The beliefs of these seventeenth-century settlers proved lasting, as some of their attitudes have remained dominant in American life. These include honesty, moderation, hard work, and other qualities that help define a successful, moral life and assist in establishing and sustaining a stable society.

Despite the primacy of the Puritans and their progeny during the entirety of the colonial era in New England, this period was not religiously homogenous in British North America. Other religions became established in New England and dominated different sections of America.

Perhaps the first new group in New England was the Baptists, established in Providence, Rhode Island, in the late 1630s by Roger Williams and soon thereafter in Newport by John Clarke. Both men had encountered religious difficulties in Massachusetts Bay. Williams, Clarke, and others disagreed with the Puritans on several issues, including baptism (the Baptists insisted that believers be baptized), state involvement in religion (the Baptists were against it), and other matters. Demonstrating the power of their convictions, the Baptists made Rhode Island a colony open to religious dissenters. Baptists residing outside the colony often were persecuted in the seventeenth century.

The Puritans treated the Quakers more harshly than they did the Baptists. From their arrival in New England in the mid seventeenth century, the Quakers' rejection of state control of religion and their refusal to swear oaths, as well as their belief in Inner Light, which they defined as "that of God in everyone," threatened the Puritans to the degree that the Quakers were forbidden to settle in Massachusetts Bay; when they entered the colony, they were forced to leave. As a result of their continued refusal to stay away, the colony enacted a law, in 1658, which permitted the execution of Quakers. After some were killed, including Mary Dyer, popular opinion turned against executions, and the law was repealed in 1661. In time the Quakers, under William Penn, founded Pennsylvania; in so doing, they created, in an enormous area, a home for a religion not only alien to but rejected by the Puritans of New England. Like Rhode Island, Pennsylvania welcomed dissenters; it forbade persecution of any believing person. The seventeenth-century establishment of Baptists in the small colony of Rhode Island and Quakers in the vast expanse of Pennsylvania—and these faiths' acceptance of dissenting religious opinions—anticipates the religious pluralism that would characterize the United States of America.

Because the Puritans migrated to North America largely in order to flee religious persecution in England, they were reluctant to accept the establishment of the Anglican Church in New England. Their refusal to do so led, in 1684, to the revocation of the 1629 charter under which the Bay colony operated. The first Anglican church in Boston was established in 1688, and Anglicans gained a full voice in Massachusetts governmental affairs, including religious ones, when the next charter, that of 1691, made land ownership, not church membership, the requirement for voting.

The Puritans objected to the Church of England for several reasons, including its similarity to Roman Catholicism. Reaction against Catholicism, after all, led to the Protestant Reformation. Therefore, while the Puritans did not welcome Anglicans to Massachusetts Bay, they were even more reluctant to accept Catholics. A 1647 law prohibited the presence of priests in the colony. The first Catholic church in Boston was not established until 1783.

Religion was also important in colonies other than Massachusetts Bay, Rhode Island, and Pennsylvania. The first permanent English settlement in North America, at Jamestown, Virginia, was established for political and commercial reasons, yet its residents were required to attend church, which was Anglican. Under the Calverts, Maryland was established as a Catholic colony, though in the first years of the eighteenth century it became Anglican, with mandatory church attendance and with the church supported by taxes. Despite this development, Maryland remained the colony with the greatest number of Catholics. New Netherlands, later New York, was religiously pluralistic from the beginning, partly because of its cosmopolitan populace; it was the only colony to welcome Jews. Elsewhere, Connecticut and New Hampshire were mostly Congregational; the Carolinas, Anglican. Lutherans settled in New York and New Jersey but soon found Pennsylvania and other colonies attractive as well. Presbyterians gravitated to Delaware, Maryland, and New York. John Wesley introduced Methodism to Georgia. By the end of the seventeenth century the Congregationalists had the greatest number of churches in the colonies, most of them located in New England; the group with the second greatest number was the Anglicans, most of whose churches were located in Maryland and Virginia.

An important aspect of eighteenth-century American religion was, slightly before midcentury, the Great Awakening. Drawing on the writings of Jonathan Edwards as popularized by George Whitefield, this period was characterized by an emotional response to religion, and evangelicalism emerged as an important factor in religious life. Also during the eighteenth century, Enlightenment ideas—the valuing of reason above all else—influenced some Americans to become religious skeptics to the degree that Benjamin Franklin and others became deists, an unofficial group of thinkers who viewed mankind as rational and believed in human perfectability. Such concepts helped inspire politically revolutionary thoughts in the second half of the eighteenth century, thoughts that led to the American Revolution and that are expressed in the Declaration of Independence.

TOPICS FOR DISCUSSION AND RESEARCH

1. During the colonial period, the major New England figures were Puritans and members—often ministers—of the Congregational Church. As the seventeenth century progressed, the religious intensity of the first generation of English settlers in New England diminished, for understandable reasons. With increasing immigration came people of different faiths, for example, and generations after the first were generally less dedicated to religious purity than the initial English settlers. In order to understand the declension of Puritanism during this century, students should identify a few important events that might have influenced or reflected its decline and understand why they were significant. Students might consider such a document as the Half-Way Covenant of 1662 and such an action as Solomon Stoddard's considering of the Lord's Supper as a converting ordinance beginning in the 1670s. For information about these two events in particular, consult *The Encyclopedia of American Religious History*.

2. During the seventeenth century different religions predominated in various parts of British North America, such as Congregationalism in New England and Anglicanism in the South. Why were there these sectional differences? Within this context, how significant were the charters that governed various areas? What was the general nature of the people who settled them? From where did they originate? What caused them to reside in North America? How important were colonial governors to the religions of their areas? Answers to many of these questions may be found in such books as Richard Beale Davis, *Intellectual Life in the Colonial South*, A. James Reichley, *Faith in Politics*, William Warren Sweet, *Religion in Colonial America*, and *Encyclopedia of the American Religious Experience* (the book generally, but especially the essay "Geography and Demography of American Religion" by Edwin S. Gaustad).

3. Enlightenment thought was inspired by the writings of several people including Sir Francis Bacon (1561–1626) and Réné Descartes (1596–1650) but especially by the scientific investigations of Sir Isaac Newton, as expressed in *Principia Mathematica* (1687), and the philosophic observations of John Locke, notably in *An Essay Concerning Human Understanding* (1690). Newton proved the ordered nature of the universe; Locke believed, among other things, that the human brain

is born empty, a blank slate that is filled as a result of experiences. In what ways did these findings influence the American deists? How did these ideas inspire people to challenge religious answers to the riddles of the universe and in some cases to abandon religion as a result? Who were some of the eighteenth-century American deists so influenced and what did their rational approach to serious issues provide to American life? Any reputable summary of the Enlightenment and American deism—such as that found in *The Encyclopedia of American Religious History*—will help answer these questions.

RESOURCES

Criticism

Richard Beale Davis, *Intellectual Life in the Colonial South, 1585–1763*, volume 2 (Knoxville: University of Tennessee Press, 1978), pp. 627–700.
Discusses religion in the colonial South.

The Encyclopedia of American Religious History, 2 volumes, edited by Edward L. Queen II, et al. (New York: Facts On File, 1996).
Provides basic information about people and movements important to American religion.

Encyclopedia of the American Religious Experience: Studies of Traditions and Movements, volume 1, edited by Charles H. Lippy and Peter W. Williams (New York: Scribners, 1988).
In a series of essays by various hands, examines American religions in a "cross-disciplinary" manner.

A. James Reichley, *Faith in Politics* (Washington, D.C.: Brookings Institution Press, 2002).
Discusses religion in American public life from the age of John Winthrop to the twenty-first century.

William Warren Sweet, *Religion in Colonial America* (New York: Scribners, 1947).
Convincingly discusses religious developments in colonial America.

Sweet, *Religion in the Development of American Culture, 1765–1840* (New York: Scribners, 1952).
Examines "the part played by organized religion in the transit of civilization westward."

PERSON OF INTEREST

George Whitefield (1714–1770)
Was an Anglican minister who was largely responsible for the Great Awakening; he published voluminously, including accounts of God's dealings with him (1740, 1747).

Women Authors

Because they were generally not educated and often not literate, because their lives were difficult, and because writing was considered the province of men, seventeenth-century American women wrote little, or little that has been preserved. Further, because paper was imported throughout the century (the first American paper mill was established in 1690), it was expensive, which means that only the relatively affluent could afford it.

One woman of social and political standing who wrote was Anne Bradstreet, who arrived from England on the *Arbella* in 1630, at the beginning of the great migration of Puritans to North America. Daughter of Thomas Dudley and wife of Simon Bradstreet, each of whom became governor of the Massachusetts Bay Colony, she had been educated in England in the library of the Earl of Lincoln, whom her father served as steward. Not only did she write, but she wrote verse. In doing so, she was possibly unique for her time and place; additionally, few English women had written poetry by the mid seventeenth century. Elizabeth Stuart, Queen of Bohemia, is one who did, and others include the aristocrats Mary Sidney Herbert, Countess of Pembroke; and Elizabeth Tanfield Cary, Viscountess Falkland. An irony of early American literature is that, given such realities, Bradstreet, a woman, became the first published poet of British North America. This happened not because she thought her verse worth sharing with a wide audience, apparently, but rather because her family admired her poems; John Woodbridge, husband of her sister Mercy, took the manuscripts to London, presumably without Bradstreet's permission or awareness, where Stephen Bowtell published them in 1650 as *The Tenth Muse Lately Sprung up in America*, with the author identified as "a Gentlewoman in those parts." Woodbridge supplied the title. Perhaps surprisingly, the book was popular, possibly because of the nature of the poems themselves but also possibly because the author was a woman, and therefore a curiosity, or because the author provided unexpected proof of the intelligence, competence, and sophistication of the Puritans who had fled England for America. In what is probably her most famous poem, "The Prologue," Bradstreet addresses the issues of women's perceived worth and of women's authorship. She finds women generally inferior to men because of their sex, going so far as to proclaim: "Men have precedency, and still excel, / It is but vaine, unjustly to wage war, / Men can doe best; and Women know it well; / Preheminence in each, and all is yours" (stanza 7). Further, she acknowledges that she has been criticized by certain unidentified people for writing: "I am obnoxious to each carping tongue, / Who sayes, my hand a needle better fits, / A Poets Pen, all scorne, I should thus wrong; / For such despight they cast on female wits" (stanza 5). In other words, her critics believe that writing poems keeps her from domestic duties, such as sewing, which demand a woman's full attention and which are more important than writing. Yet, to indicate her dissatisfaction with women's writing being rejected out of hand solely on the basis of the author's sex, after granting men's superiority she implores, "Yet grant some small acknowledgement of ours" (stanza 7), with "ours" meaning women's capability, skill. As a result of quietly protesting against the perceived inferiority of women, Bradstreet might be seen as the mother of American feminism. An enlarged edition of her poems was published posthumously in Boston as *Several Poems Compiled with Great Variety of Wit and Learning, Full of Delight* (1678), with the author identified as "a Gentlewoman in New-England."

While Bradstreet was criticized for shirking her womanly responsibilities, the domestic art of sewing served Mary White Rowlandson well. Wife of a Congregational minister, Joseph Rowlandson, in 1676 she and a daughter were abducted from her home in Lancaster, Massachusetts, by Wampanoags during King Philip's War. She sewed for her captors in exchange for food; for her needle work, she was also given a knife. Approximately ten weeks after being captured—after surviving such a harrowing event as being shot and such sorrow as that caused by the death of the daughter—she was released. Although the narrative is dramatic and presents events vividly, it is ultimately religious and instructive. Often she cites the Bible, which bolstered her during captivity; she believes that God's mercy permitted her to survive her ordeal at the hands of the Indians, whom many thought were the devil's representatives. Her *Soveraignty & Goodness of God, Together with the Faithfulness of His Promises Displayed* (1682)—published the same year in London as *A True History of the Captivity & Restoration of Mrs. Mary Rowlandson, a Minister's Wife in New England*—is the first published account of a female captured by Indians, though there are earlier accounts of captivity, as, famously, in John Smith's *Generall Historie of Virginia, New-England, and the Summer Isles* (1624). As a result, Rowlandson's book inaugurates a genre of American literature, the female Indian captivity narrative. Subsequent narratives include Hannah Dustan's, in Cotton Mather's *Magnalia Christi Americana* (1702), the Quaker Elizabeth Hanson's *God's Mercy Surmounting Man's Cruelty* (1728) and *A Journal of the Captivity of Jean Lowry and Her Children* (1760).

Bradstreet and Rowlandson are by far the most important seventeenth-century American women authors, though other women wrote during this period. They include Sarah Symmes Fiske (*A Confession of Faith; or, A Summary of Divinity*, written in 1677 but published in 1704) and Sarah Whipple Goodhue (*The Copy of a Valedictory and Monitory Writing*, 1681). The latter is a letter in which Goodhue expresses, to her husband, her love of family as she anticipates death during childbirth, which actually occurred three days after she delivered twins. Another woman whose compositions have appeared in print is Margaret Tyndal Winthrop, the third wife of John Winthrop, to whom she wrote letters during the first half of the century.

As the American population grew and the country expanded in the eighteenth century, so did the number of women writers increase. One of the first to write in the new century was Sarah Kemble Knight, who, in 1704 and 1705, kept a diary of her journey by horse from Boston to New Haven, and on to New York. It was not published until 1825, as *The Journal of Madam Knight*. Unlike Rowlandson, Knight is not concerned with religion; rather, she focuses on practical matters, such as finding appropriate lodging.

While much verse was written during the previous century, the only known female poet was Bradstreet. More women turned to verse in the eighteenth century, including Knight, six of whose poems are in her journal. A poem by Elizabeth

Sowle Bradford appears in Benjamin Keach's *War with the Devil* (1707). The earliest significant woman poet in the new century, though, was Jane Colman Turell, who died young. Her poems, some notable for their use of the religious sublime, were published in 1735, the year of her death, in *Memoirs of the Life and Death of the Pious and Ingenious Mrs. Jane Turell*, by her widower, Ebenezer Turell; this work is included in *Reliquiæ Turellæ, et Lachrymæ Paternæ. The Father's Tears over His Daughter's Remains* (1735), by her father, Benjamin Colman. Subsequent women who wrote poems include Sarah Parsons Moorhead (a 1742 poem to James Davenport upon his departing Boston); Lucy Terry, the earliest known black American poet (the 1746 "Bars Fight," handed down orally and published in 1855); Martha Wadsworth Brewster (*Poems on Divers Subjects*, 1757); Annis Boudinot Stockton (numerous poems beginning in 1758, collected in 1995 as *Only for the Eye of a Friend*); and Anna Steele (*Poems on Subjects Chiefly Devotional*, 1760). Two political poems by women appeared in 1768: Elizabeth Graeme Fergusson's "The Dream of the Patriotic Philosophical Farmer" and Milcah Martha Moore's "The Female Patriots"; another was published in 1775: Anna Young Smith's "An Elegy to the Memory of the American Volunteers." Jane Harris Dunlap published *Poems, upon Several Sermons, Preached by the Rev'd, and Renowned, George Whitefield, While in Boston* (1771). The major female poet of the 1770s was Phillis Wheatley, whose *Poems on Various Subjects, Religious and Moral* was published in 1773.

Among the spiritual narratives published during the century are Bathsheba Bowers's *An Alarm Sounded to Prepare the Inhabitants of the World to Meet the Lord in the Way of His Judgments* (1709), *The Experiences of God's Gracious Dealing with Mrs. Elizabeth White* (written in the seventeenth century, published in 1741), Sarah Haggar Osborn's *The Nature, Certainty, and Evidence of True Christianity* (1755), and Elizabeth Sampson Ashbridge's *Some Account of the Fore-Part of the Life of Elizabeth Ashbridge* (written in 1746, published in 1774).

Some women's diaries or journals have been published, including parts of one begun in 1743 in Sarah Prince Gill's *Devotional Papers* (1773), excerpts from Sarah Eve's 1772–1773 journal (published in 1881), *The Journal of Esther Edwards Burr* (written in the 1750s, published in 1984), Elizabeth Sandwich Drinker's *Not So Long Ago* (written over three decades beginning in 1758, with selections published in 1937), *Diary of Anna Green Winslow: A Boston School Girl of 1771* (1894), and Margaret Hill Morris's *Private Journal Kept During a Portion of the Revolutionary War* (written in 1776 and 1777, published in 1836). Other publications include the ailing Mercy Wheeler's recommendation for youth to find God through Christ, which appears in *An Address to Young People* (1733); Abigail Adams's letters, which she began writing in the 1770s; *Hymns and Spiritual Songs* (1773) by Bridget Richardson Fletcher; Janet Schaw's *Journal of a Lady of Quality; Being the Narrative of a Journey from Scotland to the West Indies, North Carolina, and Portugal, in the Years 1774 to 1776* (more a narrative than a journal, 1921); and, significantly, *The Adulateur* (1772, 1773), *The Defeat* (1773), and *The Group* (1775), plays by Mercy Otis Warren.

The compositions of Eliza Lucas Pinckney, a South Carolinian accomplished in agriculture, are as well documented as those of any American woman of the middle third of the century. Her writings may be found in *Journal and Letters of Eliza Lucas* (1850), in an 1896 biography by Harriott Horry Ravenel, in *Recipe Book of Eliza Lucas Pinckney, 1756* (1956), and *The Letterbook of Eliza Lucas Pinckney, 1739–1762* (1972).

TOPICS FOR DISCUSSION AND RESEARCH

1. The works of both major seventeenth-century women writers contain prefatory material by men. Anne Bradstreet's efforts are endorsed in poems by Robert Quarles, Nathaniel Ward, John Woodbridge, and others; Mary Rowlandson's book, by Increase Mather. What does the presence of such endorsements imply about women authors of the time? About the authority of men? About readers' biases? About perceptions of truth? Does it matter that Mather was an esteemed minister? If so, why? A good starting place for answering these questions is Rebecca Blevins Faery's *Cartographies of Desire*.
2. With only a few exceptions, the seventeenth-century American women whose writings were published—then or later—were residents of the Massachusetts Bay Colony. What does this indicate about the nature of the colony? About the nature of English-speaking communities elsewhere in America? For information about such questions, consult Samuel Eliot Morison's *The Intellectual Life of Colonial New England*.
3. In the realm of belles lettres, some eighteenth-century women wrote poems, and Mercy Otis Warren wrote closet plays in the 1770s. American women apparently did not write literary essays, as did such men as Mather Byles and the autodidact Benjamin Franklin, or full-scale plays that could be performed. What conditions might account for these realities? Did women have access to literary models, such as the essays of Joseph Addison or the plays of Shakespeare? Did they belong to groups or salons where literary issues could be discussed and talents fostered? Assuming that a woman wrote a play to be acted, how likely is it that it would have been performed, assuming its adequate quality? For assistance in answering these questions, consult David S. Shields, *Civil Tongues & Polite Letters in British America* and *The Cambridge History of American Theater*.
4. The major female belletrists from 1700 to 1776 were probably Jane Colman Turell, Phillis Wheatley, and Warren. What sets their work apart aesthetically from that of other women writing during this period? For guidance, consult David S. Shields, "The Religious Sublime and New England Poets of the 1720s" (Turell); Frank Shuffelton, "On Her Own Footing" (Wheatley); and Nancy Rubin Stuart, *The Muse of the Revolution* (Warren).

RESOURCES

Biography
Nancy Rubin Stuart, *The Muse of the Revolution: The Secret Pen of Mercy Otis Warren and the Founding of a Nation* (Boston: Beacon, 2008).
A modern biography that draws extensively on Warren's correspondence.

Criticism

The Cambridge History of American Theatre, Volume One: Beginnings to 1870, edited by Don B. Wilmeth and Christopher Bigsby (Cambridge, England: Cambridge University Press, 1998).
Details the development of American theater to 1870.

Rebecca Blevins Faery, *Cartographies of Desire: Captivity, Race, and Sex in the Shaping of an American Nation* (Norman: University of Oklahoma Press, 1999).
Examines how the repeated telling of women's Indian captivity narratives defends "a privileged, protected version of white American identity, subjectivity, and nationhood."

Samuel Eliot Morison, *The Intellectual Life of Colonial New England* (New York: New York University Press, 1956).
Though this book does not focus on women, it provides an authoritative account of intellectual New England during the seventeenth century.

Mary Beth Norton, *Liberty's Daughters: The Revolutionary Experience of American Women, 1750–1800* (1980; Ithaca, N.Y.: Cornell University Press, 1996).
Examines the effect of the American Revolution on women's self-perceptions.

William J. Scheick, *Authority and Female Authorship in Colonial America* (Lexington: University Press of Kentucky, 1998).
Discusses tensions in the works of such women authors as Anne Bradstreet, Esther Edwards Burr, Elizabeth Hanson, Elizabeth Ashbridge, and Phillis Wheatley.

David S. Shields, *Civil Tongues & Polite Letters in British America* (Chapel Hill: University of North Carolina Press, 1997).
Examines the discursive cultures, such as salons, of Boston, Charleston, and Philadelphia.

Shields, "The Religious Sublime and New England Poets of the 1720s," *Early American Literature,* 19 (Winter 1984/85): 231–248.
Discusses American poets of the 1720s, including Jane Colman Turell, who followed the example of Sir Richard Blackmore's *The Creation.*

Frank Shuffelton, "On Her Own Footing: Phillis Wheatley in Freedom," in *Genius in Bondage: Literature of the Early Black Atlantic,* edited by Vincent Carretta and Philip Gould (Lexington: University Press of Kentucky, 2001), pp. 175–189.
Discusses how Wheatley benefited from opening "a connection to an imperial public sphere."

PEOPLE OF INTEREST

Abigail Adams (1744–1818)
Wrote many letters, including to her husband, John Adams; in one of 1776, she famously asks him to "remember the ladies" as he and other members of the Sec-

ond Continental Congress were drafting the Declaration of Independence and Articles of Confederation.

Elizabeth Sampson Ashbridge (1713–1755)
Was reared an Anglican but converted to Quakerism and became a minister; died in Ireland, where she had been preaching.

Bathsheba Bowers (1671–1718)
A Philadelphia Quaker who moved to South Carolina, apparently wrote more than one work, though *An Alarm Sounded* is the only one to be published.

Elizabeth Sowle Bradford (1663–1731)
Daughter of the English printer Andrew Sowle, married her father's apprentice William Bradford, who became the first important American printer outside of Boston and Cambridge.

Simon Bradstreet (1603–1697)
Was active in the political life of Massachusetts Bay, including serving as governor. His first wife was Anne Bradstreet, who wrote him moving love poems.

Martha Wadsworth Brewster (dates unknown)
About whom almost nothing is known, was a resident of Lebanon, Connecticut; she is one of the few pre-Revolution American women to have a book of her poetry published.

Esther Edwards Burr (1732–1758)
Daughter of Jonathan Edwards, wife of the president of the College of New Jersey (Princeton), Aaron Burr, and mother of future vice president of the United States Aaron Burr Jr., recorded her thoughts and experiences in order to inspire other women to do so.

Elizabeth Tanfield Cary, Viscountess Falkland (1585–1639)
Wrote biographies in verse and a translation of Seneca's *Epistles,* all lost, as well as the play *The Tragedie of Mariam* (1613).

James Davenport (1716–1757)
Was a Connecticut minister active in the Great Awakening; among other titles, he published *Meditations on Several Divine Subjects* (1748).

Elizabeth Sandwich Drinker (1734–1807)
Was taught by Anthony Benezet; her journal details the life of a well-to-do Quaker family in Philadelphia and comments on the persecution of Quakers.

Thomas Dudley (1576–1653)
Was the father of Anne Dudley Bradstreet and four-time governor of Massachusetts Bay Colony; he composed at least one poem, which was discovered in his pocket following his death.

Jane Harris Dunlap (dates unknown)
Wrote as "a Daughter of Liberty and Lover of Truth"; she was married to George Dunlap, who died in 1771, shortly before the publication of her *Poems.*

Hannah Dustan (Duston, Dustin) (1657–1736)
Was captured by Abenaki Indians in 1697; her account of captivity was delivered from the pulpit by Cotton Mather, who also recorded it in his *Magnalia Christi Americana* (1702).

Sarah Eve (1750–1774)
Of Philadelphia, wrote a journal for the edification of her seafaring father; she died as the fiancée of Dr. Benjamin Rush.

Elizabeth Graeme Fergusson (1737–1801)
Was an intellectual who conducted weekly literary salons in Philadelphia and who wrote as "Laura." Anne M. Ousterhout's *The Most Learned Woman in America*, a biography of Fergusson, was published in 2004.

Sarah Symmes Fiske (1652–1692)
Was the granddaughter of noted minister Zachariah Symmes and wife of minister Moses Fiske.

Bridget Richardson Fletcher (1726–1770)
Composed hymns, published posthumously, that detail her spiritual life.

Sarah Prince Gill (1728–1771)
Daughter of the important minister Thomas Prince, recorded her thoughts and experiences in order to inspire other women to do so.

Sarah Whipple Goodhue (1641–1681)
Was a Puritan from Ipswich, Massachusetts, married to Joseph Goodhue.

Elizabeth Hanson (1684–1737)
Was a Quaker whose diary of her five-month captivity by Indians in 1724 was published, four years later, as *God's Mercy Surmounting Man's Cruelty*.

Mary Sidney Herbert, Countess of Pembroke (1561–1621)
For whom her brother, Sir Philip Sidney, wrote *The Covntesse of Pembroke's Arcadia* (1590), translated Robert Garnier's *Marc Antoine* as *The Tragedie of Antoine* (1595).

Benjamin Keach (1640–1704)
Was an English Baptist minister and controversialist whose publications include *Antichrist Stormed* and *Distressed Sion Relieved* (both 1689).

Sarah Kemble Knight (1666–1727)
Is noted for her diary of an arduous trip by horseback in 1704–1705. It depicts her as a strong, no-nonsense woman.

Jean Lowry (flourished 1756)
Taken captive with two children while she was pregnant, wrote about her experiences in a tone of self-pity.

Milcah Martha Moore (1740–1829)
A Quaker, wrote moral and instructive verse. Her commonplace book was published in 1997.

Sarah Parsons Moorhead (dates unknown)
Opposed the excesses of the Great Awakening and lamented dissension within Congregational churches.

Margaret Hill Morris (1737–1816)
A Quaker knowledgeable about medicine, tended to injured and afflicted people who needed assistance. In a journal, she recorded her observations about the American Revolution.

Sarah Haggar Osborn (1714–1796)
Resident of Newport and a follower of Nathaniel Clap, organized the Religious Female Society, hosted large prayer groups in her home, and apparently wrote voluminously, though only *The Nature, Certainty, and Evidence of True Christianity* was published during her lifetime.

Eliza Lucas Pinckney (1723–1793)
Was born in Antigua and schooled in England. In South Carolina she developed indigo into a major crop for export. She was so significant that George Washington served as a pallbearer at her funeral. Two of her sons became important military and political figures: Charles Cotesworth Pinckney and Thomas Pinckney.

Joseph Rowlandson (circa 1631–1678)
Husband of Mary White Rowlandson, published one title, *The Possibility of Gods Forsaking a People* (1682).

Janet Schaw (circa 1731–circa 1801)
Born in Scotland, was briefly a resident of North Carolina, a state whose residents she found unsophisticated. In her journal, she sympathizes with the plight of slaves.

Anna Young Smith (1756–1780)
Who wrote as "Sylvia," was a niece of Elizabeth Graeme Fergusson, whose literary salon influenced Smith positively.

Anna Steele (1717–circa 1778)
Who wrote numerous hymns and versified psalms, wrote as "Theodosia." She was an invalid whose fiancé died the day before they were to be married.

Annis Boudinot Stockton (1736–1801)
Was a prolific poet who hosted a salon that encouraged the writing of its members. She was married to Richard Stockton, who signed the Declaration of Independence.

Elizabeth Stuart, Queen of Bohemia (1596–1662)
Daughter of James I of England, wrote verses for her preceptor, Lord Harrington of Exton.

Lucy Terry (1730–1821)
Taken from Africa and sold into slavery, grew up in Deerfield, Massachusetts. A convincing speaker, she successfully argued a case before the Vermont Supreme Court and addressed the trustees of Williams College for several hours.

Ebenezer Turell (1702–1778)
Harvard College class of 1721, was minister of the church at Medford, Massachusetts, for over half a century; he was married to Jane Colman Turell, now valued as a poet.

Jane Colman Turell (1708–1735)
Daughter of Benjamin Colman and wife of Ebenezer Turell, was the most accomplished American female poet of the first half of the eighteenth century.

Mercy Wheeler (1706–1796)
Of Plainfield, Massachusetts, composed her essay while bed-bound by illness.

Elizabeth White (circa 1637–1699)
Focuses, in her narrative, on her spiritual condition and details her religious doubts.

Anna Green Winslow (1759–1779)
Wrote a diary from 1771 to 1773, beginning at age twelve; in it, she details her interests in fashion and religion.

Margaret Tyndal Winthrop (1591–1647)
Third wife of John Winthrop, corresponded with her husband; some of her letters to him have been published.

John Woodbridge (1613–1695)
Took the poems of Anne Bradstreet, his sister-in-law, to England, where they were published as *The Tenth Muse* (1650), for which he wrote a prefatory poem.

Part III
Study Guides
on Works and Writers

William Bradford
History of Plymouth Plantation . . .
edited by Charles Deane
Collections of the Massachusetts Historical Society, fourth series, no. 2 (1856).
Republished as *Of Plymouth Plantation, 1620–1647,* edited by
Samuel Eliot Morison (New York: Knopf, 1952)

William Bradford was born in Austerfield, England, in March 1590, son of William Bradford and Alice Hanson Bradford. After moving frequently following the deaths, in rapid succession, of his father (when Bradford was one), paternal grandfather, and mother, the prepubescent Bradford lived with two of his father's brothers. Following a religious conversion, he became a member of Richard Clyfton's Separatist church in nearby Scrooby, which also included William Brewster, at whose residence the group met, and John Robinson; they became major influences on young Bradford. After James I began persecuting Separatists, the church moved to Holland in 1608 and became established in Leyden the following year. Bradford accompanied it. He worked as a weaver in Holland, where in 1613 he married Dorothy May, with whom he had a son, John. Bradford and his wife, as well as Brewster, were among the passengers on the *Mayflower* during its passage from England to North America in 1620. She drowned shortly after arriving at Cape Cod, possibly a suicide. Bradford then married the widow Alice Carpenter Southworth, with whom he had three children: William, Mercy, and Joseph. Following the death of John Carver, the first governor of the Plymouth Colony, in 1621 Bradford was elected to the position, in which he ultimately served for more than thirty years. He was the most important person in the colony. He died in Plymouth, in what is now the state of Massachusetts, on 9 May 1657, and is interred at Burial Hill, Plymouth.

Because Bradford was part of the Scrooby Separatists and moved with them to Holland and then North America, he was in a position to record the group's history, which he did, despite the belief of the admired Sir Walter Raleigh that contemporary history is less desirable than that written significantly after the events being examined. Bradford was not in a position to write much after the fact. In 1630, he began his chronicle of the Pilgrims, as he called his group, in a manuscript published as *Of Plymouth Plantation* (1856; in the manuscript Bradford spells the second word "Plimmoth"). Written in a plain style, his history is the source of most of what is known about the Plymouth Colony. The manuscript served as the basis for a history published by Bradford's nephew Nathaniel Morton, *New-Englands Memoriall* (1669). Cotton Mather consulted it for *Magnalia Christi Americana* (1702), as did William Hubbard for *A General History of New England* (written in the seventeenth century but not published until 1815), Thomas Prince for *A Chronological History of New-England* (1736, 1755), and Thomas Hutchinson for *The History of the Colony of Massachusetts-Bay* (1764, 1767, 1828). These works based on Bradford's document had the effect of confirming its accuracy: if the later historians record some of the same events and reach the same conclusions as Bradford, whose work was published after theirs, then he must be reliable.

After Hutchinson finished with the manuscript, it disappeared, inexplicably. It was located in Fulham Palace in London in 1855 and was published the next year. After much negotiation, it was returned to the United States in 1897. It resides in the State Library of Massachusetts, Boston.

Edward Winslow, a *Mayflower* passenger who served as governor of the Plymouth colony, wrote *Good Newes from New-England* (1624), which explains the Plymouth experience to the English. He and Bradford contributed to a book published in London in 1622. Now known as *Mourt's Relation*, it describes the first year of the English residence in Plymouth and treats some of the personalities and events discussed in *Of Plymouth Plantation*. It includes the first publication of the Mayflower Compact, which governed life ashore. The Compact was signed by the adult males aboard the *Mayflower*, including Bradford and Winslow but excluding the crew. Precisely which parts of *Mourt's Relation* Bradford wrote cannot be determined.

In addition to chronicling the Plymouth colony, Bradford wrote poetry, at mid century, that was collected and published in 1974. In general, the poems lament the movement of Plymouth society away from its original spiritual ideals, which Bradford was instrumental in establishing. Whether the texts of these poems represent Bradford's final wishes is doubtful because most of them survive only in copies made by a fifteen-year-old following Bradford's death. Bradford's poems have not found critical favor.

TOPICS FOR DISCUSSION AND RESEARCH

1. Many people forget that the Pilgrims—originally residents of England—began their trip to America not from England but Holland, where they had lived for years. What conditions led them to leave England for Holland? Why did they leave Holland? Why did they risk everything, including their lives, to sail to America? Read selections in *Of Plymouth Plantation* to answer these questions. Guidance may also be found in Nathaniel Philbrick's *Mayflower*, as well as in other books listed below.

2. In a two-sentence introduction to *Of Plymouth Plantation*, Bradford establishes a rhetorical strategy by identifying his voice, style, and veracity: "And first of the occasion and inducements thereunto; the which, that I may truly unfold, I must begin at the very root and rise of the same. The which I shall endeavour to manifest in a plain style, with singular regard unto the simple truth of all things; at least as near as my slender judgment can attain the same." His modesty and emphasis on truth plainly told—which are sustained throughout the text—prepare the reader to accept the author's assertions and judgments without question. That Bradford writes as a believer who survived the trip on the *Mayflower* and led the Plymouth colony further enhances his credibility. While there is no reason to doubt most of his accounts of personalities and events, another document presents at least a contrasting perspective on an American situation he describes. Bradford depicts Anglican Thomas Morton and his followers at Merry Mount (now Quincy) as serious threats to the Plymouth colony. In *New English Canaan* (1637), Morton characterizes his

group, including Indians, as fun loving, as a threat to no one. Which version, if either, is correct, or more correct? For assistance in answering this question, consider the evidence presented by Minor W. Major in "William Bradford Versus Nathaniel Morton." Nathaniel Hawthorne used this dispute as the basis for the story "The May-Pole of Merry Mount."

3. Bradford began writing his manuscript in 1630, the year the great migration of non-Separatists from England to America began. John Winthrop led the first group, which arrived at Salem on the *Arbella* and established the Massachusetts Bay Colony. Dwarfing the population of the Plymouth colony, the new arrivals threatened its existence. Whether Bradford knew or sensed this cannot be determined. If he did, he might have begun his manuscript in order to record the history of his community that he feared would not long survive. His community became part of the larger colony in 1691. Students would benefit from investigating how Bradford's group of Separatists differed from the later non-Separatists. Any reputable history of early America will provide information for answering this question.

4. Bradford writes about several topics that became important in American culture. One anticipates the longtime but unofficial national motto, *e pluribus unum* (out of many, one). The Separatists ("saints") were not the only people aboard the *Mayflower*. The ship had a crew, in addition to such men as John Alden and Myles Standish, who were known as "strangers" because they did not sympathize with the Separatists' desire to separate from the Church of England. Some of the strangers were actively hostile to Bradford's group. Although only one person died during the voyage to America, approximately half the passengers died during the winter of 1620–1621, leaving Plymouth with a population of approximately fifty. As a result, saints and strangers worked together for the sake of survival. The Plymouth residents also relied on certain Indians, such as Massasoit, Samoset, and Squanto, the last of whom told the new arrivals how to plant corn, where to fish, and so forth, thereby permitting them to survive. For an account of the interaction of the Pilgrims and strangers, as well as relations between the Pilgrims and Indians, read selections from *Of Plymouth Plantation*. For an analysis of the relationship of Bradford's group with the Indians, consult Nathaniel Philbrick's *Mayflower*.

5. A reader unaware of the context would not know that six sentences in the twelfth chapter of *Of Plymouth Plantation* constitute Bradford's version of what is celebrated now as the first Thanksgiving. Bradford recounts the Pilgrims' improving health and ample provisions but does not mention sharing the group's fortunes with Indians. In the sixth sentence, though, he states that some members of the community wrote glowingly but accurately to friends in England about the Pilgrims' progress in establishing a community in Plymouth. One such letter, written by Edward Winslow in December 1621, was published in *Mourt's Relation*. In it, Winslow tells of a three-day feast with Indians, including the friendly Massasoit, leader of the Wampanoags, and ninety of his men. The precise date of this 1621 gathering is unknown. The Bradford and Winslow texts are the only extant ones about what is now

characterized as the first Thanksgiving. Everything else about it is conjectural. One might be interested in addressing the nature of Thanksgiving. When did it become a national holiday? On what basis was it made a holiday? Do the reasons for its becoming a holiday follow from what is known about the 1621 event from Bradford and Winslow? For assistance in answering these and other questions about Thanksgiving, read their accounts, as well as Godfrey Hodgson's *A Great and Godly Adventure.*

RESOURCES

Biography

Samuel Eliot Morison, Introduction, *Of Plymouth Plantation, 1620–1647,* by William Bradford (1952; New York: Knopf, 1966).
In this book that presented Bradford's work to a wide audience, Morison discusses Bradford and the history of the manuscript.

Bradford Smith, *Bradford of Plymouth* (Philadelphia: Lippincott, 1951).
The standard biography of Bradford.

Criticism

Douglas Anderson, *William Bradford's Books:* Of Plimmoth Plantation *and the Printed Word* (Baltimore: Johns Hopkins University Press, 2003).
Analyzes Bradford's work within the context of publishing and reading practices of the time.

Peter Gay, *A Loss of Mastery: Puritan Historians in Colonial America* (Berkeley: University of California Press, 1966).
Charts changes in early American culture by focusing on histories written by Bradford, Cotton Mather, and Jonathan Edwards; to Gay, Bradford's history records God's will.

Godfrey Hodgson, *A Great and Godly Adventure: The Pilgrims and the Myth of the First Thanksgiving* (New York: Public Affairs, 2006).
Discusses the Pilgrims generally and the history of Thanksgiving specifically.

H. Roger King, *Cape Cod and Plymouth Colony in the Seventeenth Century* (Lanham, Md.: University Press of America, 1994).
Shows how Cape Cod itself influenced seventeenth-century Pilgrim life.

Minor W. Major, "William Bradford Versus Thomas Morton," *Early American Literature,* 5 (Fall 1970): 1–13.
Scrutinizes Bradford's account of Morton and the Merry Mount community, concluding that Bradford is less reliable than he seems.

Nathaniel Philbrick, *Mayflower: A Story of Courage, Community, and War* (New York: Viking, 2006).
Focuses on the Pilgrims' existence in America, with special emphasis on Pilgrim-Indian relations.

David Read, *New World, Known World: Shaping Knowledge in Early Anglo-American Writing* (Columbia: University of Missouri Press, 2005).
Argues that Bradford—like John Smith, Thomas Morton, and Roger Williams—renders "an organized account of a newly experienced colonial world that will make that world distinct from the one—'Old' or just generically familiar—that previously formed the ground of knowledge."

Michael G. Runyan, Introduction, *The Collected Verse*, by William Bradford (St. Paul: John Colet Press, 1974).
Discusses Bradford's poetry and provides textual information.

Anne Bradstreet (circa 1612–1672)

Born in Northampton, England, possibly on 20 March 1612, Anne Dudley grew up in the home of the Earl of Lincoln, whom her father, Thomas Dudley, served as steward. There, she had access to a significant library, which her father presumably encouraged her to use. In 1628, she married a former assistant to her father, Simon Bradstreet, nine years her senior, who had two degrees from Emmanuel College at Cambridge University. Primarily for religious reasons—dissatisfaction with impurities in the Church of England, including Roman Catholic elements—the Dudleys and Bradstreets accompanied John Winthrop's party to America on the *Arbella* (April–June 1630), in the vanguard of the great migration of Puritans from England to America. The ship was named for Lady Arbella Johnson, a member of Winthrop's group and a childhood friend of Anne Dudley. According to legend, Winthrop gave his "Citty upon a Hill" sermon *(A Modell of Christian Charity)* aboard the ship, though he might have delivered it in England. Landing at Salem, the party established the Massachusetts Bay Colony, with Winthrop serving as governor, Thomas Dudley as deputy governor, and Simon Bradstreet as chief administrator. In time, Dudley and Bradstreet became governor. Ultimately, the Bradstreets settled in what is now Andover. Childless for the first five years of marriage, Bradstreet bore eight children from 1633 to 1652. She characterizes them in the poem "In Reference to Her Children" and addresses them in "To My Dear Children" (prose). Several poems to her husband indicate the warmth of their marriage. Four years after Bradstreet's death on 16 September 1672, Simon remarried.

Anne Bradstreet is important as a writer, primarily of poetry, though she apparently did not intend for her creations to be published. Publication occurred because John Woodbridge, husband of her sister, Mercy Dudley Woodbridge, admired the verse and, in 1647, took it to England, where Stephen Bowtell published it in 1650 as *The Tenth Muse Lately Sprung up in America*, by "A Gentlewoman in Those Parts." She comments about her poems, the book, and Woodbridge at the beginning of "The Author to Her Book," published posthumously in 1678:

Thou ill-form'd offspring of my feeble brain,
Who after birth did'st by my side remain,
Till snatcht from thence by friends, less wise than true
Who thee, abroad, expos'd to publick view.

This book that apparently embarrassed her is the first volume of original poetry published by a resident of English-speaking America. (*The Bay Psalm Book*, the first book published in British North America [1640], is a metrical version of the Psalms.) Her poems are preceded by encomia by, among others, John Woodbridge, Robert Quarles, and Nathaniel Ward, a friend of the Bradstreets whose work Bowtell published in 1647 and 1649.

The poems in *The Tenth Muse* reflect the conventions of the time and the influence especially of Guillaume Du Bartas, whom Bradstreet acknowledges in the poem "In Honour of Du Bartas" and elsewhere. The book consists mostly of the historical poem "The Foure Monarchies" and quaternions (four four-part poems)—"The Foure Elements," "Of the Foure Humours in Mans Constitution," "The Four Ages of Man," and "The Four Seasons of the Year"—poems holding little appeal for the modern reader. Yet, at least one poem appeals: "The Prologue," in which Bradstreet addresses her poetic skill (or lack thereof, according to her) in the context of men's talent, her treatment by people possibly jealous of her ("I am obnoxious to each carping tongue, / Who sayes, my hand a needle better fits"), and her desire to be judged on the basis of her work, not her sex ("If what I doe prove well, it won't advance, / [critics will] say its stolne, or else, it was by chance").

Bradstreet's *Several Poems*, by "A Gentlewoman in New-England," was published posthumously in Boston in 1678. It includes her poems published in *The Tenth Muse*, as well as verse previously unpublished. Unlike most of the poems in the earlier volume, many of those new to the later one attract the modern reader because of their personal nature: she writes about such topics as illness, childbirth, love, and death. Additional works from what are called the Andover manuscripts were published in 1867. These include "Meditations Divine and Moral" (prose) and "Here Follows Some Verses upon the Burning of Our House."

Bradstreet, Michael Wigglesworth, and Edward Taylor were the major poets of colonial America. Puritans all, each was different. Wigglesworth, a public poet, is didactic and frightening; Taylor, a private poet, wrote artful poems in preparation for administering the Lord's Supper. In the poems that inspired John Woodbridge to have *The Tenth Muse* published, Bradstreet is often derivative. Yet, in her quiet musings on personal issues, she wrote the most accessible, moving American poems before Philip Freneau or possibly Emerson.

TOPICS FOR DISCUSSION AND RESEARCH

1. Although some of Bradstreet's manuscripts survive, determining the author's final intentions about her texts is impossible because she saw nothing through the publication process. *The Tenth Muse* was published without her authorization or awareness; everything else was published posthumously, beginning with *Several Poems*, which contains verses "corrected by the author." John Harvard Ellis's

scholarly edition of Bradstreet's works (1867) reproduces the 1650 text and adds new material to it. The 1897 edition by Frank E. Hopkins modernizes the texts. Using *Several Poems* as copy text, Jeannine Hensley (1967) modernizes spelling and punctuation, in addition to rearranging the contents. Relying primarily on the 1650 edition as copy text, Joseph R. McElrath Jr. and Allan P. Robb provide the most convincing rationale for the text of Bradstreet's work (1981), though, as they acknowledge, neither they nor anyone can know for certain what Bradstreet intended. Did she, for example, intend "persever" as the last word in the penultimate line of "To My Dear and Loving Husband"? Or "persevere"? To understand textual issues surrounding Bradstreet's verse, consult McElrath and Robb's edition of Bradstreet's works.

2. That Bradstreet wrote at all is impressive. Like most Puritan women, she had numerous family responsibilities, increasingly so as the family grew in size and when her husband was away from home. Yet, she found time to write, and writing was not a lark: she worked at it, as the lengthy "Foure Monarchies" and the quaternions indicate. She also knew good poetry, with which she compared her own unflatteringly. She characterizes her art in "The Author to Her Book" and "The Prologue," in the latter of which she refers to her "mean pen," "broken strings," "main defect" (her sex), "foolish, broken, blemished Muse," "weak or wounded brain," and "lowly lines." How genuine are these phrases? Do they reflect her true thoughts? Does she diminish her verse as a tactic, one that makes her seem inadequate so as not to challenge the primacy of male poets in particular and male-dominated Puritan society in general? These questions may be answered by reading her text carefully and consulting any of the critics who have published books about Bradstreet's verse.

3. A person reading certain of Bradstreet's poems unaware of her sex would know immediately that the author is a woman, because Bradstreet writes in her own voice about issues important to her as woman. She wanted her poetry judged on its merit and not rejected out of hand because a woman wrote it, for example. She anticipates her death during childbirth in "Before the Birth of One of Her Children," wherein she expresses love for her husband and asks him to protect their children from injury by his next wife. Several poems addressed to her husband are some of her most moving creations. Among other things, they evidence such love and passion—including explicit acknowledgment of their sexual life in "A Letter to Her Husband Absent upon Public Employment"—that they negate the stereotype of Puritans as unfeeling religious zealots. In writing as a woman concerned with women's issues, Bradstreet might be seen as something of a protofeminist. For information about feminist elements in Bradstreet's poetry, consult Paula Kopacz's "'Men can doe best, and women know it well': Anne Bradstreet and Feminist Aesthetics."

4. Life was difficult for all American Puritans of Bradstreet's generation, even for Bradstreet and her family, who lived more comfortably than most. Yet, their faith helped buoy them during privation and loss. Bradstreet comforts herself at the loss of family members by believing that her granddaughter Elizabeth, for example, is "in an everlasting state," a commonplace thought seemingly deeply believed. In another poem she laments the burning of the Bradstreet home

and its contents until realizing fully that "my hope and treasure lies above." She addresses the sacred and profane in "The Flesh and the Spirit." This dialogue between twin sisters born of different fathers (Adam and God) reflects the tension Bradstreet felt between the attractions of the world and the ideal of heaven, a tension unresolved in this poem. Bradstreet resolves the issue in one of her last poems, "As Weary Pilgrim," in which she expresses world-weariness and yearns "to be at rest / And soar on high among the blest." In order to appreciate these aspects of Bradstreet's life and verse, students would benefit from learning about the realities of seventeenth-century life and how aspects of their faith sustained Puritans of the time. Claudia Durst Johnson's *Daily Life in Colonial New England* answers these questions.

5. Bradstreet occasionally used nature prominently in her verse, including in "The Four Seasons of the Year" and "In Memory of My Dear Grandchild Elizabeth Bradstreet." She employs it more effectively in the thirty-three-stanza "Contemplations," probably her most fully realized poem. In presenting the speaker walking in and pondering nature, the poem stands as possibly the first poetic expression of awe in response to the American landscape, a stance that became common in nineteenth-century American literature. Unlike the seemingly contented grasshoppers, crickets, fish, and birds, mankind is troubled ("frail," "vain," "wretched"); and unlike cyclical nature, mankind's life is brief. Despite the inadequacy of mortals in the context of nature, they ultimately can exceed nature by entering heaven if their names are "graved in the white stone," an allusion to Rev. 2:17, where a white stone indicates new, eternal life. Students would benefit from pondering the natural images in "Contemplations" and comparing their observations with those expressed by critics, such as Robert Boschman in "Anne Bradstreet and Elizabeth Bishop: Nature, Culture and Gender in 'Contemplations' and 'At the Fireshouse.'"

RESOURCES

Biography
Raymond F. Dolle, *Anne Bradstreet: A Reference Guide* (Boston: G. K. Hall, 1990).
Summarizes criticism of Bradstreet's work from 1650 to 1989.

Charlotte Gordon, *Mistress Bradstreet: The Untold Life of America's First Poet* (New York: Little, Brown, 2005).
The most modern and complete biography of Bradstreet.

Criticism
Robert Boschman, "Anne Bradstreet and Elizabeth Bishop: Nature, Culture and Gender in 'Contemplations' and 'At the Firehouse,'" *Journal of American Studies*, 26 (August 1992): 246–260.
Argues that "Bradstreet's landscape is penetrated, illuminated, and fertilized by the masculine sun, that symbol of a sky god transformed into an omnipotent, patriarchal deity."

Claudia Durst Johnson, *Daily Life in Colonial New England* (Westport, Conn.: Greenwood Press, 2001).
Investigates the daily, practical realities of colonial New Englanders, emphasizing how religion influenced many of these realities.

Paula Kopacz, "'Men can doe best, and women know it well': Anne Bradstreet and Feminist Aesthetics," *Kentucky Philological Review,* 2 (1987): 21–29.
Identifies feminist elements in Bradstreet's work.

Joseph R. McElrath Jr. and Allan P. Robb, *The Complete Works of Anne Bradstreet* (Boston: Twayne, 1981).
Establishes the best possible text of Bradstreet's poems and, in the introduction, details the poet's life and art while placing Bradstreet in historical and critical context.

Rosamond Rosenmeier, *Anne Bradstreet Revisited* (Boston: Twayne, 1991).
Examines Bradstreet's life and work by focusing on new approaches to the poet, such as gender studies.

Ann Stanford, *Anne Bradstreet: The Worldly Puritan, An Introduction to Her Poetry* (New York: Burt Franklin, 1974).
Argues that tension between the visible and invisible worlds informs Bradstreet's work.

Elizabeth Wade White, *Anne Bradstreet: "The Tenth Muse"* (New York: Oxford University Press, 1971).
Examines Bradstreet's life and work.

Mather Byles (1707–1788)

Mather Byles is probably the most notable American poet of the second quarter of the eighteenth century, a period of modest poetic achievement possibly because of the dominating, even stultifying influence of British neoclassicism, especially as expressed in the verse of Alexander Pope. Byles also wrote essays and sermons that were published, and he is known as a wit.

Byles was born on 15 March 1707 to Josias Byles and Elizabeth Mather Greenough Byles. The elder Byles, an English saddler about whom little is known, immigrated to America in the 1690s. Following the death of his wife, Sarah, in 1703 he married the widow of William Greenough, Elizabeth. A year after the birth of their only child, Mather Byles, Josias Byles died. Because Elizabeth, who never remarried, needed help rearing her son, her family helped her. The family was the Mathers, the most important and powerful American family for three generations beginning soon after the arrival of Richard Mather in America in 1635. The one who helped most was Cotton Mather, Elizabeth's brother; in his will, Increase Mather, father of Elizabeth and Cotton, bequeathed Mather Byles books and money for schooling.

Byles matriculated at Harvard in 1721 and was graduated in 1725, at age eighteen; his essay for the master's degree (1727) argues that "polite literature is an ornament to a theologian," a topic in which he obviously believed (Shipton). In 1727 he became associated with *The New-England Weekly Journal,* which began publication in March as the fourth Boston newspaper. It featured literature. To this publication Byles, John Adams (died 1740), and Matthew Adams contributed a fifty-two-week series of essays (including some poems, such as Byles's "Eternity" and "To a Friend") titled Proteus Echo. Following Benjamin Franklin's Dogood papers published in James Franklin's *New-England Courant,* it is the second essay series published in American newspapers. Although Byles wrote the first and last essays in the series, his best-known contribution to it is one about bombastic and grubstreet style in the third Proteus Echo (24 April 1727). In it, he details how to write incorrectly. In addressing moral and literary issues in a refined style, Byles, Adams, and Adams aspire to urbanity, to the sophistication of the essays published in *The Spectator* and *The Tatler* in England. That is, these men were inspired by and attempted to write in the manner of Joseph Addison in particular. Their essays may be seen as documenting the evolution of American culture from primarily religious to increasingly secular.

Byles was most active poetically in the late 1720s, but he also composed verse subsequently, as late as the 1740s. He and such other writers as John Adams and Jane Colman Turell were in the vanguard of introducing neoclassical elements to American poetry, elements that would inform American verse for most of the rest of the century. Though he and the others were not adept at such techniques as antithesis, balance, and parallelism—techniques mastered by Pope and John Dryden, for example—they often wrote in heroic couplets, as may be illustrated by the opening lines of Byles's "The Conflagration": "In some calm Midnight, when no whisp'ring Breeze / Waves the tall Woods, or curls th' undimpled Seas." Byles wrote several poems to Governor Jonathan Belcher ("An Elegy Address'd to His Excellency Governour Belcher: on the Death of his Brother-in-Law, the Honourable Daniel Oliver, Esq.," "To His Excellency Governour Belcher, on the Death of His Lady," and "On the Death of the Queen"), one to Belcher's predecessor ("To His Excellency Governour Burnet, on His Arrival at Boston"), two about the death of royalty ("A Poem on the Death of King George I. and Accession of King George II" as well as "On the Death of the Queen"), and one to Isaac Watts ("To the Reverend Dr. Watts, on His Divine Poems"). His most notable poems include "The Conflagration," "Eternity," "Written in Milton's *Paradise Lost,*" "The Comet," and "Hymn at Sea." In 1744 Byles left poetry with a flourish. That year appeared two volumes of verse: *A Collection of Poems,* which includes poems mainly by and about Byles and which is arguably the first anthology of American verse, and Byles's *Poems on Several Occasions,* which includes over thirty of his poems. He concludes his preface to the latter volume by stating, accurately, that with these poems he "bids adieu to the airy Muse." In the remaining forty-four years of his life, he published no more poems.

Unlike his illustrious forebears, Byles was not a major theologian, though his decades-long tenure in one church indicates that he satisfied his parishioners. One writer goes so far as to claim that Byles, on the basis of his sermons, was possibly "the best and most popular preacher of his generation" (Shipton). Over the years, some of his sermons were published. These include *A Discourse on the Present Vileness of the Body, and Its Future Glorious Change by Christ* and *A Sermon on the Nature and Importance of Conversion*, both delivered at Dorchester in 1732; some were so valued that they were published decades after he initially delivered them. He became, in 1732, the first minister of the Hollis Street Church in Boston. In the Province House in 1734, he married Anna Noyes Gale, widow of Azor Gale and niece of royal governor Belcher, who helped found the Hollis Street Church and was instrumental in securing Byles's appointment as its minister. Neither Byles nor his church participated in the frenzy accompanying the Great Awakening. As a result of being friendly with and indebted to Belcher and marrying into his family, Byles was predisposed to like the English; his continued affection for and friendships with them positioned him well in society for years but caused him problems at the time of the American Revolution. He and his wife had six children; she died in 1744. In 1747 he married Rebecca Tailer, whose father, William Tailer, held various governmental positions, including that of acting governor of Massachusetts. Byles and his second wife had three children. At the suggestion of Benjamin Franklin, the University of Aberdeen, Scotland, awarded Byles an honorary degree in 1765. All the while, he remained with the Hollis Street Church, to which he continued ministering until being dismissed, in 1776, for acting on his Tory sympathies by permitting British troops to quarter there. Although a civil court ordered him deported, because of his age, seventy, this punishment was reduced to two years of house arrest (lightly enforced), after which he was free to move about as he wished. This confinement led to two of his famous puns. He identified the sentinel guarding him as "my observe-a-Tory." When the guard was removed, returned, and finally dismissed, Byles said that he had "been guarded, re-guarded, and disregarded." His wife died in 1779; he suffered a paralytic shock in 1783 and died on 5 July 1788. He figures in later American literature as a character in Nathaniel Hawthorne's "Howe's Masquerade," one of four stories in "Legends of the Province-House."

TOPICS FOR DISCUSSION AND RESEARCH

1. In both prose and poetry, Byles was typical of his time by being derivative, inspired in the first genre primarily by Addison and in the second principally by Pope. One may get a sense of the aesthetics of the age and the accomplishment of Byles and other American writers by reading a few essays by Addison and some poems by Pope and comparing them with Byles's essays and poems. One will probably conclude that Byles is inferior to the English masters. If so, why is he? What are their similarities and differences? Does the subject matter of the essays influence one's response to them? If so, what are the differences in subject matter? Is the prose of one author more sophisticated than that of the other? Byles idolized Pope. Students would benefit from identifying the characteristics of neoclassical verse, which may be done

by consulting any book that reliably defines literary terms and movements. Then, identify these characteristics in poems by Pope and Byles, determining their relative effectiveness.

2. During the decade of the 1720s, American culture was changing from primarily religious to increasingly secular. This change may be documented in several ways, one of which is by examining the nature of the newspapers of the time. Following *The Boston News-Letter, The Boston Gazette,* and *The New-England Courant, The New-England Weekly Journal* was the fourth Boston newspaper. At its beginning in 1727 and at least into 1728, Byles was involved with it as an editor and contributor. Students interested in cultural history, the development of American newspapers, and public response to literature would benefit from reading random issues of these newspapers and comparing the nature of their contents. To what extent are the contents religious in nature? Commercial? Literary? Where in the papers does literature appear? What does its presence indicate about the publishers' and editors' impressions of readers' interests? For guidance in answering these questions, one might consult Charles E. Clark, *The Public Prints,* Elizabeth Christine Cook, *Literary Influences in Colonial Newspapers,* and Benjamin Franklin V, *The Other John Adams.*

3. Byles and Benjamin Franklin were almost exact contemporaries: Byles was born the year after Franklin and died two years before him. Their lives spanned most of the eighteenth century. They began their literary careers with Boston newspapers in the 1720s and were longtime friends. Byles was a college graduate and a Congregational minister; Franklin, an autodidact and not religious. In order to get a sense of various aspects of eighteenth-century America, students would benefit from comparing the lives, beliefs, and accomplishments of these men, especially in the contexts of public service and attitudes toward the American Revolution. On what issues do these men agree? Disagree? Reading biographies of them will provide answers to these questions.

4. Despite the early death of his father, Byles was a child of privilege; Franklin was not. Might their lives suggest themes that developed in American literature, such as the tainted nature of the privileged, as in Hawthorne's *The House of the Seven Gables,* and the poor-boy-makes-good stories of someone like Horatio Alger? What are other examples of these themes in American literature?

RESOURCES

Biography

Arthur W. H. Eaton, *The Famous Mather Byles* (Boston: Butterfield, 1914). The only full-scale biography of Byles.

Clifford K. Shipton, "Mather Byles," *Biographical Sketches of Those Who Attended Harvard College in the Classes 1722–1725,* volume 7 of *Sibley's Harvard Graduates* (Boston: Massachusetts Historical Society, 1945), pp. 464–493. A detailed, wittily written survey of Byles's life based in part on archival material.

Criticism

George Leonard Chaney, *Hollis Street Church from Mather Byles to Thomas Starr King. 1732–1861* (Boston: George H. Ellis, 1877).
Details Byles's long association with the Hollis Street Church.

Charles E. Clark, *The Public Prints: The Newspaper in Anglo-American Culture, 1665–1740* (New York: Oxford University Press, 1994).
Examines newspapers as a means of understanding the larger culture.

Elizabeth Christine Cook, *Literary Influences in Colonial Newspapers, 1704–1750* (New York: Columbia University Press, 1912).
Surveys the literature appearing in American newspapers to the mid eighteenth century.

Benjamin Franklin V, Introduction, *Works,* by Byles, compiled by Franklin (Delmar, N.Y.: Scholars' Facsimiles and Reprints, 1978).
Surveys Byles life and writings; focuses on "To My Friend: Occasioned by His Poem on Eternity," later titled "To an Ingenious Young Gentleman, on His Dedicating a Poem to the Author."

Franklin, *The Other John Adams, 1705–1740* (Madison, N.J.: Fairleigh Dickinson University Press, 2003).
Discusses Byles's participation in the Proteus Echo series of essays.

Austin Warren, "To Mr. Pope: Epistles from America," *PMLA,* 48 (March 1933): 67–73.
Reproduces Byles's four letters to Alexander Pope.

William Byrd II (1674–1744)

Aristocrat, Anglican, Anglophile, botanist, planter, book collector, diarist, historian, government official, traveler, linguist, ladies' man, and more, William Byrd II was born in Virginia to William Byrd and Mary Horsmanden Byrd on 28 March 1674; the couple bore three other children, all girls. His father, a goldsmith who left his native England for Virginia, became wealthy in America as a planter and trader. He sent his son, age seven, to England to live with relatives so he could be educated. Young Byrd resided there for almost two decades, during which time he attended the Felsted Grammar School in Essex, learned about business in Holland and London, and, beginning in 1692, studied law for three years at the Middle Temple, one of the Inns of Court. As a result of his legal training, in 1695 he was admitted to the bar. In London, he became cosmopolitan and made notable friends, including Sir Robert Southwell, who, having served as president of the Royal Society from 1690 to 1695, was instrumental in the twenty-two-year-old Byrd's becoming a member of this prestigious group in 1696.

Upon returning to Virginia in 1696, Byrd was elected to the House of Burgesses. He was back in England the following year and returned to Virginia in 1705, following the death of his father. The next year he married Lucy Parke, with whom he had two daughters. In 1709 he succeeded his father on the Governor's Council and began writing his secret diary, which was published in 1941 as *The Secret Diary of William Byrd of Westover, 1709–1712*. The following, dated 7 February 1709, is from this diary and gives the flavor of his entries:

> I rose at 7 o'clock and read a chapter in Hebrew and 200 verses in Homer's *Odyssey*. I said my prayers and ate milk for breakfast. I sent a boat and two hands to Appomattox for the pork. Daniel returned again to Falling Creek this morning. I ate nothing but beef for dinner. I read French. I walked about the plantation in the evening. I said my prayers. I had good thoughts, good health, and good humor, thanks be to God Almighty.

In 1710 he accepted responsibility for the debts of his late father-in-law in exchange for Daniel Parke's vast land holdings, an agreement that had long-term negative repercussions for Byrd because the debts proved onerous. A few years later he returned to London, where his wife died of smallpox in 1716 and where he kept a diary that was published in 1958 in *The London Diary (1717–1721) and Other Writings*. Back in Virginia, he presumably wrote *A Discourse Concerning the Plague, With Some Preservatives against It*, which was published in London in 1721 and is credited to "a Lover of Mankind." To avoid the disease, the author recommends heavy use of tobacco: smoking it, chewing it, wearing it, and generally surrounding oneself with it. During his final residence in London, which began in 1721, he married Maria Taylor in 1724; together, they had four children, three girls and a boy. Byrd kept a commonplace book from possibly 1722 until approximately 1726; it was published in 2001 as *The Commonplace Book of William Byrd II of Westover*. Soon after returning to Virginia in 1726, he led a team that surveyed the line that divides Virginia and North Carolina; his account of this experience was published in 1841 as *The History of the Dividing Line betwixt Virginia and North Carolina*. Byrd wrote another version of this history that was published in 1929 as *The Secret History of the Line*. He built a grand house at Westover in the early 1730s that still stands. In 1732 he visited the new mines in Germanna, Virginia, and at an uncertain date wrote about his experiences on this trip; his account was published in *A Progress to the Mines* in 1841. He surveyed his frontier land in 1733 and wrote about the expedition, also at an unknown date, in a manuscript ultimately published as *A Journey to the Land of Eden, A.D. 1733* (1841). During this trip he established, on his land, the towns of Richmond and Petersburg. In the late 1730s and early 1740s he kept another diary that was published in *Another Secret Diary of William Byrd of Westover, 1739–1741, with Letters & Literary Exercises, 1696–1726* (1942). While president of the Governor's Council, Byrd died, at age seventy, at his Westover plantation on 26 August 1744.

If Byrd wrote *A Discourse Concerning the Plague, With Some Preservatives against It*, it is his only book published during his lifetime. He was jealous of his other manuscripts, not wanting to publish until they were as he wanted them.

This time apparently never came. His major writings—*The Secret Diary of William Byrd of Westover*, *The London Diary*, and *The Secret History of the Line*—are often witty and reveal much about colonial life in Virginia, the southern landscape, an American in London, and Byrd generally. Primarily on the basis of these works, he is now considered a major colonial American author and the most important pre-Revolution southern writer.

TOPICS FOR DISCUSSION AND RESEARCH

1. In his diary, Byrd records his frequent and unsuccessful efforts to overcome deficiencies, such as lusting after another man's wife, failing to say his prayers, and so forth. Benjamin Franklin, of the next generation, is famous for recording his imperfections in the hope of overcoming them. Students would benefit from reading random selections from Byrd's diary and Franklin's *Autobiography* and comparing this tendency in the two men. Is one of them more genuine in the effort to improve himself than the other? Is one more successful in improving himself? Does either have a religious or moral reason for pursuing self-improvement? Or does one—or do both—strive for improvement mainly in order to satisfy himself? Is one more methodical than the other in attempting to rid himself of faults? Are the deficiencies of one man more serious than those of the other? One might also ask why Franklin's efforts to improve himself are well known while Byrd's are not.

2. Byrd wrote two different versions of his experiences surveying the line that separates Virginia and North Carolina. Robert Bain suggests that Byrd wrote *The History of the Dividing Line* with a British audience in mind, and *The Secret History of the Line* for reading by friends in the American South. Even though these manuscripts were not published during his lifetime, why might Byrd have written about the same events for different audiences? How dissimilar are the two versions? Differences may be observed by comparing passages in the two texts for the same date. The entry for 7 October 1728 in *The Secret History of the Line*, for example, is much longer than the version in *The History of the Dividing Line*, partly because it alone includes two lengthy letters. In *The Secret History of the Line*, Byrd comments negatively on North Carolinians, as he does not in *The History of the Dividing Line*. Consider why he omitted this information from the latter work. What is the nature of other differences between the two texts? One might benefit from reading additional selections from these books and asking if one is more formal and less revealing than the other. Is one more dramatic? For guidance in analyzing the two texts, one should consult William K. Boyd's introduction to *William Byrd's Histories of the Dividing Line betwixt Virginia and North Carolina* and Louis B. Wright's introduction to *The Prose Works of William Byrd of Westover*.

3. At the beginning of *The History of the Dividing Line*, Byrd comments about the nature of settlers' relations with Indians. After observing that earlier settlers had, after hostilities, made peace with Indians, he notes that Indians remained distrustful of the settlers because the whites were reluctant to marry

Indian women. Byrd believes that it was in the settlers' interest—converting Indians to Christianity and gaining protection from them—to intermarry. Further, even though Byrd owned slaves and generated much of his wealth because of their labor, late in life he believed that slavery ultimately benefited neither race. What do Byrd's attitudes toward darker races indicate about him? How do his thoughts compare with those of other southern aristocrats of the time, and of southerners generally in later times? Might Byrd have been influenced on the Indian issue by the thoughts expressed in *The History and Present State of Virginia* (1705) by the husband of his sister Ursula, Robert Beverley, who believed that miscegenation is desirable because of the problems it would solve? Information about these and other such issues raised by Byrd may be gleaned from histories of Indian-white and slave-white relations, especially in the South and particularly in Virginia.

4. Like Byrd, Cotton Mather, his contemporary in Massachusetts, was also a member of the Royal Society, though his membership resulted from scientific writings rather than from personal connections, as was largely the case with Byrd. In time, though, Byrd contributed to science in several writings, including making observations about natural America in his histories of the dividing line. How similarly or differently did the two men approach science? What were their motivations for scientific observation? Were their contributions significant? Substantial information about Mather may be found in Otho T. Beall Jr. and Richard H. Shryock, *Cotton Mather: First Significant Figure in American Medicine;* details about Byrd's interests are available in Pierre Marambaud, *William Byrd of Westover, 1674–1744*, chapter 6, and in *The Commonplace Book of William Byrd II of Westover*, chapter 7.

RESOURCES

Biography

Robert Bain, "William Byrd of Westover," in *The History of Southern Literature*, edited by Louis D. Rubin Jr., et al. (Baton Rouge: Louisiana State University Press, 1985), pp. 48–56.
Surveys the life of Byrd and focuses on him as a southern writer.

Richard Croom Beatty, *William Byrd of Westover* (Boston: Houghton Mifflin, 1932).
The first full-scale biography of Byrd.

Alden Hatch, *The Byrds of Virginia* (New York: Holt, Rinehart & Winston, 1969). Provides biographies of five Virginia Byrds, including William Byrd I ("The First William"), William Byrd II ("The Black Swan of Virginia"), and William Byrd III ("The Wastrel").

Pierre Marambaud, *William Byrd of Westover, 1674–1744* (Charlottesville: University Press of Virginia, 1971).
The second full-scale biography of Byrd.

Louis B. Wright, Introduction, *The London Diary (1717–1721) and Other Writings*, edited by Wright and Marion Tinling (New York: Oxford University Press, 1958).
Details the life of Byrd, emphasizing his years in England.

Criticism

Percy G. Adams, Introduction, *William Byrd's Histories of the Dividing Line betwixt Virginia and North Carolina*, edited by William K. Boyd (New York: Dover, 1967).
Updates William K. Boyd's introduction to an earlier edition of this book.

Otho T. Beall Jr. and Richard H. Shryock, *Cotton Mather: First Significant Figure in American Medicine* (Baltimore: Johns Hopkins University Press, 1954).
Argues that Mather "provides an almost unique mass of evidence concerning early American medicine, with all its implications for the social and cultural history of the times."

Kevin Berland, et al., Introduction, *The Commonplace Book of William Byrd II of Westover*, edited by Berland, et al. (Chapel Hill: University of North Carolina Press, 2001).
In a lengthy introduction, Berland, Jan Kirsten Gilliam, and Kenneth A. Lockridge discuss the nature of commonplace books, focus on Byrd's book, and comment on Byrd's observations about religion and women, among other topics.

William K. Boyd, Introduction, *William Byrd's Histories of the Dividing Line betwixt Virginia and North Carolina*, edited by Boyd (Raleigh: North Carolina Historical Commission, 1929).
Compares and contrasts Byrd's two manuscripts about the dividing line, provides a history of the border dispute between the two colonies, and offers a brief biography of the author.

Louis B. Wright, Introduction, *The Prose Works of William Byrd of Westover: Narratives of a Colonial Virginian*, edited by Wright (Cambridge: Belknap Press of Harvard University Press, 1966).
Discusses Byrd as man of letters by analyzing and providing contexts for four of his works: *The Secret History of the Line, The History of the Dividing Line, A Progress to the Mines*, and *A Journey to the Land of Eden Anno 1733*.

Wright, Introduction, *The Secret Diary of William Byrd of Westover, 1709–1712*, edited by Wright and Marion Tinling (Richmond: Dietz Press, 1941).
Discusses Byrd's manuscript diary, the shorthand in which Byrd wrote it, and its intimacy.

Charles Chauncy (1705–1787)

Best known as the major opponent of the Great Awakening and therefore as an adversary of Jonathan Edwards, Charles Chauncy, whose life spanned most of the eighteenth century, also was interested and involved in events leading to the American Revolution. His ancestry is impressive: he was the great-grandson of the second president of Harvard College, Charles Chauncy, the grandson of an English minister, Isaac Chauncy, and, on his mother's side, a judge of the Massachusetts supreme court, John Walley. He was born in Boston on 1 January 1705 to Charles Chauncy, a merchant, and Sarah Walley Chauncy. After attending the Boston Latin School, at age sixteen he was graduated from Harvard with the class of 1721. Among his classmates were John Adams, minister, poet, and essayist; Isaac Greenwood, the initial Hollis Professor of Mathematics at Harvard; Ebenezer Pemberton, a founder of the College of New Jersey (now Princeton University); Stephen Sewall, Harvard librarian and later chief justice of the Massachusetts supreme court; and Ebenezer Turell, a minister who wrote a biography of his father-in-law, Benjamin Colman. After completing his degree, Chauncy remained at Harvard, studying religion, until 1727. This year, he married Elizabeth Hirst, with whom he had three children; he also became an associate of Thomas Foxcroft at the First Church in Boston, to which he ministered for the remainder of his life. (Following the death of his wife in 1737, he married Elizabeth Phillips Townsend, who died in 1757; then, in 1760 he wed Mary Stoddard, who died in 1783.) He assumed the First Church position at a time of change, when Bostonians were less religiously intense than previously and were embracing Enlightenment ideas from Europe; in other words, they were valuing reason more than religious doctrine. Generally wealthy and cosmopolitan, the First Church congregation reflected this development. So did Chauncy, as indicated by such a sermon as *Early Piety Recommended and Exemplify'd* (1732).

Chauncy began presenting his thoughts to an audience beyond his congregation in 1731 with the publication of his sermon *Man's Life Considered under the Similitude of a Vapour, That Appeareth for a Little Time, and Then Vanisheth Away.* Thereafter, his sermons and other writings appeared frequently until 1785, two years before his death. His most important publications appeared during the first half of the 1740s, when he commented on issues relating to the Great Awakening. He felt uneasy about this movement from the beginning, primarily because its heightened emotionalism—caused by feeling God's presence within—rendered a reasoned consideration of the Bible irrelevant. He eased his way into the debate with *An Unbridled Tongue a Sure Evidence, That Our Religion is Hypocritical and Vain* and *The New Creature Describ'd, and Consider'd as the Sure Characteristick of a Man's Being in Christ* (both 1741). Then, the next year, he became more pointed in *Enthusiasm Described and Caution'd Against,* in which he characterizes people moved to emotional frenzy as delusional. Chauncy expressed himself most fully in *Seasonable Thoughts on the State of Religion in New-England* (1743), his most significant work. Here, he attacks and rebuts the points Jonathan Edwards makes about the legitimacy of emotional conversion in *Some Thoughts Concerning the Present Revival of Religion in New-England* (1742). Chauncy argues that reason should guide one in all things; he also posits that unbridled emotion is unacceptable in religion but also in society generally where, if unchecked by reason, it would threaten the social order. Further, he objects to revivalists preaching in areas already served by a minister. In so stating, Chauncy reveals his fear that such revivalists as George Whitefield and Gilbert Tennent will attract members of his and other traditionalists' congregations, thereby threatening their ecclesiastical and social power, as well as their purse. Chauncy published more attacks on the Great Awakening as its fervor waned in 1744–1745.

Chauncy was not reluctant to take a stand. He joined Jonathan Mayhew in opposing the establishment of Anglicanism in America and published several works arguing his position; these two men and others feared that its establishment would lead to the suppression of dissenting religious views, ones that were then well established in America and that they, themselves, believed and promulgated. Their fear of oppressive English rule was heightened when, in 1765, George III dictated to the colonies with the Stamp Act. Partly because of the efforts of Chauncy, Mayhew, and others, the act was repealed.

Military issues interested Chauncy. Understanding the French threat during the French and Indian War, he tried to rally support for the war from his disinterested congregation. After analyzing the British defeat near Fort Duquesne, he recommended using colonial commanders—not British ones, like Edward Braddock—as well as local combatants to fight the French and Indians.

As the English presence in Boston and New England became increasingly onerous and as revolution was in the air, Chauncy was involved, on the Patriot side. When George III established the Coercive Acts following the Boston Tea Party, for example, Chauncy wrote against them in *A Letter to a Friend. Giving a Concise, but Just, Representation of the Hardships and Sufferings the Town of Boston Is Exposed to, and Must Undergo in Consequence of the Late Act of the British Parliament* (1774). He also corresponded about events with such an activist as Samuel Adams and went so far, shortly after the publication of the Declaration of Independence, as to force the removal of the Tory Mather Byles from his position as minister of the Hollis Street Church.

Late in life, Chauncy resumed writing about religious issues, including detailing his beliefs in *The Mystery Hid from Ages and Generations* (1784). He died in his parsonage on 10 February 1787, at age eighty-two.

TOPICS FOR DISCUSSION AND RESEARCH

1. Using Chauncy as an example of the religious establishment at the time of the Great Awakening, one could reasonably ask why worshipers found a rational approach to religion limiting to the degree that they were prepared to receive the message of preachers such as George Whitefield and others, men who inspired them to emotional frenzy and helped them feel that God resided within them. Alternatively, why might many of Chauncy's congregation in particular have stayed with him and found the new religious emotional-

ism unappealing, if not troubling and offputting? Help in answering these questions may be found in any serious study of the Great Awakening and of American religion generally during the 1740s. Perry Miller's *Jonathan Edwards* and Patricia U. Bonomi's *Under the Cope of Heaven* would be good places to begin.

2. Chauncy was not the first American clergyman to fear the establishment of Anglicanism in America, nor would he be the last. What is the historical background for this attitude? What was the relationship between the Puritans and Anglicans in England in the late sixteenth and early seventeenth century? Why did this relationship lead, ultimately, to the sailing of the *Mayflower* in 1620 and the populating of New England by English men and women soon thereafter? In other words, one would benefit from asking if Chauncy's concern was justified. Any decent book treating the history of the Pilgrims—or books dealing with the history of religion in America—would help provide answers to these and collateral questions.

3. As Chauncy fought against the encroachment of Anglicanism on American religion, he also argued strongly against the heavy-handed establishment of unfair acts and laws in the colonies. The Stamp Act was the first to draw his ire. What aspects of the Stamp Act particularly irritated him? Why? Might his stands against Anglicanism and the imposition of the Stamp Act have stemmed from a common belief? If so, what is it? Edward M. Griffin's *Old Brick* provides information for answering these questions.

4. In arguing for the use of colonial soldiers in fighting the French and Indians, Chauncy, without military training, was prescient. Consider his recommendation in the context of the American Revolution, when the British, the enemy, fielded troops unfamiliar with the local terrain. The American troops knew the geography. Why was such awareness important? How significant was this knowledge in the execution of the Revolution? Any reputable history of the American Revolution will answer these questions.

RESOURCES

Biography

Edward M. Griffin, *Old Brick: Charles Chauncy of Boston, 1705–1787* (Minneapolis: University of Minnesota Press, 1980).
The only full-scale biography of Chauncy.

Charles H. Lippy, *Seasonable Revolutionary: The Mind of Charles Chauncy* (Chicago: Nelson-Hall, 1981).
A brief but compelling intellectual biography of Chauncy.

Clifford K. Shipton, "Charles Chauncy," *Biographical Sketches of Those Who Attended Harvard College in the Classes 1713–1721*, volume 6 of *Sibley's Harvard Graduates* (Boston: Massachusetts Historical Society, 1942), pp. 569–571.
Presents a factual biography of Chauncy and places his thoughts and writings in context.

Criticism

Patricia U. Bonomi, *Under the Cope of Heaven: Religion, Society, and Politics in Colonial America* (New York: Oxford University Press, 1986).
Avers that instead of declining during the eighteenth century, as is generally believed, American religious life grew to the degree that it was "more or less equivalent to processes in the economic and political realms as an influence on the formation of early American culture."

John Corrigan, *The Hidden Balance: Religion and the Social Theories of Charles Chauncy and Jonathan Mayhew* (Cambridge, England: Cambridge University Press, 1987).
Argues that during the period between the Great Awakening and the American Revolution, there was a "contest between (1) new ideas about and evidences of personal virtue and effort and (2) traditional social institutions grounded in an essentially elitist view of society, skeptical of human capability," and that Chauncy and Jonathan Mayhew "struggled to fashion elements drawn from each side of the conflict into coherent statements about God, man, and the world."

Perry Miller, *Jonathan Edwards* (New York: William Sloane Associates, 1949).
Discusses Chauncy's role as Jonathan Edwards's antagonist during the Great Awakening.

Benjamin Colman (1673–1747)

A voice of moderation during a transitional time in American Congregationalism, Benjamin Colman was born in Boston on 19 October 1673 to William and Elizabeth Colman, who had emigrated from England two years earlier. After being taught by his mother and the famous Ezekiel Cheever, he matriculated at Harvard College in 1688 and received his degree four years later. The president of the college, Increase Mather, was in England during the entirety of Colman's undergraduate career. John Leverett, who succeeded Mather as president, tutored Colman. After preaching for six months in Medford, Massachusetts, Colman returned to Harvard, from which he received a master's degree in 1695.

Following his second degree, Colman sailed for England. En route, his ship was attacked by pirates, who took him and others to France, where they were jailed for several months. Upon release, he went to London. He boarded with the family of Thomas Parkhurst, a bookseller through whom he met various religious dissenters. Colman preached in England, including in Bath for over two years. While in England, he absorbed urbanity, including the attention of the poet Elizabeth Singer (later, Rowe); his refusal to live permanently in England led, apparently, to their decision not to marry.

At this time, some Bostonians desired a church less restrictive than that of the Second Church of Increase Mather and Cotton Mather. As a result, Thomas Brattle gave land for what became known as the Brattle Street Church, which liberalized certain aspects of the Mathers' church, including the requirements for membership. The new church detailed the nature of its government in a document known as the Brattle Street Manifesto (1699), to which Colman probably contributed. Although the Mathers ultimately accepted this church, initially they opposed it, as evidenced by Increase Mather's *The Order of the Gospel* (1700); the new church responded in *Gospel Order Revived* (1700), to which Colman was probably the major contributor. Colman became the first minister of the church in 1699. His importance dates from this appointment.

Colman married Jane Clark in 1700; together they had three children: a son who died in infancy; Jane, whose husband, Ebenezer Turell, became her father's biographer; and Abigail. Following the death of his wife in 1730, Colman married the widow Sarah Clark in 1732; the second of her three previous husbands was John Leverett. Sarah Colman died in 1744, and the next year Colman married the widow Mary Frost, sister of Sir William Pepperrell, merchant and noted soldier about whom Nathaniel Hawthorne wrote a sketch published in 1833. Colman outlived his children and died on 28 August 1747.

A masterful preacher, Colman wrote voluminously—letters, sermons, tracts on social issues, and more—in a sophisticated style inspired by the English essayist Joseph Addison. He also wrote poems, an early example of which is *A Poem on Elijah's Translation* (1707), which commemorates the life of Samuel Willard, minister of Boston's Third Church and acting president of Harvard. Later, he would deliver sermons at the funerals of such notables as John Leverett (*The Master Taken Up from the Sons of the Prophets*, 1724), Cotton Mather (*The Holy Walk and Glorious Translation of Blessed Enoch*, 1728), and Solomon Stoddard (*The Faithful Ministers of Christ Mindful of Their Own Death*, 1729). One of his initial publications was *Faith Victorious* (1702), a sermon preached to the Artillery Company, later known as the Ancient and Honorable Artillery Company of Massachusetts, which dates from 1638 and is the oldest military group in what is now the United States. Five years later he published the first of his series of sermons as *Practical Discourses upon the Parable of the Ten Virgins*. As Teresa Toulouse observes, in the sermon on Matt. 25:2-4 Colman proposes that reason and common sense inspire religious behavior and that such behavior is in individuals' best interest. The terms he uses constitute a break from seventeenth-century concepts.

A smallpox epidemic struck Boston in 1721. The new procedure of inoculation caused heated debate. One group, including Dr. William Douglass and all but one of the other Boston doctors, railed against it, while the other, including Colman, Cotton Mather, and Dr. Zabdiel Boylston, argued in its favor. Boylston did the inoculating. Colman wrote about this issue in *Some Observations on the New Method of Receiving the Small-Pox by Ingrafting or Inoculation* (1721). This document shows his enlightened thinking and demonstrates his interest in topics other than religion.

Although the Puritans and later Congregational ministers believed that one should not lament the death of loved ones too profoundly because one should not be too attached to things of the world, Colman deeply laments the death of his daughter, Jane, in *Reliquiæ Turellæ, et Lachrymæ Paternæ. The Father's Tears over His Daughter's Remains* (1735). This work memorializes Jane Colman Turell, but it also humanizes Colman. That same year Ebenezer Turell's biography of his wife was published as *Memoirs of the Life and Death of the Pious and Ingenious Mrs. Jane Turell,* which is the source of all her extant poems.

Colman's ministry coincided with a general decline in religious fervor that lasted until the Great Awakening, and his well-written and -delivered sermons were inadequate to stop the increasing lassitude. Therefore, he welcomed the Great Awakening, characterized by an emotional approach to religion that swept the Atlantic seaboard. The Great Awakening was inspired by the thoughts, writings, and preaching of Colman's friend Jonathan Edwards, who wrote about the early stages of the movement in a work ultimately known as *A Faithful Narrative of the Surprising Work of God* (1737). Edwards composed it as a letter to Colman, who later wrote positively about the preaching of George Whitefield, who popularized the movement, in *Soul's Flying to Christ Pleasant and Admirable to Behold* (1740). His position allied him with Edwards and Whitefield and positioned him against Charles Chauncy, the influential minister of Boston's First Church.

Colman preached to Indians and supported missionaries to them. He was also involved in issues that were not strictly religious in nature but that were for the common good. In 1713 he proposed establishing two charity schools, one for boys and one for girls. He wanted markets created, as he details in *Some Reasons and Arguments Offered to the Good People of Boston, and Adjacent Places, for the Setting Up of Markets in Boston* (1719). He served Harvard as overseer and fellow and was instrumental in securing the significant donations—money and books—to the college by the London merchant Thomas Hollis. Although Colman was elected to succeed John Leverett as president of Harvard, he declined the position. Despite his long association with and dedication to his alma mater, Colman also supported Yale College. In 1731, the University of Glasgow awarded him the degree Doctor of Divinity.

TOPICS FOR DISCUSSION AND RESEARCH

1. When Colman proposes that reason and common sense inspire religious behavior and that such behavior is in people's best interest, he uses concepts that became standard in the eighteenth century. Probably the most important American of the century, Benjamin Franklin, valued similar concepts, though in a secular, not a religious manner or context. Students would benefit from reading Teresa Toulouse's discussion of Colman's sermons and pertinent selections from Franklin's *Autobiography* in order to consider Colman as expressing, early in the century, eighteenth-century values that became standard later, perhaps most obviously in Franklin's presentation of his own life. How do Colman's religious concerns inform the minister's concepts of "reason," "common sense," and "best interest"? What is the significance of Franklin's secular use of these same terms?

2. Inoculation works by giving someone a small dose of a disease being fought, thereby causing immunity to it. In Boston, Zabdiel Boylston inoculated people in a generally successful effort to protect the population during the smallpox

epidemic of 1721. Yet, the concept of inoculation caused great debate. Why did it? By reading about the Boston epidemic of 1721–1722 (as in John B. Blake, "The Inoculation Controversy in Boston"), students can understand the issues that Colman and others had to address when formulating their positions on this life-or-death issue. History has proven Colman and the supporters of inoculation correct. On what basis did he and they form their opinions? What were some of the arguments against inoculation?

3. Unofficial groups known as the Old Lights and New Lights responded differently to the Great Awakening, with the primary issue being the appropriateness of the movement's emotionalism. The rationalist Old Lights, Charles Chauncy paramount among them, objected to the emotionalism, but the New Lights, such as Gilbert Tennent and James Davenport, favored it. Though a New Light in the sense that he welcomed George Whitefield and approved the increased focus on religion, Colman adopted a more moderate stance than other New Lights, such as Davenport. How is his attempted moderation consistent with other aspects of his life? Students would benefit from reading any summary of the Great Awakening and considering the positions of the Old Lights and New Lights. What did the Old Lights find so offensive about emotionalism? Did it cause people to lose sight of other important aspects of the religious experience? Did the New Lights embrace emotionalism for political reasons, in the sense that many people became passionate about religion, as they had not been for several decades? What biblical reasons might the New Lights have had for not only supporting but encouraging emotionalism?

4. Colman was hardly the first minister to preach to the Indians. The early Puritans, though, found them generally hostile and viewed them as agents of the devil. Only a few Puritans, such as John Eliot, attempted to convert them. Over time, attitudes changed. Students would benefit from charting this evolution in perception from the early seventeenth century, including King Philip's War and a consideration of Roger Williams, until Colman's age, a period of roughly a century. Did the decreasing Indian population make these adversaries less threatening? Did religious attitudes become less extreme, thereby permitting English-speaking people generally to consider Indians as people, not fiends? William S. Simmons's "Cultural Bias in the New England Puritans' Perception of Indians" provides a good starting place for answering these questions.

RESOURCES

Biography

Christopher R. Reaske, Introduction, *The Life and Character of the Reverend Benjamin Colman, D.D. (1749)*, by Ebenezer Turell (Delmar, N.Y.: Scholars' Facsimiles and Reprints, 1972).

Reliably examines Colman's career and places it in historical perspective.

Clifford K. Shipton, "Benjamin Colman," *Biographical Sketches of Those Who Attended Harvard College in the Classes 1690–1700*, volume 4 of *Sibley's Harvard Graduates* (Cambridge, Mass.: Harvard University Press, 1933), pp. 120–137.

A succinct, authoritative account of Colman's career, based partly on archival material and including a list of the minister's publications.

Ebenezer Turell, *The Life and Character of the Reverend Benjamin Colman, D.D., Late Pastor of a Church in Boston New-England Who Deceased August 29th 1747* (Boston: Rogers & Fowle, and J. Edwards, 1749).
A biography, by Colman's son-in-law, that includes poems and letters by the subject, as well as a list of his publications.

Criticism

John B. Blake, "The Inoculation Controversy in Boston: 1721–1722," *New England Quarterly*, 25 (December 1952): 489–506.
Examines the issues involved in the 1721–1722 inoculation controversy in Boston.

William S. Simmons, "Cultural Bias in the New England Puritans' Perception of Indians," *William and Mary Quarterly*, 38 (January 1981): 56–72.
Examines why the New England Puritans thought that Indians "worshipped devils, that Indian religious practitioners were witches, and that the Indians themselves were bewitched."

Teresa Toulouse, *The Art of Prophesying: New England Sermons and the Shaping of Belief* (Athens: University of Georgia Press, 1987).
Discusses how four preachers, including Colman, theoretically and practically blended prophesying and art.

Ebenezer Cook (circa 1667–circa 1732)

Little is known about the life of the poet Ebenezer Cook (sometimes spelled Cooke). He was born around 1667—possibly in England, possibly in America—to Andrew Cook and Anne Bowyer Cook. He had at least one sibling, Anna. From no later than 1694 he lived in Maryland until removing to London circa 1701. After another absence from London, he returned there before 1708. No later than 1720 he revisited Maryland, where he worked as land agent and lawyer. His subsequent biography is unknown, including the year and place of death, though he possibly died around 1732.

For two reasons, Cook is best known as author of a poem printed and sold in London by Benjamin Bragg in 1708: *The Sot-Weed Factor: Or, a Voyage to Maryland. A Satyr. In Which Is Describ'd the Laws, Government, Courts and Constitutions of the Country; and also the Buildings, Feasts, Frolicks, Entertainments and Drunken Humours of the Inhabitants of That Part of America. In Burlesque Verse.* First, it is by far his major literary achievement and is an important document in the history of American letters; second, a significant novel is based on it and has Ebenezer

Cook as its protagonist: John Barth's *The Sot-Weed Factor* (1960). Cook and the title are probably better known from the novel than from Cook's poem.

Cook's father was a sot-weed factor. A "sot" is a drunkard, "weed" means tobacco, and a "factor" is an agent or merchant. Therefore, the elder Cook sold besotting tobacco, as the speaker sells it in the poem titled for him.

After a three-month trip to Maryland from England, where the penurious speaker was friendless, he recounts his experiences in America, as well as his impressions of its people, geography, and institutions, as is indicated by the lengthy subtitle. Although Cook himself was not new to Maryland at the time the poem was published, the speaker has never before been there, which makes his natural naiveté all the more pronounced. He arrives with incorrect perceptions of Americans and Marylanders, and does not become much enlightened as events unfold. These events range from having his clothing burned to being cheated by a Quaker. At the conclusion of the poem, the speaker, looking back on his experiences from ship or England, levels a broadside at the Americans. He hopes they will be eaten by cannibals, be shut out from trade and therefore starve, become as savage as Indians, and have their country made a wasteland by God. The speaker will doubtless not return to this place that treated him badly and that he has just cursed.

Cook, however, was not finished with the (or a) factor, for more than two decades later William Parks in Annapolis printed Cook's *Sotweed Redivivus: Or the Planters Looking-Glass. In Burlesque Verse. Calculated for the Meridian of Maryland* (1730). ("Redivivus" means revived.) If the speaker is the same as that of the earlier poem, his residence in Maryland indicates that the previous rage of this now old man dissipated long ago. Unfortunately, this later poem lacks the liveliness and satiric edge of its predecessor and by almost any measure is inferior to it. Because the factor addresses the crisis caused by Maryland's reliance on one crop, tobacco, much of the poem concerns economic issues of the time that are of little interest to the contemporary reader. The poem is modern in at least one way, however, and that is in its brief ecological lament that trees are cut indiscriminately; this implies that a day might come when the virgin forests will become imperiled.

Cook wrote a few other poems, all of little note. A book titled *The Maryland Muse* (1731) contains two poems. One is "The History of Colonel Nathaniel Bacon's Rebellion in Virginia. Done into Hudibrastick Verse, from an old MS." This, the longest of Cook's poems, recounts the 1676 events involving Indians, Governor William Berkeley of Virginia, and rebels led by Nathaniel Bacon in what was probably the first uprising by colonists against English rule. Cook disapproves of Bacon's actions. The other poem is a revised version of Cook's most important poem, now titled *The Sotweed Factor, or Voiage to Maryland*, which has a milder conclusion than the 1708 version. *An Elogy on the Death of Thomas Bordley, Esq.* (1726), which memorializes the late Maryland attorney general, is, according to J. A. Leo Lemay, "the earliest extant belletristic work printed in the colony." It is also the first of Cook's works to identify the author as the poet laureate of Maryland, a title that was probably never bestowed on Cook. Two years later in *The Maryland Gazette* (24 December 1728), Cook acknowledged the death of the brother of Henry Lowe and Bennett Lowe, who had aided Cook professionally ("An Elegy on the Death of the Honourable Nicholas Lowe"). One other elegy (on William Lock) was published in an unreliable text long after Cook's death, and another one (on Leonard Calvert) has been attributed to Cook.

TOPICS FOR DISCUSSION AND RESEARCH

1. Although we cannot know how accurately Cook describes Maryland in *The Sot-Weed Factor*, though surely he exaggerates for effect, his depiction of it is negative: he criticizes it in order to alert possible émigrés to the unattractiveness of the territory they might sometime inhabit. His poem constitutes a warning; it discourages settlement. It is the opposite of works by William Penn, for example, that promote immigration. Why might Cook have created a speaker who assumes such a stance? In answering this question, one might consider that Cook's satire is double-edged, that the author's ultimate goal is something other than discouraging immigration. Cook presents the speaker as an Englishman with preconceived but incorrect notions of what he will experience in Maryland. This seeming sophisticate is duped and insulted by the rustic Americans. The two major critics of this poem, Edward H. Cohen and J. A. Leo Lemay, comment on this aspect of it. If this interpretation is correct, then *The Sot-Weed Factor* stands at the beginning of a long tradition in American literature, especially in Southern humor, that depicts rubes besting their supposed superiors. Within this context, students would benefit from comparing Cook's poem with perhaps the most famous work in this tradition, Mark Twain's "The Celebrated Jumping Frog of Caleveras County" (1865). Twain's story focuses on Jim Smiley's gambling but really is about the duping of the frame narrator, an educated but unwitting easterner, by Simon Wheeler, a garrulous, uneducated story-teller in a Western mining camp.

2. Cook frequently wrote Hudibrastic verse, so called because of the popularity of English poet Samuel Butler's seventeenth-century *Hudibras*. This poem has lines of iambic tetrameter; rhymes *aa, bb, cc,* and so forth; and uses feminine rhymes. In a feminine rhyme, the two final syllables rhyme and the last syllable is usually unaccented. These rhymes create humor, as is evident in *Hudibras* and limericks, which is why they are sometimes used in satiric verse. Consider Cook's use of feminine rhymes in *The Sot-Weed Factor*. Do they in fact create humor? If so, in which instances, and how? (Lemay believes that this poem is "the best hudibrastic poem of colonial America.") Also Hudibrastic, *Sotweed Redivivus* is less humorous than *The Sot-Weed Factor*. Is this because the feminine rhymes are less effective than in the earlier poem? Does it result from the drier subject matter? From Cook's desire to be more persuasive than satirical, as Cohen suggests?

3. The 1708 edition of *The Sot-Weed Factor* concludes bitterly and hostilely as the speaker curses Maryland for having treated him badly. He wants the people destroyed and sent to hell, as may be observed in the concluding lines:

May Canniballs transported o'er the Sea
Prey on these Slaves, as they have done on me;
May never Merchant's, trading Sails explore
This Cruel, this Inhospitable Shoar;
But left abandon'd by the World to starve,
May they sustain the Fate they well deserve;
May they turn Savage, or as Indians Wild,
From Trade, Converse, and Happiness exil'd;
Recreant to Heaven, may they adore the Sun,
And into Pagan Superstitions run
For Vengence ripe------------------
May Wrath Divine then lay those Regions wast
Where no Man's Faithful, nor a Woman Chast.

The 1731 version ends as follows:

If any Youngster cross the Ocean,
To sell his Wares—may he with Caution
Before he pays, receive each Hogshead,
Lest he be cheated by some Dogshead,
Both of his Goods and his Tobacco;
And then like me, he shall not lack-woe.
And may that Land where Hospitality,
Is every Planter's darling Quality,
Be by each Trader kindly us'd,
And may no Trader be abus'd;
Then each of them shall deal with Pleasure,
And each encrease the other's Treasure.

The 1731 edition did not change much of the 1708 text other than these concluding lines. This means that the double-edged satire remains. Does the revision weaken the poem? Strengthen it? How? Why might Cook have revised
the conclusion from an imprecation to a wish for, essentially, good manners
and fair dealing? One should consult Cohen for guidance in answering these
questions.

4. While historically, culturally, and artistically important, *The Sot-Weed Factor* is
not well known. Yet, John Barth appropriated it and Cook for *The Sot-Weed
Factor*, a novel that became popular and critically acclaimed. What qualities
about the poem and author might have appealed to Barth? The novel is fiction,
but do aspects of it more-or-less faithfully render parts of the poem and what
is known about Cook? If so, which aspects? Turn to David Morrell's article for
guidance in answering these questions and others relating to Barth's use of the
poem and Cook.

RESOURCES

Criticism

Edward H. Cohen, *Ebenezer Cooke: The Sot-Weed Canon* (Athens: University of Georgia Press, 1975).
Examines Cook's poems as art and concludes that in them "one may discern the roots of an American culture."

J. A. Leo Lemay, *Men of Letters in Colonial Maryland* (Knoxville: University of Tennessee Press, 1972), pp. 77–110, 357–361.
Convincingly analyzes Cook's poems, putting them in historical and artistic perspective.

David Morrell, "Ebenezer Cook, Sot-Weed Factor Redivivus: The Genesis of John Barth's *The Sot-Weed Factor*," *Bulletin of the Midwest Modern Language Association*, 8 (Spring 1975): 32–47.
Examines the degree to which Cook's life and *The Sot-Weed Factor* influenced John Barth's composing of the novel *The Sot-Weed Factor*.

John Cotton (1584–1652)

On 4 December 1584, John Cotton was born in Derby, England, to Roland Cotton, a lawyer, and Mary Hurlbert Cotton. He received a bachelor of arts degree (1602) at Trinity College, Cambridge University. For six years following his master's degree (1606), he served as fellow at Emmanuel College, Cambridge. During his last year there (1612), he received a bachelor of divinity degree, whereupon he became vicar of St. Botolph's church in Boston, England. Over the years, many of his English sermons were collected and published in five volumes. He and his wife, Elizabeth Horrocks, whom he married in 1613, had no children. In 1630 he delivered the sermon *Gods Promise to His Plantation* to John Winthrop and others before they departed Southampton, England, for America in the vanguard of the great migration. His wife died in 1631, and the next year he married the widow Sarah Hawkridge Story, with whom he had six children. In 1633 he and his wife sailed for America; en route, their son Seaborn was born. In September they arrived in Boston, where Cotton became teacher of the Boston church that John Wilson served as minister. The next year, Anne Hutchinson arrived in Boston. Her beliefs (partly drawn from Cotton, whose sermons she heard in England) and teachings led to the Antinomian Controversy of 1636–1638, in which Cotton played an important part. In 1642 his daughter Mariah was born; she later married Increase Mather and became the mother of Cotton Mather, named for Cotton. Also in 1642 he declined an invitation to participate, in London, in the Westminster Assembly of Divines, which the Long Parliament appointed to reform the Church of England. Cotton became involved, in the 1640s, in a published debate with Roger Williams over several issues, including those of liberty of conscience and the separation of church and state. He participated in the Cambridge Synod (1646–1648) that adopted the Cambridge Platform, which he influenced significantly. Cotton, who defined and was the leading proponent of the New England Way, died in Boston, Massachusetts, on 23 December 1652.

A 1611 discourse about when the Sabbath should begin, at sunset on Saturday or on Sunday morning, is the earliest of Cotton's writings to be published, though it did not appear until 1982. Other than a preface to a book of lectures by Arthur Hildersam (1629), the 1630 sermon to Winthrop's group is the first of Cotton's works to be published more or less at the time of composition. At the end of the sermon, Cotton justifies taking land from the Indians while urging their conversion. He is the first person to describe the Puritans' form of church organization as Congregational, a concept he explains in *The True Constitution of a Particular Visible Church*, written in the mid 1630s but not published until 1642, the year he declined an invitation to attend the Westminster Assembly of Divines. Cotton is the probable author of the preface to a book known as *The Bay Psalm Book* (1640), the earliest American publication of which a copy is known to exist. A little later, he wrote *The Keyes of the Kingdom of Heaven* (1644), a tract intended to convince the Assembly to adopt Congregationalism in England; he defended his position in *The Way of Congregational Churches Cleared* (1648). Also in 1648, Cotton wrote a preface for *A Platform of Church Discipline Gathered out of the Word of God* (better known as the Cambridge Platform), a document that established Congregational principles and that remains the basis of Congregational government; although Richard Mather wrote the text, he used many of Cotton's ideas.

The Antinomian Controversy revolved around Anne Hutchinson, who expressed religious views that resonated with a substantial number of Boston church members but that ultimately caused her trouble with the authorities. Cotton wrote about the matter, especially in the pamphlet *Sixteene Questions of Serious and Necessary Consequence* (1644). It contains the questions posed to him by other ministers and his responses to them, one of which—that good works (sanctification) constitute evidence of saving grace (justification)—represents an apparent change of position. His revised opinion undercut the theological basis of an important aspect of Hutchinson's beliefs.

Cotton engaged in a written debate with Roger Williams, who argued, among other things, for the separation of church and state in a society that was essentially theocratic. Cotton began the discussion innocently by writing a letter to Williams, encouraging him to alter his views. It was published in London in 1643 as *A Letter of Mr. John Cottons . . . to Mr. Williams*. Williams responded to it the next year in *Mr. Cottons Letter Lately Printed, Examined and Answered*. Also in 1644, Williams published *The Bloudy Tenent, of Persecution, for Cause of Conscience, Discussed*. Cotton responded to Williams in *A Reply to Mr. Williams His Examination* and *The Bloudy Tenent, Washed and Made White in the Bloud of the Lambe* (both 1647). Williams had the last word in *The Bloody Tenent Yet More Bloody* (1652).

One of Cotton's most influential publications is probably the shortest, *Milk for Babes* (1646), a catechism for children. In it, Cotton presents the tenets of Puritan belief, emphasizing mankind's innate depravity yet offering the possibility of salvation. It went through at least seven editions in the seventeenth century (plus one in the Indian language Massachusett) and beginning no later than 1690 was included in many editions of *The New-England Primer*.

TOPICS FOR DISCUSSION AND RESEARCH

1. In England, one of Cotton's parishioners was Anne Hutchinson, who so valued his preaching that she and her large family followed him to America. There, she took seriously what she understood to be his belief that faith, not works, is the sign of saving grace. After observing that Boston ministers other than Cotton seemed to preach that good works constitute evidence of saving grace, she began expressing her and Cotton's views to ever-increasing numbers of people. She emphasized the indwelling of the Holy Spirit, which implies that people possessing it need not obey the Ten Commandments because they are already assured of salvation. Such a thought not only was at variance with what most ministers believed and taught, but, taken to an extreme, it threatened the smooth functioning of Boston society by eliminating sacred instructions for moral living. In an effort to understand the source of Hutchinson's beliefs, ministers asked Cotton to explain his; in responding to them, he modified his previously held views somewhat. Hutchinson was then tried, excommunicated, and expelled from Massachusetts Bay. One might beneficially examine the documents and ask to what degree Cotton believed that sanctification is evidence of justification and how much, if at all, he altered his position when asked about it by the other ministers. Were his comments self-serving? Did he owe allegiance to Hutchinson, who expressed views derived from his teaching? If he modified his views in order to remain in good standing with other ministers and if he abandoned Hutchinson, how might these actions affect his reputation as perhaps the most important Boston cleric of his generation? Larzer Ziff's *The Career of John Cotton* discusses these and other issues relating to the Antinomian Controversy.

2. Cotton, John Winthrop, and others had problems with Roger Williams, a Puritan minister who held some beliefs inimical and threatening to the fundamental religious and civil principles of the Massachusetts Bay Colony. The basic issue was the relationship between church and state. The colony was essentially a theocracy, but Williams believed in separating the two institutions. As a believer in and spokesman for the New England Way, Cotton responded negatively to Williams's views, which threatened what Cotton and others perceived as the necessity of having a unified society in order to attain the Puritan ideal in America. Not immediately but in time, Williams won the debate, as evidenced by the First Amendment to the Constitution of the United States (1791). One might beneficially examine the decline of Cotton's position and the elevation of Williams's. Because the proper relationship between government and religion continues to be disputed, one could examine current debates and legal cases about this issue by using Cotton's and Williams's views as starting points. Students would also benefit from consulting Irwin H. Polishook's *Roger Williams, John Cotton and Religious Freedom*.

3. Beginning at approximately age five, children had catechism lessons with catechists and sometimes with parents. In the second half of the seventeenth century and into the eighteenth, Cotton's *Milk for Babes* was the catechism used most frequently in America. As a result, it shaped the religious thinking of generations of American children. In sixty-four sets of questions and answers, it presents the basic Puritan beliefs. It emphasizes mankind's sinful nature, interprets the Ten Commandments, specifies that failure to honor all the commandments means that salvation is available only through Christ, asserts that one attains Christ through His word and spirit, defines such words as "faith" and "prayer," details the nature of the Lord's Supper, and explains that on Judgment Day the righteous will enter heaven and the wicked will go to hell. By comparing Cotton's catechism with other children's catechisms of the time, such as the Westminster Assembly's shorter catechism (1648), one might consider why Cotton's was so popular. Is style an issue? Length? Content? Wilberforce Eames's *Early New England Catechisms* is the best starting place for any study of early American catechisms.

RESOURCES

Criticism

Sargent Bush Jr., Introduction, *The Correspondence of John Cotton* (Williamsburg, Va.: Omohundro Institute of Early American History and Culture; Chapel Hill: University of North Carolina Press, 2001).
Examines the world of John Cotton and evaluates his letters, including those relating to the Antinomian Controversy.

Wilberforce Eames, *Early New England Catechisms: A Bibliographical Account of Some Catechisms Published before the Year 1800, for Use in New England* (1898; New York: Burt Franklin, 1971).
Details the catechisms used in America before the nineteenth century.

Everett Emerson, *John Cotton*, revised edition (Boston: Twayne, 1990).
Provides a contextual reading of Cotton's works.

Irwin H. Polishook, *Roger Williams, John Cotton and Religious Freedom: A Controversy in New and Old England* (Englewood Cliffs, N.J.: Prentice-Hall, 1967).
Reproduces documents by Cotton and Williams relating to the separation of church and state.

Teresa Toulouse, *The Art of Prophesying: New England Sermons and the Shaping of Belief* (Athens: University of Georgia Press, 1987).
Discusses how four preachers, including Cotton, theoretically and practically blended prophesying and art.

Larzer Ziff, *The Career of John Cotton: Puritanism and the American Experience* (Princeton: Princeton University Press, 1962).
Presents biographical information, but mostly examines Cotton's perception of the world he inhabited.

John Dickinson (1732–1808)

Born at Croisadore estate in Talbot County, Maryland, in November 1732, John Dickinson was the first of three children of Samuel Dickinson and his second wife, Mary Cadwalader Dickinson. A child of privilege, he was tutored at home. At eighteen he moved to Philadelphia, where he worked for and learned from the distinguished attorney John Moland. Following Moland's example, in 1753 Dickinson matriculated at the Inns of Court in London, studying law at the Middle Temple. Back in America in 1757, he began practicing law in Philadelphia. Because he worked and lived in Philadelphia and owned land in Delaware, Dickinson served both states, being elected to the Delaware Assembly in 1759 and to the Pennsylvania legislature in 1762, where he served alongside Benjamin Franklin, with whom Dickinson often disagreed. Discontent with English colonial rule began percolating around 1764 when the British Parliament passed the Sugar Act, which taxed various commodities imported to America and tightened English control of colonial trade; the next year, dissatisfaction came to a boil when the Stamp Act was imposed on the colonies, adding to the taxation. Dickinson argues against these two acts in *The Late Regulations Respecting the British Colonies on the Continent of America, Considered* (1765), suggesting that both England and the colonies will suffer from the Sugar Act in particular, but also warning—presciently, as it turned out—that serious colonial dissatisfaction with England could lead to the colonies desiring political independence. Also in 1765, Dickinson participated in the Stamp Act Congress in New York and was the major author of its final document, "The Declaration of Rights and Grievances," which urged repeal of the Stamp Act and posited that the colonies would not accept taxation without representation. The next year in *An Address to the Committee of Correspondence in Barbados*, Dickinson continued his opposition to the Stamp Act by arguing that the colonists are justified in challenging it.

With such a background, Dickinson was well qualified to comment boldly and authoritatively about the increasing colonial discontent with English rule. Within the context of various restrictive acts imposed on the colonies, this is precisely what Dickinson did in a series of twelve letters published in *The Pennsylvania Chronicle* in 1767 and 1768. Titled *Letters from a Farmer in Pennsylvania, to the Inhabitants of the British Colonies* when published in pamphlet form (1768), they encourage vigilant monitoring of British rule. In the third letter, Dickinson's speaker, a farmer, explains his purpose: "to convince the people of these colonies that they are at this moment exposed to the utmost dangers; and to persuade them immediately, vigorously, and unanimously, to exert themselves in the most firm, but most peaceable manner, for obtaining relief." Two key words are "firm" and "peaceable," which ultimately proved irreconcilable. For these letters, Dickinson is best known.

The letters caused a sensation. They were published in other newspapers, such as *The Boston Evening Post;* after the first pamphlet of the letters was published, other editions followed. The letters were successful for two main reasons: the messenger and the message. The fictional persona Dickinson created, an unnamed farmer, is believable, appealing, and nonthreatening. Though educated, this man of adequate but modest means is not aristocratic. A lover of mankind, he believes that freedom is the condition most important for one's well-being; and because he sees that the colonists' liberty is threatened, he writes his letters. They warn Americans about the increasing excesses of British rule, mainly concerning taxation. He encourages his countrymen to protest the various unacceptable acts that have been imposed upon them, which they did, though the tax on tea remained in place, and this tax became significant. Tensions between the colonies and England eased after the punitive acts were repealed. During this period, in 1770, Dickinson married Mary Norris, with whom he had two daughters.

In 1773 the issue of the tea tax (and the right of the East India Company to be the sole importer of tea) loomed large; passions against it ran high. Dickinson joined others in arguing that this tax could be avoided by refusing to permit the unloading of tea. At the same time he urged caution against excessive enthusiasm in this endeavor. This moderate attitude was consistent with his desire, in the third of the farmer's letters, for people to resist English misrule firmly, but peaceably. Although Boston had its tea party in December, this same month Philadelphia prohibited the landing of a British ship bearing tea without incident.

The next year, 1774, Dickinson made the major address at a convention in Philadelphia that was charged with advising the Continental Congress, which would soon be formed; he served in the First and Second Continental Congresses. Armed conflict between colonies and the English began in Lexington and Concord, Massachusetts, in 1775. The next year, the Second Continental Congress approved the Declaration of Independence. Dickinson, who had argued strenuously against English tyranny, refused to sign the document, partly because he thought that internecine conflicts would keep the united colonies from governing themselves. At the same time, he was temperamentally inclined toward reconciliation with England, not war. Eight days after the signing of the Declaration of Independence, Dickinson, who chaired the committee charged with drafting the Articles of Confederation, presented a draft of the Articles to Congress. Although they were altered before being sent to states for ratification, upon ratification they became the first constitution of the United States. They remained in force until the present constitution was adopted in 1789. After resigning from Congress, Dickinson served in the Pennsylvania militia.

Subsequently, Dickinson provided more significant governmental service and continued writing: *The Letters of Fabius, in 1788, on the Federal Constitution; and in 1797 on the Present Situation of Public Affairs* (1797), *A Caution; or Reflections on the Present Contest between France and Great Britain* (1798), and *An Address on the Past, Present, and Eventual Relations of the United States to France* (1803). *The Political Writings of John Dickinson* was published in two volumes in 1801. At age seventy-five, Dickinson died on 14 February 1808. Dickinson College in Pennsylvania is named for him.

TOPICS FOR DISCUSSION AND RESEARCH

1. *Letters from a Farmer in Pennsylvania* was instrumental in generating support for colonial rights during a time of serious political unrest. Students would benefit from investigating why this was so. Was it merely a case of Dickinson commenting about topical events in the right way at the right time? The nature of the events and the specificity of the time are obvious, but "the right way" is not. What was Dickinson's manner of writing? Does it matter that he wrote in epistolary form? That he characterizes the speaker as a farmer, as something of an American everyman? Do the style and content seem appropriate to a Pennsylvania farmer of the day? What is the farmer's audience? Is the letter writer primarily concerned with influencing decision makers? Or is he interested in convincing ordinary people, like himself, of the justness of colonial objections to the injustices of British rule? Or both? On the issue of audience, one might consider the full title of the letters as they were first published in pamphlet form in 1768. Pierre Marambaud discusses Dickinson's artfulness in "Dickinson's *Letters from a Farmer in Pennsylvania* as Political Discourse."

2. Dickinson and Thomas Paine are often perceived as temperamental and stylistic opposites, despite their dedication to a common cause. Dickinson was calm and moderate, reasoned and not inflammatory in his prose; Paine was a firebrand. Yet, each profoundly influenced American opinion about the Revolution. One would benefit from reading selected passages from *Letters from a Farmer in Pennsylvania* and *Common Sense* in order to understand the two men's styles. Do the styles help account for Americans' enduring awareness of Paine and general unawareness of Dickinson? Do their current general reputations result partly from when they wrote—Dickinson years before hostilities began and Paine after they had begun? In "Paine and Dickinson," A. Owen Aldridge examines these two men. What is the significance of Aldridge's title, which places first the name of Paine, who was younger and wrote about the American cause later than Dickinson?

3. Aside from writing *Letters from a Farmer in Pennsylvania*, Dickinson is probably best known for refusing to sign the Declaration of Independence. Given his strong advocacy of colonial rights, his not signing might seem odd, even contradictory. Yet, Dickinson did not refuse to sign out of pique or because he wished to be difficult. His decision was principled; he had reasons for not signing. In determining his reasons—among them, colonial disunity and a desire for peace, not war—students might conclude that the issues surrounding the Declaration of Independence were not black and white, were not as easy or obvious, at least to someone like Dickinson, as they might seem centuries later. A full discussion of his thoughts about the Declaration, as well as the context of them and the Declaration itself, may be found in David L. Jacobson's *John Dickinson and the Revolution in Pennsylvania, 1764–1776.*

4. In the perfectly titled *John Dickinson, Conservative Revolutionary*, Milton E. Flower states that Dickinson was not only "the best-known politician and writer in the decade leading to the Revolution but also, subsequently, . . . an intellectual force in the nation's development." What was Dickinson's post-Revolution influence? How significant was it? Did any of his thoughts

became ingrained in the American political and social fabric to the degree that contemporary Americans benefit from them while being unaware of Dickinson's contributions to their lives? One might consider, for example, the ideas Dickinson expressed at a 1787 convention in Philadelphia called to revise the Articles of Confederation. After deciding that the national legislature should have two branches, the delegates needed to decide how the representatives to the branches would be determined. What was Dickinson's involvement in this discussion? What was his position? Flower's book answers these questions.

RESOURCES

Criticism

Owen Aldridge, "Paine and Dickinson," *Early American Literature*, 11 (Fall 1976): 125–138.

Examines *Letters from a Farmer in Pennsylvania* and Thomas Paine's *Common Sense,* concluding that Dickinson and Paine—the great propagandists of the American Revolution and of the time immediately before it—are more similar than not, that in these two works "they share essentially the same political principles" and that in their later writings "the ideology of the two authors is identical."

Milton E. Flower, *John Dickinson, Conservative Revolutionary* (Charlottesville: University Press of Virginia, 1983).

Focuses on Dickinson's political career and writings, emphasizing the subject's political moderation within a radical context.

David L. Jacobson, *John Dickinson and the Revolution in Pennsylvania, 1764–1776* (Berkeley: University of California Press, 1965).

Examines "Dickinson's contribution to the coming of the American Revolution" and analyzes "his political system and methods."

Pierre Marambaud, "Dickinson's *Letters from a Farmer in Pennsylvania* as Political Discourse: Ideology, Imagery, and Rhetoric," *Early American Literature*, 12 (Spring 1977): 63–72.

Argues that *Letters from a Farmer in Pennsylvania* has an intentional, sophisticated structure; characterizes Dickinson as "one of the ablest American prose-writers that took part in the pre-revolutionary debate."

Jonathan Edwards
Sinners in the Hands of an Angry God. A Sermon Preached at Enfield, July 8th 1741. At a Time of Great Awakenings; and Attended with Remarkable Impressions on Many of the Hearers

(Boston: Printed and sold by S. Kneeland & T. Green, 1741)

The major American religious thinker of the eighteenth century, Jonathan Edwards was born in East Windsor, Connecticut, on 5 October 1703, the fifth child of Timothy and Esther Stoddard Edwards and the only son among their eleven children. His father was a minister; his mother, the daughter of Solomon Stoddard, who was one of the most important American theologians of the late seventeenth century. His parents taught him at home. He matriculated at Yale College, at age twelve, as a member of the class of 1720. He was an accomplished student. After remaining at Yale to study theology and after experiencing a spiritual conversion, he affiliated with a Presbyterian church in New York in 1722, though he left it the following year to become the initial minister of the Congregational church in Bolton, Connecticut. Also in 1723, Edwards received a master's degree from Yale and submitted a paper on flying spiders to Paul Dudley, a Massachusetts member of the British Royal Society, which Edwards hoped would publish his work. Although it did not, this effort documents Edwards's early interest in nature and science, which would continue. Edwards left Bolton in 1724 to serve Yale as tutor, a position he resigned in 1726, upon becoming an associate of his grandfather Stoddard in the Congregational church at Northampton, Massachusetts. The following year he was ordained and married Sarah Pierpont, great-granddaughter of the Puritan minister Thomas Hooker, a founder of the Connecticut colony, and the daughter of James Pierpont, a founder of Yale. The couple had eleven children.

Upon Stoddard's death in 1729, Edwards became minister of the Northampton church, and soon the first of his many works was published: *God Glorified in the Work of Redemption, by the Greatness of Man's Dependence upon Him* (1731). This sermon, delivered in Boston, addresses God's sovereignty and individuals' inability to influence salvation. In asserting that mortals' actions have no bearing on the disposition of the soul, Edwards hews to Calvinist orthodoxy and counters the belief of a growing number of ministers that human actions do in fact have influence. While reiterating this point in *A Divine and Supernatural Light, Immediately Imparted to the Soul by the Spirit of God, Shown to Be Both a Scriptural, and Rational Doctrine* (1734), delivered during a religious revival in Northampton, Edwards focuses on the nature of conversion. People are redeemed, he argues, by perceiving the divine greatness of things not rationally but rather by means of something akin to a new, sixth sense, which God provides to the soul, replacing its darkness with light. God dwells in true believers. He extends this point in *A Treatise Concerning Religious Affections* (1746). Here, he argues that unregenerate people do not possess and cannot comprehend this new sense, which is available only to the regenerate, the true believers. Here, as in *A Divine and Supernatural*

Light, Edwards likens the difference to perceptions of honey: one may understand its qualities, but one needs a sense of taste in order to comprehend its sweetness.

Edwards ponders the nature of the Northampton revival of 1733–1734 in *The Duty and Interest of a People, Among Whom Religion Has Been Planted, to Continue Stedfast and Sincere in the Profession and Practice of It* (1736), revised and published the next year as *A Faithful Narrative of the Surprising Work of God in the Conversion of Many Hundred Souls in Northampton, and the Neighbouring Towns and Villages,* by which title it remains known, in abbreviated form. After commenting on the revival, he details the steps necessary for conversion. They range from church attendance to saving grace, with several steps in between. Edwards warns, though, that people cannot be certain of salvation, and that believing they are saved is presumptuous.

Revivalism became a larger issue later in the 1730s and especially in the 1740s, when people generally felt the need for a renewed religious fervor, which Edwards inspired, most notably in his famous and frightening sermon, *Sinners in the Hands of an Angry God* (1741), delivered more than once, including at Enfield, Massachusetts (though later in Connecticut). In it, he states that God dangles sinners by a thread over hell and that only His pleasure keeps them aloft. The evangelist George Whitefield popularized Edwards's ideas, spreading them along the Atlantic seaboard as far south as Georgia. This widespread emotional revival is known as the Great Awakening.

Edwards details the evolution of his own spiritual life in "Personal Narrative" (written circa 1739 but not published until 1765). He tells of the ebb and flow of religious feelings during his youth, a process that culminated in his perceiving God in everything, especially nature. Yet, as he aged he internalized nature and God, with only his obstinate will separating him from God. He embraces the Calvinist notion of mankind's sinfulness. While believing that mortals must look for signs of salvation, they—including Edwards—can never be assured of it; certainty of it is possible only in death.

Edwards wrote most importantly about abstruse theological issues, such as freedom of the will, the nature of virtue, and the legitimacy of emotion in religion. He also wrote and preached about salvation, never more vividly and effectively than in his 1741 *Sinners in the Hands of an Angry God.* In focusing unrelentingly on mankind's depravity and helplessness, however, it is atypical of his work, which makes the reality of its being by far Edwards's best-known work ironic and unfortunate. Yet, there are valid reasons for its renown. For one, it is artfully written, with its images being particularly effective. For another, it is highly dramatic, with much at stake for people who believe Edwards's description of them as dangling over the fiery pit of hell. For yet another, it reflects the spirit of the time, the Great Awakening, when revivals were a regular feature of American life and resulted in the conversion or religious awakening of an enormous number of people. Edwards hoped that the sermon would inspire his auditors not only to understand realities relating to heaven and hell, but to sense them, to be moved by them to the degree that they would admit their depravity and open themselves to God, thereby becoming eligible to accept salvation. In other words, while the sermon threatens throughout, it is ultimately hopeful, optimistic, because it allows for the possibility of an eternal life in heaven.

As the 1740s progressed, Edwards alienated his Northampton parishioners by publicly announcing the names of people who had behaved immorally and by restricting the Lord's Supper to people who professed their faith. As a result, he was dismissed in 1750. The next year, he became pastor at Stockbridge, Massachusetts, and ministered to the Indians until being elected president of the College of New Jersey, later named Princeton University. Five weeks after his inauguration, he died, on 22 March 1758, as a result of being inoculated against smallpox.

During the last fifteen years of his life, Edwards continued grappling with significant religious issues in numerous publications. These include *An Humble Inquiry into the Rules of the Word of God Concerning the Qualifications Requisite to a Compleat Standing and Full Communion in the Visible Christian Church* (1749), *True Grace, Distinguished from the Experience of Devils* (1753), and *A Careful and Strict Enquiry into the Modern Prevailing Notions of That Freedom of Will, Which Is Supposed to Be Essential to Moral Agency* (1754).

TOPICS FOR DISCUSSION AND RESEARCH

1. Edwards delivered *Sinners in the Hands of an Angry God* calmly, unemotionally. Although this manner of presentation probably reflected Edwards's temperament, it also might have been strategic. Why might this method of conveyance have been more effective than a passionate one? How did this sermon so delivered affect the parishioners who heard it? What was the nature of Edwards's audience? How significant is the fact that Edwards delivered the sermon during the Great Awakening? For help in answering these questions, consult Thomas S. Kidd's *The Great Awakening*, especially page 104, and Philip F. Gura's *Jonathan Edwards*, pages 117–119.

2. In *Jonathan Edwards's Philosophy of History*, Avihu Zakai states "that no single work in American religious history caused such great fear and trembling and none captured the imagination of so many generations as" *Sinners in the Hands of an Angry God*. What reasons does Zakai give to support this bold statement? Are the reasons convincing? Zakai's most important point about this sermon, though, is that its "main theme, the imminent approach of God's judgment on those who refuse to receive his gospel of salvation, can only be understood within Edwards's philosophy and theology of history." Read Zakai's discussion of the sermon to understand what he means by "Edwards's philosophy and theology of history." How convincing is Zakai?

3. Kidd begins *The Great Awakening* with these words: "To expect revival, one had to experience despair, a mood in which the New England Puritans specialized. Puritan church leaders began lamenting the decline of their godly experiment beginning in the 1660s and 1670s. Michael Wigglesworth's poem 'God's Controversy with New England' (1662) featured God warning formerly devout New Englanders" that they will be punished if they do not soon repent. Students would benefit from reading Wigglesworth's poem and *Sinners in the*

Hands of an Angry God to gain a sense of the American jeremiad tradition. Precisely what do the authors of these jeremiads lament? What events or perceptions inspired these works? Is one work more effective than the other? If so, why? Does the fact that Wigglesworth's jeremiad is in verse and Edwards's is in prose influence how one responds to these works?

4. Attributing the rhetorical success of *Sinners in the Hands of an Angry God* largely to the minister's deft use of imagery is a critical commonplace. Students could partly understand why the sermon is effective by reading it straight through for meaning, and then reading it to chart imagery. Are there patterns of imagery? If so, what are they? Why are they appropriate in this sermon? How do they augment Edwards's goal? What is the minister's goal? For assistance with imagery in the sermon, consult William J. Scheick's *The Writings of Jonathan Edwards*.

5. Even students who do not share Edwards's religious beliefs will probably find *Sinners in the Hands of an Angry God* frightening. Yet, it may also be read as encouraging, as hopeful, as positive. How? Scheick offers helpful information for reading the sermon in such a manner, especially on pages 78–79.

6. Edwards and Benjamin Franklin (born 1706) were contemporaries, though Franklin lived decades longer than Edwards. Each influenced American thought profoundly. Generally speaking, what were their philosophies? What were the effects of their ideas? Students would benefit from contrasting the interests and views of these men. Both were concerned with moral perfection. In what ways do their views differ? Does the fact that Edwards was well schooled and Franklin was an autodidact help explain why they saw the world as they did? Did family assist in shaping their views? Were they influenced by their places of residence: the small towns and villages of Edwards and the cities of Franklin? Both men had a relationship with George Whitefield, as well as with the Mather family. How did the relationships of Edwards and Franklin with these people differ? Though their styles are dissimilar, the prose of both Edwards and Franklin is clear and easy to read. What are their stylistic differences? Are there stylistic similarities? Reputable biographies and literary studies of the two men will provide information for answering these questions.

RESOURCES

Criticism

Philip F. Gura, *Jonathan Edwards, America's Evangelical: An American Portrait* (New York: Hill & Wang, 2005).

Details the response of the auditors to *Sinners in the Hands of an Angry God*, the emotionalism of which Edwards soon regretted.

Thomas S. Kidd, *The Great Awakening: The Roots of Evangelical Christianity in Colonial America* (New Haven: Yale University Press, 2007).

Discusses the interconnectedness of various revivals and argues that the Great Awakening lasted for several decades; details the context of Edwards's deliveries of *Sinners in the Hands of an Angry God*.

Wilson H. Kimnach, et al., Introduction, *The Sermons of Jonathan Edwards: A Reader*, edited by Kimnach, et al. (New Haven: Yale University Press, 1999). Argues that *Sinners in the Hands of an Angry God* represents neither all that Edwards believed nor the central tenets of his faith; yet, it is "one of the most affecting sermons ever preached in the English language."

M. X. Lesser, *Jonathan Edwards* (Boston: Twayne, 1988). Explains the structure of *Sinners in the Hands of an Angry God* and posits that the application is the most significant part of the sermon.

George M. Marsden, *Jonathan Edwards, A Life* (New Haven: Yale University Press, 2003). Discusses the context of *Sinners in the Hands of an Angry God*, focusing on it as an "awakening sermon."

William J. Scheick, *The Writings of Jonathan Edwards: Theme, Motif, and Style* (College Station: Texas A&M University Press, 1975). Analyzes the structure of *Sinners in the Hands of an Angry God*, with a particular focus on its imagery.

Avihu Zakai, *Jonathan Edwards's Philosophy of History: The Reenchantment of the World in the Age of Enlightenment* (Princeton: Princeton University Press, 2003). Argues that *Sinners in the Hands of an Angry God* is best understood within the context of Edwards's philosophy of history.

Benjamin Franklin
Poor Richard. An Almanack

Published by Franklin from 1733 to 1758 under various titles and imprints.
Collected as *The Complete Poor Richard Almanack*, 2 volumes,
edited by Whitfield J. Bell Jr. (Barre, Mass.: Imprint Society, 1970)

One of the essential Americans, Benjamin Franklin was born in Boston on 17 January 1706 to Josiah Franklin, who made candles and soap, and Abiah Folger Franklin. They had ten children, of which Benjamin was the eighth; Josiah had seven children by his first wife. Although Benjamin received little formal schooling, he was an autodidact who valued books and read as many as possible. He also received an early education from many youthful experiences, including as an apprentice to his brother James, a printer who published *The New-England Courant*, the third newspaper in Boston. Without his brother's knowledge, sixteen-year-old Benjamin submitted essays to the paper, which James published. Inspired by the *Spectator* essays of Joseph Addison and Richard Steele, Franklin's satirical and often witty creations are known as the Dogood papers (or essays) because they were ostensibly composed by the widow Silence Dogood. So began Franklin's long, distinguished career in letters.

Upon leaving his apprenticeship and his sometimes overbearing brother in 1723, Franklin fled Boston, alone, stopping in New York before settling in Philadelphia. The next year, he sailed to England where, when promised support was not forthcoming, he was on his own. While there, he published *A Dissertation on Liberty and Necessity, Pleasure and Pain* (1725), in which he responds to a work by the Anglican William Wollaston by, among other things, denying the existence of evil. Back in Philadelphia the next year, Franklin quickly succeeded as a printer. In 1729 he and a partner bought a bankrupt publication and retained part of its title, *The Pennsylvania Gazette*, which, under their ownership, was well written primarily because of Franklin's own contributions to it. Following the dissolution of the partnership the next year, Franklin ran this newspaper for two decades. In 1728 or 1729 he fathered a child, William, who became an ardent Loyalist and the last colonial governor of New Jersey. In 1730, Franklin married Deborah Read Rogers, with whom he had two children, Francis Folger, who died young, and Sarah; Deborah died in 1774.

While writing for, printing, and publishing *The Pennsylvania Gazette*, Franklin was involved in other activities. He founded the Library Company of Philadelphia (1731); began compiling *Poor Richard*, an almanac (1732); established the Union Fire Company, the first in Philadelphia; became clerk of the Pennsylvania Assembly (1736); became postmaster of Philadelphia (1737); published *The General Magazine, and Historical Chronicle*, the second magazine in colonial America (1741); invented a stove—the Franklin stove—that improved the safety of heating a house (1742); founded the American Philosophical Society (1744); was the major force behind the founding of what became the University of Pennsylvania (1749); co-founded the Pennsylvania hospital in Philadelphia (1751); invented the lightning rod and helped establish the Philadelphia Contributionship, the first successful colonial fire-insurance company (1752); was made deputy postmaster general of the colonies for the Crown; received honorary master's degrees from Harvard and Yale, and from the Royal Society received the Copley Medal for distinguished scientific achievement (1753); and became a member of the Royal Society and received an honorary master's degree from the College of William and Mary (1756).

During this same period, Franklin wrote tracts published independent of the newspaper, almanac, and magazine. Among his publications are several 1735 defenses of the recently arrived Irish Presbyterian preacher Samuel Hemphill; the anonymous *Plain Truth: or, Serious Considerations on the Present State of the City of Philadelphia, and Province of Pennsylvania* (1747); *Proposals Relating to the Education of Youth in Pensilvania* (1749); the first part of *Experiments and Observations on Electricity, Made at Philadelphia in America* (1751; the second part was published two years later); and *Some Account of the Pennsylvania Hospital* (1754). These and other writings indicate the breadth of Franklin's interests.

Because of his contributions to science and the betterment of society, Franklin's recognition not only continued but increased after 1758, including internationally. As the Revolution approached, Franklin was of great importance to the American cause: he was a delegate to the Second Continental Congress, and he helped compose the Declaration of Independence (1776), which he signed. Additionally, he became postmaster for the United Colonies in 1775.

Also in the 1770s, Franklin began writing the first of four parts of his memoirs. This most engaging section (1771) deals with his youth. Here, he details most of what is known about his early years: a young man making his way—through intelligence, hard work, and perseverance—in a difficult world, someone dedicated to self-improvement, one who labored to refine his prose style, and so forth. By the time of his death in Philadelphia on 17 April 1790, he was respected if not revered in the United States he helped create, as well as abroad. (Because the *Autobiography*, as the memoirs became known, was not completed until after 1776, the year this volume of *Research Guides to American Literature* ends its coverage, it will be treated fully in the second volume.)

Franklin's evolution from solitary youth to accomplished adult and indispensable citizen is similar to the evolution of colonial America into the United States and its ultimate position in the world. Both he and his country began modestly but succeeded beyond reasonable expectations. One could argue that he is the quintessential American.

TOPICS FOR DISCUSSION AND RESEARCH

1. Although Benjamin Franklin might be the most famous almanac maker in American history, he was not the first one. His initial *Poor Richard* was for the year 1733 (the last was for 1758); the first American almanac, compiled by William Peirce, was published almost a century earlier, in 1639, though no copy of it is known to exist. Many American almanacs were published after Peirce's and before Franklin's first one. They are all practical in nature, providing astrological and other information that was invaluable to farmers in particular, though as time passed they also included verse, medical advice, and other items that appealed to a large readership. Students might wonder, then, what differentiates Franklin's almanac from other almanacs and why *Poor Richard* is, with the possible exception of *The Farmer's Almanac*, the best-known American almanac. (*The Farmer's Almanac*, initially published in 1793, is still being published.) Students should, therefore, read selected volumes of Franklin's almanac and compare their contents with those of other almanacs of the time, such as those by Nathaniel Ames and Titan Leeds. Students would probably best be served in determining the uniqueness of Franklin's almanac by focusing on Richard Saunders, the putative compiler of Franklin's almanacs. What is the nature of Saunders's personality? In what ways does Saunders seem similar to people who might be expected to consult the almanac? Why did Franklin create a persona—Saunders—rather than write as himself? For assistance in answering these questions, consult the third chapter of Bruce Ingham Granger's *Benjamin Franklin* and the second volume of J. A. Leo Lemay's *The Life of Benjamin Franklin*, pages 179–180 and 190–191.

2. Franklin borrowed much material for *Poor Richard*, including many sayings, including some famous ones. He might even have fashioned Richard Saunders after a character created earlier. John F. Ross suggests John Partridge, in

Jonathan Swift's *Bickerstaff Papers* (1708–1709), as the inspiration for Saunders. Students interested in Franklin's borrowings should acquaint themselves with Partridge and Saunders and then read Ross's essay. What similarities does Ross observe between the two fictional characters? How convincing is he? If he is convincing, does Franklin's borrowing from Swift—and other authors—lessen Franklin's artistry? If so, in what manner and to what degree? If not, why not? For assistance in answering these questions, read the third chapter of Richard Amacher's *Benjamin Franklin*.

3. Students might wonder why Richard Saunders's sayings are so pithy. One reason is the context in which they appear in the various almanacs, a context that might surprise the uninitiated. Consult a few volumes of *Poor Richard* and locate some of Saunders's sayings. Consider, for example, the saying *"An empty Bag cannot stand upright"* on the page for January 1740. Where on the page does the saying appear? Why is it positioned there? On the page for May 1750, Saunders expands the saying to *"Tis hard (but glorious) to be poor and honest: An empty Sack can hardly stand upright; but if it does, 'tis a stout one!"* Why does Saunders lengthen the saying? Why is reading it in the almanac difficult? For help in answering these questions, to see photographs of the pages in question, and to examine evidence that Franklin borrowed this saying from Thomas Fuller's *Gnomologia*, see the sixth chapter of James N. Green and Peter Stallybrass's *Benjamin Franklin*; Granger's *Benjamin Franklin* will also prove helpful.

4. For the last volume of the almanac, that for 1758, Franklin composed an essay that became one of his most famous creations, known as both *The Way to Wealth* and *Father Abraham's Speech*. It is included in many if not most anthologies of American literature. In the essay, after lamenting that he is ignored by authors other than almanac compilers, Saunders recounts a speech he heard Father Abraham give in response to a question about how to survive in a time of onerous taxation. Father Abraham's lengthy response consists largely of sayings from previous volumes of *Poor Richard*, which delights Saunders. Despite its seeming simplicity, though, the essay is complex. Who is the narrator of the speech? Is it Father Abraham? Richard Saunders? Benjamin Franklin? How does the answer to this question affect meaning? For example, if Father Abraham narrates, what do his words indicate about him and Saunders? If Saunders is responsible for the speech, to what degree, if any, does his seeming immodesty detract from his character? If Franklin controls everything, why does he establish two narrators? Further, Saunders's sayings constitute good advice, individually and collectively. Why, then, of all the people listening to Father Abraham, is Saunders the only one to heed it? What does this indicate about the influence of Saunders's sayings? If it suggests that they are easily disregarded, what must Saunders think about the words attributed to him, as spoken by Father Abraham? Why does he recount a speech that ostensibly praises him but, as judged by the response to it, ultimately indicates that his sayings are well known but ultimately ignored? What is Franklin's point?

5. The influence of *Poor Richard* has been significant in several ways. One way concerns military history. When, in 1779, John Paul Jones declared that "I have not yet begun to fight," he did so aboard the *Bonhomme Richard* while fight-

ing the British ship *Serapis*. Jones named his ship *Bonhomme Richard* in honor of Benjamin Franklin, his patron then serving as American commissioner in Paris. Why did he select this name rather than another one? What does the French name of the ship mean in English? To answer these and collateral questions, consult H. W. Brands's *The First American* and Walter Isaacson's *Benjamin Franklin*. Why was the battle with the *Serapis* so important? Why has the U.S. Navy named other ships *Bonhomme Richard*? When was the most recent *Bonhomme Richard* commissioned?

RESOURCES

Biography

H. W. Brands, *The First American: The Life and Times of Benjamin Franklin* (New York: Doubleday, 2000).
Discusses *Poor Richard* and argues that of the men who made American independence possible, only George Washington was Franklin's equal.

Walter Isaacson, *Benjamin Franklin: An American Life* (New York: Simon & Schuster, 2003).
A richly detailed, authoritative biography that discusses *Poor Richard*.

J. A. Leo Lemay, *The Life of Benjamin Franklin, Volume 2: Printer and Publisher, 1730–1747* (Philadelphia: University of Pennsylvania Press, 2005).

Lemay, *The Life of Benjamin Franklin, Volume 3: Soldier, Scientist, and Politician, 1748–1757* (Philadelphia: University of Pennsylvania Press, 2008).
These two volumes of a planned seven-volume biography examine various aspects of *Poor Richard*, including controversies surrounding it, Franklin's use of Richard Saunders as a persona, and its astronomical predictions.

Criticism

Richard E. Amacher, *Benjamin Franklin* (New York: Twayne, 1962).
Convincingly examines Franklin's writings, including *Poor Richard*.

Benjamin Franklin V, "The Origins of American Almanacs," in *American Literary Almanac: From 1608 to the Present*, edited by Karen L. Rood (New York: Facts On File, 1988), pp. 3–6.
Discusses early American almanacs, including *Poor Richard*.

Bruce Ingham Granger, *Benjamin Franklin: An American Man of Letters* (Ithaca, N.Y.: Cornell University Press, 1964).
Assesses Franklin's literary accomplishments by focusing on belletristic writings, including *Poor Richard*.

James N. Green and Peter Stallybrass, *Benjamin Franklin: Writer and Printer* (New Castle, Del.: Oak Knoll Press, 2006).
Examines Franklin's career as writer and printer and devotes two chapters to *Poor Richard*.

Lorraine Smith Pangle, *The Political Philosophy of Benjamin Franklin* (Baltimore: Johns Hopkins University Press, 2007).
Discusses the humor in *Poor Richard.*

John F. Ross, "The Character of Poor Richard: Its Source and Alteration," *PMLA,* 55 (September 1940): 785–794.
Indicates that Franklin modeled Richard Saunders on Jonathan Swift's John Partridge.

Robb Sagendorph, *America and Her Almanacs: Wit, Wisdom & Weather, 1639–1970* (Dublin, N.H.: Yankee, 1970).
Discusses *Poor Richard* within the context of other American almanacs.

Marion Barber Stowell, *Early American Almanacs: The Colonial Weekday Bible* (New York: Burt Franklin, 1977).
Discusses *Poor Richard* in the context of the development of the American almanac.

Cotton Mather (1663–1728)

The most famous member of the illustrious Mather family, Cotton Mather was the son of Increase Mather and grandson of Richard Mather, major figures in seventeenth-century American life. His mother, Maria Cotton Mather, was the daughter of John Cotton, a figure at least as important as the Mathers. Born in Boston on 12 February 1663, Cotton Mather, something of a prig, studied as a child with the noted schoolmaster Ezekiel Cheever. In 1674, at age eleven, he matriculated at Harvard College, from which he received a bachelor's degree in 1678 and a master's two years later. He was awarded the second degree by his father, who oversaw the commencement proceedings. Cotton Mather's initial publication—the first of over four hundred published works—is a 1681 poem (published in 1682) dedicated to Urian Oakes, the Harvard president who died two days before Mather was to receive his master's degree.

After preaching in 1680 at the Boston Second Church, also known as the North Church, he was invited to assist his father there in ministerial duties, which he did. He was finally ordained in 1685 and remained with the church for the remainder of his life. In 1686 he married fifteen-year-old Abigail Phillips, with whom he had nine children, the first being born in 1687. While Increase Mather was in England from 1688 to 1692, Cotton Mather was solely responsible for the Second Church. In 1689 he helped overthrow Sir Edmund Andros, who had been appointed governor by James II. Also that year he published his first important book, *Memorable Providences, Relating to Witchcrafts and Possessions,* which helped establish a climate in which the witchcraft frenzy of 1692 could develop. When the witchcraft trials were held in Salem, Mather, while urging the judges' caution, recommended, in *The Return of Several Ministers* (1692), that the judges prosecute witches fully. In 1690 he was elected Fellow of Harvard, which means that he became a member of the Harvard Corporation, which governs the college. Following the 1702 death of his wife, the next year Mather married the widow Elizabeth Clark Hubbard, with whom he had six children. He was disappointed when not he but John Leverett, a man with Anglican leanings, was made president of Harvard in 1708; and he was again hurt when Benjamin Wadsworth, not he, was selected to succeed Leverett. By approximately 1710, Mather's political influence began to wane. He received an honorary doctor of divinity degree from the University of Glasgow in 1710; three years later, in recognition of his observations about various scientific phenomena, he was elected to the Royal Society. Also in 1713 his wife died; Mather married Lydia Lee George two years later. As a result of his having persuaded Elihu Yale to make a substantial gift to the college in New Haven, Connecticut, the school was named for Yale in 1718. Mather, his father, and Zabdiel Boylston were proponents of inoculation during the Boston smallpox epidemic of 1721–1722. Mather died on 13 February 1728, the day following his sixty-fifth birthday.

Mather was one of the most voluminous writers in American history. The following books are among the most significant of his many important publications. Following by three years Mather's discussion of witches in *Memorable Providences, The Wonders of the Invisible World* is Mather's account of the Salem witchcraft trials. In it, Mather emphasizes the devil's threat to New England and justifies the court's convictions of witches, despite the judgments having been made on the basis of spectral evidence, which Mather opposed. His most important work is probably *Magnalia Christi Americana: Or, the Ecclesiastical History of New-England, from Its First Planting in the Year 1620, unto the Year of Our Lord, 1698* (1702). The subtitle accurately characterizes the book, though it does not indicate that the book includes Mather's important biographies of many American Puritan divines. In his translation of *Psalterium Americanum* (1718), Mather was the first American to write in blank verse in a sustained manner. In *The Christian Philosopher: A Collection of the Best Discoveries in Nature, with Religious Improvements* (1720), Mather insists that natural science implies a divine creator. *The Angel of Bethesda, Visiting the Invalids of a Miserable World* (1722) offers medical remedies and information while raising scientific questions. As Increase Mather wrote a biography of his father, Richard Mather, so did Cotton Mather write one of his father, Increase Mather, in *Parentator* (1724). He provides instruction to young ministers in *Manuductio ad Ministerium* (1726).

TOPICS FOR DISCUSSION AND RESEARCH

1. While Cotton Mather strove to uphold the seventeenth-century religious values of his father and grandfathers, he demonstrated advanced thinking in several areas, including science. How is it possible that someone who believed in the devil's actions on earth could make significant contributions to science? Did his thinking reflect the changing nature of the times? Or were some of his thoughts in the vanguard of progressive thinking, setting an example for others to follow? Why might the prestigious Royal Society have honored Mather with membership only eleven years after the Salem witchcraft trials,

with which he was associated in the popular mind? Any comprehensive study of Mather will provide information for answering these questions; one such study is David Levin's *Cotton Mather.*

2. Although Mather's prose style is not consistent, it is often florid, with lengthy sentences; Latin and Greek words, phrases, and sentences; italicized words; and other elements that make his prose different from and more difficult than that of most writers of the time. To get a sense of his style, compare selections from his writings with the relatively plain prose of someone like Jonathan Mayhew. Mather himself referred to his style as massy. How easily can one understand him? Why might he have written in such a manner? What does his style indicate about him? About his perception of his readers?

3. In America, Puritans generally viewed the Indians as the devil's people and were ostensibly eager to convert the natives to their version of Christianity, though few actually made a serious, sustained effort to do so. By the end of the seventeenth century, the Indian population had been greatly reduced by disease and war, including the Pequot War of 1636–1637 and King Philip's War of 1675–1676, the latter fought when Mather was a student at Harvard. Although he was accepting of the Indians who had already been converted, he became antagonistic toward unconverted ones, going so far as, in *Souldiers Counselled and Comforted* (1689), to encourage troops to kill them. Yet, in the last years of the seventeenth century he began working as missionary to the Indians, a responsibility he took seriously. How might Mather's different attitudes toward Indians be understood? Reconciled? Might events in American life have influenced his views? Could his hostile attitude be related to his perception of witches, as expressed in the late 1680s and early 1690s? Kenneth Silverman addresses these issues in *The Life and Times of Cotton Mather.*

4. Mather's acceptance of witchcraft, as expressed in *Memorable Providences,* helped establish a context for the witchcraft frenzy of three years later that resulted in the hanging of nineteen supposed witches and the pressing to death of one. In addition to writing about witchcraft, he also preached about it on several occasions. His exact involvement in the trials, however, is unclear. Illness kept him from attending the early stages of them. While he favored the execution of people (witches) convicted of serious crimes, he warned about the dangers of accepting spectral evidence, or evidence based on actions of the appearance of the accused, not of the actual person. He believed that the confession of witchcraft constituted the best evidence of it. Although he criticized the court for convicting people on the basis of inadequate evidence, he encouraged the continuance of the trials. In August 1692, Mather attended the hangings of six people. On what basis might he have condoned the executions of these and apparently other witches? His religious beliefs obviously influenced his attitude. Could his friendship with some of the judges similarly have affected him? Among the numerous sources for information about these issues and the witchcraft trials is Robert Middlekauff's *The Mathers.*

5. In 1710, Mather published *Bonifacius. An Essay upon the Good, That Is to Be Devised and Designed, by Those Who Desire to Answer the Great End of Life,*

and to Do Good While They Live. In it, he addresses three types of doing good: spreading the word of Christ, correcting evil manners, and aiding the needy. From the beginning of Puritan presence in America, people's good works were important; they even helped demonstrate evidence of saving grace. Mather's book directly influenced young Benjamin Franklin, who gave the name of Silence Dogood to one of his most engaging fictional creations and who devoted his life to doing good. How similar are the Mather and Franklin approaches to what might be called philanthropy? How do they differ? Babette M. Levy addresses this issue in *Cotton Mather.*

RESOURCES

Biography

David Levin, *Cotton Mather: The Young Life of the Lord's Remembrancer, 1663– 1703* (Cambridge, Mass.: Harvard University Press, 1978).
A biography of Mather to age forty.

Robert Middlekauff, *The Mathers: Three Generations of Puritan Intellectuals, 1596–1728* (New York: Oxford University Press, 1971).
An "intellectual history of Puritanism" that focuses on the lives and works of Richard Mather, Increase Mather, and Cotton Mather.

Kenneth Silverman, *The Life and Times of Cotton Mather* (New York: Harper & Row, 1984).
The most comprehensive biography of Mather.

Two Mather Biographies: Life and Death *and* Parentator, edited by William J. Scheick (Bethlehem, Pa.: Lehigh University Press; London: Associated University Presses, 1989).
Scheick compares and reprints the biographies of their fathers by Increase Mather and Cotton Mather.

Criticism

Otho T. Beall Jr. and Richard H. Shryock, *Cotton Mather: First Significant Figure in American Medicine* (Baltimore: Johns Hopkins University Press, 1954).
Argues that Mather "provides an almost unique mass of evidence concerning early American medicine, with all its implications for the social and cultural history of the times."

Mitchell R. Breitwieser, *Cotton Mather and Benjamin Franklin: The Price of Representative Personality* (Cambridge, England: Cambridge University Press, 1984).
Examines the continuity between Puritanism and the American Enlightenment by showing Benjamin Franklin's indebtedness to Mather.

Alan Heimert, Introduction, *Cotton Mather, The Puritan Priest,* by Barrett Wendell (New York: Harcourt, Brace & World, 1963).
Defends Wendell's 1891 biography of Mather against its several critics.

David Levin, *What Happened in Salem? Documents Pertaining to the Seventeenth-Century Witchcraft Trials* (New York: Harcourt, Brace & World, 1960).
Reproduces documents from five of the witchcraft trials, contemporary commentary about the trials (including some by Mather), documents providing legal redress, and fiction by Nathaniel Hawthorne and Esther Forbes.

Babette M. Levy, *Cotton Mather* (Boston: Twayne, 1979).
A consideration of Mather's works.

Constance J. Post, *Signs of the Times in Cotton Mather's* Paterna: *A Study of Puritan Autobiography* (New York: AMS Press, 2000).
Attempts to increase awareness of *Paterna* by considering it from several perspectives.

Increase Mather (1639–1723)

Born on 21 June 1639 in Dorchester, in what is now the state of Massachusetts, Increase Mather was the last child of Richard Mather, one of the most important of the early American church fathers, and Katharine Hoult Mather. Schooled at home by his parents during his early years, Increase Mather matriculated at Harvard College in 1651 at age twelve and received his degree in 1656. He was in Ireland and England from 1657 to 1661, first studying at Trinity College, Dublin, from which he received a master's degree, and then preaching, at more than one location in both countries. When Charles II assumed the English throne in 1660 and Anglicanism again became the official religion, nonconformists such as Mather became personae non gratae. As a result, he returned to America in 1661, settling in Dorchester. The next year he married Maria Cotton, his stepsister by virtue of Richard Mather having married Sarah Cotton, widow of John Cotton; Maria was the daughter of Sarah and John Cotton. Cotton Mather was the most notable of Mather and his wife's ten children. Also in 1662, Increase Mather attended the synod that produced the Half-Way Covenant. Two years later in Boston, he became teacher at the Second Church, also known as the North Church, an affiliation that lasted for the remainder of his life. He was religiously conservative, defending the ways of his father's generation and objecting to liberalizing actions by the likes of Solomon Stoddard, who offered the Lord's Supper to anyone who subscribed to the articles of faith and lived more-or-less uprightly, whether or not the person demonstrated evidence of saving grace.

In 1681, Mather was elected to succeed Urian Oakes as president of Harvard, though he declined the position. When elected to succeed John Rogers in 1685, he accepted and served in this position until 1701, when he was forced from office for refusing to live in Cambridge, where Harvard is located, a requirement not imposed on his successor, Samuel Willard. Among his accomplishments as president were establishing discipline among the students, encouraging the mastery of Greek and Hebrew as well as Latin, and introducing the study of physics.

By 1688, citizens were angry at the heavy-handed rule of Massachusetts Bay Colony governor Sir Edmund Andros, an Anglican who challenged their titles to lands and imposed taxes. That year Mather sailed to London to thank James II for issuing the Declaration of Indulgence, which suspended laws against dissenters, thereby granting the Congregationalists some protection from Andros. While in England, Mather succeeded in securing a new charter for Massachusetts Bay, the charter of 1629 having been revoked in 1684 by the Committee of Trade and Plantation in London. The new one, that of 1691, allowed for colonial governors but also permitted an elected legislature. It put an end to Puritan governance and replaced it with secular rule. For this Mather deserves major credit. He writes about the negotiations for the new charter in *A Brief Account Concerning Several of the Agents of New-England* (1691). Upon returning to Boston from England in 1692, Mather faced issues relating to the Salem witchcraft trials. The year following the 1714 death of his wife, Maria, Mather married Anne Lake Cotton, the widow of John Cotton, son of Maria's brother, Seaborn Cotton. Increase Mather died in Boston on 23 August 1723.

Mather wrote voluminously, ultimately publishing more than one hundred titles. Among the more notable ones are the following. In 1670 appeared *The Life and Death of That Reverend Man of God, Mr. Richard Mather*, a biography glorifying his late father. As Michael G. Hall notes, this work is the first biography written by someone born in America and the initial one published there (in Cambridge). Mather helped establish himself as a significant preacher by delivering two sermons published as *The Day of Trouble Is Near* (1674), a jeremiad intended to encourage regeneration among his listeners and readers. He explained his changed position about baptism in two works: *The First Principles of New-England, Concerning the Subject of Baptisme & Communion of Churches* and *A Discourse Concerning the Subject of Baptisme*, both published in 1675. Mather wrote about the Indians in *A Brief History of the War with the Indians in New-England* (1676), which concerns King Philip's War, and *A Relation of the Troubles Which Have Hapned in New-England, By Reason of the Indians There* (1677), an account of Indian-white relations that focuses on the Pequot War. In time, Mather was named an Indian commissioner, which meant that he was responsible for helping convert the Indians to Christianity. He evidenced his scientific interest in several sermons and in *Kometographia. Or a Discourse Concerning Comets* (1683), probably the first study of comets published in English. Although Mather was hardly the first Puritan to interpret unusual occurrences as God's handiwork, he details his beliefs about them in *The Doctrine of Divine Providence* and the powerfully written *An Essay for the Recording of Illustrious Providences* (both 1684). Although he thought the witchcraft trials should be held, he believed that reliance on spectral evidence alone was inadequate for convicting someone, an opinion fully expressed in *Cases of Conscience Concerning Evil Spirits* (1692), enlarged and published the next year in London as *A Further Account of the Tryals of the New-England Witches*. In 1702 he published another major jeremiad, *Ichabod. Or, a Discourse, Shewing What Cause There Is to Fear That the Glory of the Lord, Is Departing from New-England*. In 1721, Boston suffered a smallpox epidemic, which inspired debate over the advisability of inoculation. That year, he wrote in favor of the procedure in two works published on one broadside, *Several Reasons Proving That Inoculating or Transplanting the Small Pox, Is a Lawful Practice, and That It Has Been Blessed by God for the Saving of Many a Life* and *Sentiments on the Small Pox Inoculated.*

TOPICS FOR DISCUSSION AND RESEARCH

1. In 1662, Increase Mather represented the church of Dorchester at a synod called to discuss the issue of baptism. The issue was basically as follows. Children of church members were baptized, but what should happen when these children became adults and had their own offspring without having become church members? The synod resolved the issue by allowing the baptism of these children, but permitting them only halfway membership in the church: they could be baptized and disciplined but could not partake of the Lord's Supper or vote. As a result, this is known as the Half-Way Covenant. Mather did not approve of this decision, though his father, Richard Mather, did. Thirteen years later Increase Mather changed his mind, arguing in favor of half-way church membership, partly, he said, in order to respect the Fifth Commandment by honoring his father. Mason I. Lowance Jr. offers another reason for this changed position: the greater the number of people in the church, even as half-way members, the larger the number of people Mather could control. If Lowance is correct, then Mather altered his position for political reasons. Students might reasonably ask how convincing Mather is in explaining his new position, as he does in "To the Reader" in *The First Principles of New-England, Concerning the Subject of Baptisme & Communion of Churches.* Lowance offers guidance for answering this question.

2. In 1689, Mather's son Cotton Mather published, in Boston, *Memorable Providences, Relating to Witchcrafts and Possessions,* republished two years later in London as *Late Memorable Providences Relating to Witchcrafts and Possessions.* In it, he writes about a case of supposed witchcraft that occurred in Boston in 1688. The book gained popularity and therefore introduced the topic of witchcraft to general conversation. Early in 1692 the erratic behavior of some children was blamed on witchcraft. Soon, a court that included Samuel Sewall and John Hathorne, ancestor of Nathaniel Hawthorne, found various people guilty of witchcraft and sentenced them to death by hanging. Ultimately, nineteen people were hanged and one person, Giles Cory, was pressed to death. Increase Mather was concerned about one aspect of the trials in particular: the use of spectral evidence, evidence based on the actions of the appearance of the accused, not of the actual person. In *Cases of Conscience Concerning Evil Spirits* he writes, "To take away the life of any one, merely because a *Spectre* or Devil, in a Bewitched or Possessed person does accuse them, will bring the Guilt of Innocent Blood on the Land, where such a thing will be done." In this same work, he expresses his belief that "it were better that Ten Suspected Witches should escape, than that one Innocent Person should be Condemned." One might ask why Massachusetts society of the late seventeenth century, including the Mathers, respected the accusa-

tions of witchcraft. Why would the learned members of the court convict accused witches? Why would the judges sentence the witches to death? What might have caused the end of the witchcraft frenzy? Any reputable study of the witchcraft trials will provide information for answering these questions.

3. A smallpox epidemic that struck Boston in April 1721 did not subside until spring 1722. It so frightened people that approximately 700 of the 10,500 residents left town. Although different sources give different numbers, William Douglass, a doctor who was there at the time and opposed inoculation, notes that 844 of the 5,989 people who contracted the disease died, or one in seven; 6 of the 286 people who were inoculated died, or one in forty-eight. In other words, inoculation, while not perfect, worked. Mather was immune to the disease because he had contracted it in the 1650s; thus, he was able to visit and tend to the afflicted. Following the lead of Cotton Mather, Increase Mather argued for inoculation. In general, the clergy favored inoculation while the citizenry and doctors opposed it. One might reasonably expect doctors and potential victims to approve of inoculation and ministers possibly to oppose it. Why might these different groups have viewed inoculation differently? For direction in answering this question, one should consult Ola Elizabeth Winslow's *A Destroying Angel*.

RESOURCES

Biography

Michael G. Hall, *The Last American Puritan: The Life of Increase Mather, 1639– 1723* (Middletown, Conn.: Wesleyan University Press, 1988).
A thorough biography of Increase Mather.

Robert Middlekauff, *The Mathers: Three Generations of Puritan Intellectuals, 1596–1728* (New York: Oxford University Press, 1971).
An "intellectual history of Puritanism" that focuses on the lives and works of Richard Mather, Increase Mather, and Cotton Mather.

Kenneth B. Murdock, *Increase Mather: The Foremost American Puritan* (Cambridge, Mass.: Harvard University Press, 1925).
A full examination of Increase Mather's life and career.

Criticism

Zabdiel Boylston, *An Historical Account of the Small-Pox Inoculated in New England* (London: S. Chandler, 1726).
An account of the 1721–1722 smallpox epidemic by the doctor who inoculated residents of Boston.

William Douglass, *A Summary, Historical and Political, of the First Planting, Progressive Improvements, and Present State of the British Settlements in North-America,* 2 volumes (Boston: Daniel Fowle, 1751).
A discussion of the smallpox epidemic by a doctor who was there at the time.

Mason I. Lowance Jr., *Increase Mather* (New York: Twayne, 1974).
Examines the life and works of Increase Mather and places him in cultural context; considers him "the most vitally representative Puritan of his age."

Williston Walker, *A History of the Congregational Churches in the United States* (New York: Scribners, 1893).
A history of Congregationalism, including detailed analysis of the Half-Way Covenant.

Ola Elizabeth Winslow, *A Destroying Angel: The Conquest of Smallpox in Colonial Boston* (Boston: Houghton Mifflin, 1974).
An analysis of the smallpox epidemic.

Richard Mather (1596–1669)

In 1596, Richard Mather was born to Thomas Mather and Margrett Abrams Mather in Lowdown, Lancashire, England, near Liverpool. The parents were of the yeoman class; records do not indicate if they had other children. Little information about Richard Mather's childhood exists, though around age six he began attending grammar school in Winwick. There he learned Greek and Latin, which he began teaching at a new grammar school in Toxteth Park at age fifteen. While living in Toxteth Park with the family of Edward Aspinwall, he absorbed his hosts' nonconformist views to the degree that he yearned to become one of God's elect, which, in 1614, he believed he became. Four years later he left Toxteth Park to enroll at Brasenose College at Oxford University. After a few months he accepted a call from Toxteth Park to return as minister of the village church, thereby concluding his Oxford education. Ordained by the Church of England, he ministered to Toxteth Park until 1633, when church officials removed him from his ministry because of his nonconformist ways. Through connections, he was reinstated later that year, though he was soon removed again, ostensibly for never having worn a surplice. By that time he was the father of four sons by his wife Katharine Hoult, whom he married in 1624. They lived in Much-Woolton, near Toxteth Park. With a family and with no prospects for preaching in England, Mather immigrated to America with his wife and children aboard the *James,* arriving in Boston in August 1635.

Mather was denied membership in the Boston church because he provided inadequate evidence of his salvation, though later he was granted membership. Then, when called to minister to the community of Dorchester in 1636, he was initially unable to establish a church because his parishioners were found unworthy. Later that year the church was established, and Mather served it until his death thirty-three years later. Mather's son Eleazar was born in 1637; Increase, in 1639. In 1643, Mather delivered the annual election sermon. Mather was esteemed by his fellow ministers to the degree that he became significantly involved in several important undertakings, including the Cambridge Synod of 1646–1648 that produced the Cambridge Platform.

Following the 1655 death of Katharine Mather, in 1656 he married Sarah Cotton, widow of John Cotton. In time, Mather's son Increase married Sarah and John Cotton's daughter Maria; one of their children was Cotton Mather, who bore the surnames of both his grandfathers. Richard Mather died at his Dorchester home on 22 April 1669.

Mather's first publication is one of his most important works. He was a translator of the Hebrew psalms into English, a work published as *The Whole Booke of Psalmes Faithfully Translated into English Metre* (1640), better known as *The Bay Psalm Book*. The first publication of British North America of which a copy is known to exist, it was widely used until supplanted by a new translation in 1651. The translators of the later edition attempted to make the psalms more poetic than those of the more literally translated earlier work. Mather was long considered the author of the preface of the 1640 edition, though it is now generally considered the work of John Cotton.

When aspects of the New England Way were criticized, Mather was called upon to defend it, which he did in *An Apologie of the Churches in New-England for Church-Covenant* and *Church-Government and Church Covenant Discussed*, both published in London in 1643. The former defends the Congregational nature of church organization; the latter explains other aspects of church polity. He continued defending the New England Way in *A Modest & Brotherly Answer to Mr. Charles Herle His Book, Against the Independency of Churches* (1644), written with William Tompson, and *A Reply to Mr. Rutherfurd* (1647), both published in London. Though the Cambridge Synod asked Mather, John Cotton, and Ralph Partridge to draft what amounts to a constitution for Congregational churches, Mather was the major author of *A Platform of Church Discipline Gathered out of the Word of God* (1648), better known as the Cambridge Platform.

Some of Mather's sermons about justification by faith were published in 1652 as *The Summe of Certain Sermons upon Genes: 15.6.*

Mather was one of twenty clergymen attending a 1657 conference that addressed issues relating to baptism. The ministers liberalized the traditional church position on this sacrament, a decision Mather endorsed. He explained this development in *A Disputation Concerning Church-Members and Their Children, in Answer to XXI. Questions* (1659), the contents of which his own church members found unconvincing. Undaunted, Mather continued supporting the relaxed requirements for baptism, as may be seen in his last volume published during his lifetime, *A Defence of the Answer and Arguments of the Synod Met at Boston in the Year 1662. Concerning the Subject of Baptism, and Consociation of Churches* (1664).

TOPICS FOR DISCUSSION AND RESEARCH

1. *The Bay Psalm Book* is one of the most important American books. Not only is it the first publication in English-speaking North America of which a copy is known to exist, but it raises important issues. One concerns the nature

of translation. The last paragraph of the introduction states that "if . . . the verses are not always so smooth and elegant as some may desire or expect; let them consider that God's altar needs not our polishings: *Ex. 20.* for we have respected rather a plain translation, than to smooth our verses with the sweetness of any paraphrases, and so have attended conscience rather than elegance, fidelity rather than poetry. . . ." That is, the translators, including Mather, knew that their version of the psalms would lack euphony and grace, qualities they sacrificed in favor of what they perceived as fidelity to the Hebrew original. What does this attitude indicate about them and about their understanding of the people who would use their book? What does the ostensibly more poetic 1651 translation indicate about the accuracy of the 1640 translators' principles of translation and their attitude toward their audience? What is the effect of citing Exodus 20 in the 1640 statement about translation? For information about these issues, students should consult Zoltán Haraszti's *The Enigma of the Bay Psalm Book*.

2. Fearing involvement in their affairs by English authorities and concerned about dissident clergy in their own ranks, ministers convened a synod, which met at Cambridge off and on from 1646 to 1648, to discuss ecclesiastical issues. Ultimately, the group produced what is known as the Cambridge Platform, one of the major American religious documents of the seventeenth century. Written largely by Mather, it established what amounts to a constitution for Congregationalism. It asserts, among other things, that each church is autonomous, though it encouraged cooperation among churches. It stipulates that ministers are called (requested) by individual churches and that a personal relationship with Christ is required for church membership. It limits the Lord's Supper to people evidencing saving grace. It requires that the Westminster Confession of Faith be used in all churches, and it encourages magistrates to be involved in church matters. One might beneficially consider the realities in England that interested the American ministers to the degree that they felt compelled to establish church polity at the Cambridge Synod. As the synod was meeting in Cambridge, the Westminster Assembly of Divines in London was restructuring the Church of England with a Presbyterian form of government. Why might this English reform have influenced the ministers attending the Cambridge Synod? At this same time, the English Civil War was being fought. Why might the synod participants have been interested in this conflict? For information about the Cambridge Synod and Cambridge Platform, consult Williston Walker's *The Creeds and Platforms of Congregationalism* and *A History of the Congregational Churches in the United States*.

3. The Cambridge Synod was held in large part to resolve the important issue of children's baptism: which children should be permitted to receive the sacrament? Ignored by the synod, the question was addressed at a 1657 ministerial assembly and again at a 1662 synod, where it was resolved. Until this time, Congregationalists limited baptism to children of at least one church member, which implied that the parent had satisfactorily demonstrated evidence of saving grace; on the basis of their parent's church membership,

these children also became members. As time passed, the number of such baptized children who in adulthood failed to attain assurance of salvation presented church leaders with a problem: how should the children of these now-adult but unregenerate parents be treated? The officials decided to make them half-way members of the church. "Half-way" meant that they could be baptized and subjected to discipline, but could not receive Holy Communion or vote. Before this time, Mather believed that baptism should be limited to children of regenerate parents. At the meetings of 1657 and 1662, however, he argued in favor of the new guidelines for baptism, a position not shared by his son, the notable Increase Mather. Because these guidelines were not binding, each church needed to resolve the issue itself, which Mather's church did by rejecting the proposal of the synod. Although there were religious reasons for rejecting it, there were social reasons for accepting it. What might be an example of a social reason? One of many sources of information about the Half-Way Covenant and the Cambridge Platform is Robert Middlekauff's *The Mathers*.

RESOURCES

Biography
Robert Middlekauff, *The Mathers: Three Generations of Puritan Intellectuals, 1596–1728* (New York: Oxford University Press, 1971).
An "intellectual history of Puritanism" that focuses on the lives and works of Richard Mather, Increase Mather, and Cotton Mather.

Criticism
B. R. Burg, *Richard Mather of Dorchester* (Lexington: University Press of Kentucky, 1976).
Examines Mather's life, career, and writings.

Zoltán Haraszti, *The Enigma of the Bay Psalm Book* (Chicago: University of Chicago Press, 1956).
Discusses *The Bay Psalm Book* in detail.

Williston Walker, *The Creeds and Platforms of Congregationalism* (1893; Boston: Pilgrim Press, 1960).
Reproduces and discusses the major documents of Congregationalism, including the Cambridge Platform.

Walker, *A History of the Congregational Churches in the United States* (New York: Scribners, 1893).
A history of Congregationalism, including detailed analysis of the Cambridge Platform and the Half-Way Covenant.

Jonathan Mayhew (1720–1766)

Gadfly of the religious establishment and one of the significant American thinkers from the late 1740s until his death in 1766, Jonathan Mayhew was born on
8 October 1720 to Experience Mayhew and Remember Bourne Mayhew in
Chilmark, Martha's Vineyard, Massachusetts, which was owned by the Mayhew family. There, he was taught by his father, a missionary to the Indians. He
matriculated at Harvard College in 1740 and received his degree four years later.
Soon after arriving at Harvard, he and other students were electrified by the
preaching of evangelist George Whitefield, who, along the Atlantic coast as far
south as Georgia, soon inspired an emotional approach to religion that blossomed
into the Great Awakening. Mayhew was, however, unimpressed with Whitefield's
farewell sermon in 1747, the year Mayhew received his master's degree from
Harvard. His disenchantment with religious emotionalism led to his adopting
a rational approach to religion, which was in keeping with the intellectual spirit
of the times: Enlightenment thought in America and Europe. At the same time,
Mayhew allowed that sermons should stir the emotions, as long as the sermons
faithfully represented the word of God, as expressed in the Bible. Mayhew's
valuing of rationality led to the minister's embracing of what might be called a
plain prose style, similar in conception to that of William Bradford, writing a
century earlier. That is, he wanted his (and others') prose to be transparent, easily understood. Also in 1747, Mayhew became minister of the newly established
West Church in Boston, in which position he remained for the remainder of his
relatively brief life.

Though influenced by John Locke and others, Mayhew was an independent
thinker, one not reluctant to challenge accepted thoughts and practices. At the
beginning of his ministerial career, he was treated as something of a pariah by
most of the established Boston ministers for failing to invite them to participate
in his ordination; he was soon ostracized also because of his religious hetero-
doxy: essentially, he believed that traditional Calvinism was irrelevant to people's
lives. He thought that the goal of religion was to encourage people to live a life
of goodness and not to concern themselves with abstract, abstruse theological
concepts or doctrines. He further believed that most people conclude rationally
that goodness is the desired goal of life; as a result, he wanted people to act freely
and not be dictated to by ministers who preach doctrines that are irrelevant to
people's lives. Among the doctrines Mayhew challenged were those of original
sin, irresistible grace, and the Trinity. Despite his questioning of and rejecting
such ideas, Mayhew retained some attitudes of his forebears. In particular, he
interpreted unfortunate events—such as defeats during the French and Indian
War, an earthquake, and a devastating fire—as signs of God's displeasure.

Mayhew's career began auspiciously with the publication of *Seven Sermons
upon the Following Subjects* (1749), in which he asks, among other things, how one
determines religious truth. One does not find it through creeds and doctrines, he
argues, because they could be wrong, but also because they, if honored, prevent
people from questioning and possibly improving on received religious knowledge:
if one believes only what one has been taught, there is no probing that could lead

to greater religious truths. Nor is truth found by believing as do others, even the majority of people. Rather, Mayhew thought that religious truth is discovered within each person, who, through reason, however imperfect, is capable of determining truth on his own. Such thoughts, as well as his rejection of original sin and other doctrines, struck at the foundation of Calvinism, the dominant religious belief in America from the Pilgrims to Mayhew's time and beyond, and helped alienate him from most Boston ministers. The next year Mayhew's book was published in England, where it received a generally warm response from groups such as the Arminians, who approached religion more rationally than did American Calvinists of the time. Because Mayhew's thoughts were so well received abroad, in 1750 the University of Aberdeen awarded the young Boston minister the honorary degree Doctor of Divinity.

On the anniversary of the execution of Charles I, Boston Anglicans typically reaffirmed their belief in the divine right of kings. In 1750, Mayhew responded to their views in a sermon published as *A Discourse Concerning Unlimited Submission and Non-Resistance to the Higher Powers*. Here he argues that a citizenry should obey and support a government that performs as it should, for the betterment of the lives of the governed; alternatively, reason dictates that people resist a government that disserves them, as was the case during the reign of Charles I. As a result, the English Puritans were right to overthrow him. This attitude—a desire for freedom from tyranny—is similar to that Mayhew expresses about religion in *Seven Sermons upon the Following Subjects*. The 1750 sermon was widely read (it was republished in London two years later) and generated much discussion.

In 1755, Mayhew's *Sermons upon the Following Subjects* was published in Boston and the next year in London. One of the sermons, "On Hearing the Word," is among Mayhew's most provocative and notorious works because in it he rejects the doctrine of the Trinity. This sermon caught the immediate attention of other ministers, who were dumbstruck. Jonathan Edwards, in the frontier village of Stockbridge, urged a quick response to Mayhew's position lest people think the denunciation of the Trinity could not be refuted. None was forthcoming until 1757, when Edwards's son-in-law, Aaron Burr, presented the position of the religiously orthodox.

In 1756, a decade before his death, Mayhew married Elizabeth Clarke; together, they had three children, only the oldest of whom, Elizabeth, survived childhood. During the next five years he published several discourses. His *Observations on the Charter and Conduct of the Society for the Propagation of the Gospel in Foreign Parts* was published in 1763 in response to the Anglican East Apthorp's defense of the Society for the Propagation of the Gospel in Foreign Parts, an Anglican organization intended to minister to Indians and blacks in sparsely populated areas but that attempted to establish Anglicanism in various settled communities already well populated with churches, in violation of the society's charter. To Mayhew and others, the Anglican effort to eradicate established churches or make them Anglican was similar to the Anglican persecution of Puritans in early-seventeenth-century England, a persecution that led—ultimately—to the Pilgrims leaving England on the *Mayflower* and establishing a permanent English settlement in America. Various writers published tracts on both sides of the issue, pro-Apthorp and pro-Mayhew. This debate is known as the Mayhew Controversy. It is important because Americans generally objected to the society's attempt to impose its will on American religion. Soon this fervor against English intervention in American religious life was redirected to politics when George III imposed the Stamp Act of 1765 on America. The forty-five-year-old Mayhew died on 9 July 1766; that year, his last work was published: *The Snare Broken*, which celebrates the repeal of the Stamp Act, an action for which he was ultimately partly responsible because of his position in the Mayhew Controversy.

TOPICS FOR DISCUSSION AND RESEARCH

1. Mayhew championed religious and political liberty. The latter, in particular, became a defining issue in eighteenth-century America. How similar are Mayhew's ideas about freedom to those of a contemporary such as Benjamin Franklin? Does it matter that Mayhew's views were influenced by his religious beliefs, while those of Franklin were secular in nature? If this difference in origin of thought matters, why does it? If it does not, why not? Further, Mayhew believed that religion is ultimately about living a life of goodness, of behaving well. One might beneficially apply this view to Franklin's life, which was largely one of good works. According to Mayhew's perception of religion, was Franklin religious? For help in answering these questions, one might read selected sermons of Mayhew, and Franklin's *Autobiography*.

2. Most of Mayhew's Calvinist predecessors believed that church membership and the partaking of sacraments provided evidence of salvation. This view was modified during the Great Awakening when Jonathan Edwards and others believed that God comes to one through the senses. The first view is highly formal; the second, emotional. Mayhew accepted neither position, arguing, rather, for a rational, nondoctrinaire approach to the issue, one that opposes both the rigidity of the former and the irrationality of the latter. Students might reasonably ask, though, if Mayhew's belief constitutes a synthesis of the two views. If so, what elements of traditional Calvinism and emotionalism did he retain? If his belief is not a synthesis, is he therefore an original thinker on this issue? Charles W. Akers's biography of Mayhew can help answer these questions.

3. In arguing for freedom from tyranny in *A Discourse Concerning Unlimited Submission and Non-Resistance to the Higher Powers*, Mayhew expresses a sentiment that resonated with many Americans both then and later as English rule grew increasingly onerous, reaching a climax of sorts with the Stamp Act of 1765. Ultimately, this desire for freedom—political independence—led to the American Revolution and the establishment of the United States of America. Mayhew's desire for freedom seems innate, but he expressed it first in the context of religion. How might ideas detailed in *Seven Sermons upon the Following Subjects* have influenced his political position as presented in *A Discourse Concerning Unlimited Submission and Non-Resistance to the Higher Powers*? One might beneficially demonstrate how ideas expressed in the first work (religious) are similar to those presented in the second (political). One

might also ask how this application of religious thought to politics anticipated a similar shift in the larger population. To answer this question, one could beneficially consult George Bancroft's thoughts as quoted in and commented on in Akers's biography.

4. Mayhew was not the first American to argue against tyranny: he was part of a tradition that stretches at least from the 1630s (Thomas Morton at Merry Mount, as well as Anne Hutchinson during the Antinomian Controversy) to the present day. One would benefit from considering Mayhew within the context of this tradition, comparing his thoughts with those of others who actively opposed governmental injustices, such as Henry David Thoreau ("Civil Disobedience") in the nineteenth century and Martin Luther King Jr. ("Letter from Birmingham Jail") in the twentieth.

5. Because Mayhew approached religion rationally and rejected the doctrine of the Trinity, he is sometimes considered a forefather of Unitarianism, which began flourishing in New England in the nineteenth century, with Ralph Waldo Emerson as its most famous member. Mayhew and Emerson were ministers who challenged Calvinist doctrines and were discontent with church formalism generally. Mayhew was so radical that he incurred the antipathy of most of his Boston colleagues; Emerson was so troubled by doctrines that he gave up his ministry. Compare Mayhew's and Emerson's religious thought. What views do they share? Is it correct, therefore, to consider Mayhew a precursor of Unitarianism? Students could answer these questions by reading selected sermons by Mayhew and then such an Emerson essay as "Divinity School Address" (1838) and such an Emerson poem as "Brahma" (1857), as well as commentary on these works.

RESOURCES

Biography

Charles W. Akers, *Called unto Liberty: A Life of Jonathan Mayhew, 1720–1766* (Cambridge, Mass.: Harvard University Press, 1964).

A thorough, authoritative biography that examines Mayhew's writings and analyzes his thought.

Bernard Bailyn, "Religion and Revolution: Three Biographical Studies," *Perspectives in American History*, 4 (1970): 111–124.

Argues that *The Snare Broken* "marks the struggle of the eighteenth-century radical seeking to maintain in an explosive situation the balance between political authoritarianism and social stability that is the essence of the libertarian creed."

Clifford K. Shipton, "Jonathan Mayhew," in *Biographical Sketches of Those Who Attended Harvard College in the Classes 1741–1745*, volume 11 of *Sibley's Harvard Graduates* (Boston: Massachusetts Historical Society, 1960), pp. 440–472.

Discusses Mayhew's life and works.

Criticism

John Corrigan, *The Hidden Balance: Religion and the Social Theories of Charles Chauncy and Jonathan Mayhew* (Cambridge, England: Cambridge University Press, 1987).

Argues that during the period between the Great Awakening and the American Revolution there was a "contest between (1) new ideas about and evidences of personal virtue and effort and (2) traditional social institutions grounded in an essentially elitist view of society, skeptical of human capability," and that Mayhew and Charles Chauncy "struggled to fashion elements drawn from each side of the conflict into coherent statements about God, man, and the world."

Thomas Morton (circa 1579–1647)

Little is known about the early years of Thomas Morton. Probably in the late 1570s, he was born of unknown parents (though his father was reportedly a soldier) in an unknown location in England. A lawyer, Morton prepared for his profession at Clifford's Inn, London. He married Alice Miller, a widow, in 1621. He spent a few months exploring America in late 1622 and early 1623. Morton sailed to America aboard the *Unity* in early 1624, landing at Passonagessit, which the party named Mount Wollaston, after the captain of the ship. This area is now part of Quincy, Massachusetts. When Wollaston removed to Virginia in 1626 and his partner Humphrey Rasdall soon followed him, first a Lieutenant Filcher and then Morton became sole leader of Mount Wollaston, which Morton renamed Merry Mount. Because of its friendly relationship with the Indians, the community had been and continued being in conflict with the settlers of Plymouth, so much so that Morton was arrested by Myles Standish and forced back to England in 1628. The Puritans renamed the community Mount Dagon. Returning to America the next year on the *Lyon*, Morton again encountered difficulty, quarreling with authorities to the degree that in late 1630 he was, for a second time, arrested and shipped back to England. In his native country he complained to officials, including colonizer Sir Ferdinando Gorges, about his treatment in the Plymouth and Massachusetts Bay colonies. Morton's actions in England were partly responsible for the request by Archbishop Laud's Commission for Regulating Plantations that the Massachusetts Bay charter be returned to England for the purpose of invalidating it, though the request was not honored. For reasons that cannot be determined—though possibly to represent Gorges in Maine, which Gorges controlled—in 1643, Morton returned to America, landing at Plymouth. The next year, he was again arrested, probably because in England he was involved in the effort to recall the charter and also probably because he wrote a book that depicts the colonists in an unfavorable light. After being jailed for a year in Boston, fined, and freed, Morton settled in Agamenticus (now part of York, Maine), where he died in 1647.

Morton wrote but one book, *New English Canaan,* which he composed in England and which was published in Amsterdam in 1637. It contains three distinct parts. The first deals with the Indians; the second, with natural New England; the third, with the Puritans and their interaction with Morton and his community. Unlike the first two sections, the last is partly satirical. In it, for example, Morton calls Myles Standish "Captain Shrimpe," while identifying his adversary John Endecott as "Captain Littleworth." The book is important for several reasons: it was written by an Anglican who lived in proximity to the anti-Anglican Puritans; it is occasionally witty, even bawdy; and it details Morton's sympathetic observations about the Indians. It is most famous for presenting Morton's perspective on the dispute with the Puritans over the existence of the Merry Mount community. His views contrast with those expressed by William Bradford in *Of Plymouth Plantation,* an account generally believed because of Bradford's importance as the longtime governor of the Plymouth colony, his plain writing style (Morton's is not plain), and his professed desire to tell the truth. Basically, the Pilgrims considered Morton and the Merry Mount community threats because they provided guns to the Indians, thereby compromising the Puritans' security; further, Bradford and his group disliked the Merry Mounters' licentious ways, which included dancing around a maypole, drinking to excess, and consorting with Indian women. In the end, *New English Canaan* serves best as a defense of Morton and the Merry Mounters, outsiders who threatened the Pilgrims of Plymouth.

TOPICS FOR DISCUSSION AND RESEARCH

1. In an article published in 1970, Minor W. Major carefully examines Bradford's account of Morton and the Merry Mounters. As a result of finding reasons for doubting Bradford, Major implies that Morton's rendering of events might be credible, or at least ought not to be dismissed out of hand. Among other things, Major provides evidence for questioning, if not refuting, Bradford's charges that the Merry Mounters did not respect Morton, that they drank excessively, that Morton was the first European to trade guns to the Indians, that the Merry Mounters became prosperous because of arms transactions with the Indians, that other plantations joined Plymouth in bringing charges against Morton, and that Morton and his group violated English law in dallying with Indian women. Furthermore, Morton was acquitted when tried in England for selling guns to the Indians, which was Bradford's main charge against him. After reading Bradford's account of Morton and Morton's treatment of the same events, ask which author seems more convincing, and why. Then, consult Major's article and determine if his conclusions appear to be accurate. Karen Ordahl Kupperman addresses similar issues in "Thomas Morton, Historian."

2. As Edward M. Griffin has shown, historians generally dismiss the conflict between Morton and the Puritans as too insignificant for serious study because few people were involved in it (there were only seven men at Merry Mount when Morton was in charge), too little happened between the two parties, and there are too few documents relating to it. Yet, while historians tend to ignore this incident, artists have found it compelling. Most famously, Nathaniel Haw-

thorne writes about it in "The May-Pole of Merry Mount."The third sentence of the story—"Jollity [Morton] and gloom [Puritans] were contending for an empire"—indicates why the author found the conflict appealing: it permitted him to examine and possibly resolve contrasting attitudes toward life in early America. Among the other artists who use Morton in their work are John Lothrop Motley (*Merry Mount*, an 1849 novel), Howard Hanson and Richard L. Stokes (*Merry Mount*, a 1933 opera), Stephen Vincent Benét ("The Devil and Daniel Webster," a 1937 story), Robert Lowell (*Endecott and the Red Cross*, a 1965 play revised in 1968), and L. S. Davidson Jr. (*The Disturber*, a 1964 novel). One might beneficially consider why these artists were attracted to the conflict and how they transformed historical events into art. For information about Morton as historian, see Kupperman's "Thomas Morton, Historian." For a discussion of how artists have used Morton and Merry Mount in their work, consult John P. McWilliams Jr.'s "Fictions of Merry Mount."

3. Despite contemporary opinion to the contrary, Puritans were not opposed to sex. In fact, sex was desirable within marriage, which is one reason why many of them married soon after the death of a spouse. Fornication was another matter, which is largely why the Puritans so objected to the Merry Mounters' dalliances with Indian women. Morton treats such relations as harmless, as may be observed in the lines *"Lasses in beaver coats come away, / Ye shall be welcome to us night and day,"* which are from the second of two poems he wrote about the Merry Mount festivities. Even though such activity violated the Puritans' moral code, one might reasonably question why this group objected so strenuously to the mingling of the Merry Mount men and Indian women, especially since no Puritans were involved in the revelries. Did they think that such apparent licentiousness would ultimately migrate to and contaminate their community? Or did they object less to sexual promiscuity than to the establishment of the pagan English tradition of dancing around a maypole, which they cut down? For information about Puritan attitudes toward sex, consult *The Puritan Origins of American Sex*.

4. The prose styles of Morton and Bradford differ. The occasionally humorous, rococo, and unintelligible Morton is less disciplined than Bradford, who writes prose that is often elegant in its plainness. How do the styles influence one's reading of the two texts? Do they suggest that one author is more believable than the other? That one is more likable? Read the authors' accounts of their conflict for help in answering these questions.

5. Morton wrote *New English Canaan* partly as propaganda, as a tract for promoting the New World to Englishmen who might be willing to settle there. He characterizes natural America glowingly, as in this passage written in 1622 about his first impressions of the country: "For in mine eye, 'twas Nature's Masterpiece: Her chiefest Magazine of all, where lives her Store. If this land be not rich, then is the whole world poor." He prefers the Indians to the Puritans: he found the Indians "most full of humanity, and more friendly than the other." In other words, he portrays America and its native inhabitants positively and directs his criticism mainly to his adversaries, the Puritans. To what degree, if any, does Morton's doubtlessly idealistic picture of America

compromise the value of the book as history? For information about Morton as historian, consult Kupperman's "Thomas Morton, Historian" and Major's "William Bradford Versus Thomas Morton."

RESOURCES

Biography

Jack Dempsey, *Thomas Morton of "Merrymount": The Life and Renaissance of an Early American Poet* (Scituate, Mass.: Digital Scanning, 2000).
A comprehensive biography.

Criticism

Charles Edward Banks, "Thomas Morton of Merry Mount," *Massachusetts Historical Society Proceedings*, 58 (1925): 147–193.
Reproduces documents by and relating to Morton.

Donald F. Connors, *Thomas Morton* (New York: Twayne, 1969).
Analyzes Morton and *New English Canaan* within the context of Morton's experiences and times.

Edward M. Griffin, "Dancing around the Maypole, Ripping up the Flag: The Merry Mount Caper and Issues in American History and Art," *Renascence*, 57, no. 3 (Spring 2005): 177–202.
Discusses how historians and creative writers treat *New English Canaan* differently.

Karen Ordahl Kupperman, "Thomas Morton, Historian," *New England Quarterly*, 50, no. 4 (December 1977): 660–664.
Argues for Morton's worth as a historian.

Minor W. Major, "William Bradford Versus Thomas Morton," *Early American Literature*, 5, no. 2 (Fall 1970): 1–13.
Scrutinizes Bradford's account of Morton and the Merry Mount community, concluding that Bradford is less reliable than he seems.

John P. McWilliams Jr., "Fictions of Merry Mount," *American Quarterly*, 29, no. 1 (Spring 1977): 3–30.
Discusses how various artists have used Morton and Merry Mount in their work.

The Puritan Origins of American Sex: Religion, Sexuality, and National Identity in American Literature, edited by Tracy Fessenden, et al. (New York: Routledge, 2001).
Fifteen essays by various hands discuss Puritan attitudes toward sex and illustrate how these attitudes affected later ones.

David Read, *New World, Known World: Shaping Knowledge in Early Anglo-American Writing* (Columbia: University of Missouri Press, 2005).

Argues that Morton—like John Smith, William Bradford, and Roger Williams—renders "an organized account of a newly experienced colonial world that will make that world distinct from the one—'Old' or just generically familiar—that previously formed the ground of knowledge."

Samson Occom
"S. Occom's Account of Himself, Written Sept. 17, 1768" ("A Short Narrative of My Life")

Initially published in *The Elders Wrote: An Anthology of Early Prose by North American Indians, 1768–1931*, edited by Bernd Peyer (Berlin: Dietrich Reimer Verlag, 1982), pp. 12–18

Samson Occom is, with Phillis Wheatley, among the least-likely authors of colonial America. A Mohegan, or Mohican, Indian born in New London, Connecticut, to nomadic parents in 1723, Occom was inspired to learn English by missionaries. Converted to Christianity by James Davenport, he was educated by Eleazar Wheelock in Lebanon and Hebron, Connecticut, for four years beginning in 1743; poor health and weak eyesight caused him to end his studies. He became proficient enough in languages to tutor students in Hebrew, Latin, and Greek, as well as English. Around 1751 he married the Montauk Indian Mary Fowler, an action that exacerbated his already difficult financial situation. The couple had ten children.

Wheelock figures prominently in one of Occom's major undertakings. In 1765, Occom and Nathaniel Whitaker traveled to England to raise funds for Wheelock's school for Indians. They succeeded, which is ironic in the context of Occom's own poverty. It is further ironic because, over Occom's objections, Wheelock moved his school from Lebanon to Hanover, New Hampshire, an action that led, as Occom foresaw, to the school's decreased attention to Indian students. This school became Dartmouth College, established partly because of Occom's efforts that ultimately did little to improve the education of Indians. As a result of this disagreement with Wheelock, the men's relationship deteriorated. Doubtless feeling abused, Occom attempted to explain himself in an autobiography. This brief document—twenty-six pages in manuscript and five pages in anthologies of American literature—constitutes Occom's major contribution to letters.

Like many other spiritual narratives, Occom's recounts the process by which the author became aware of and involved in Christianity. It also relates the process by which Occom learned to read and write, as well as the methods he used to teach Indian children to read English. Occom describes his family's way of life, which was largely that of other Indians, such as residing in a wigwam and living off the land. He describes financial difficulties that were caused primarily by insufficient support from Boston commissioners. Occom defends himself against the charge of extravagance and observes that he is paid far less than a young, presumably white missionary whose services are not needed. Reluctantly, Occom concludes that he is treated unfairly because he is an Indian.

Although the autobiography remained unpublished for over two centuries (the manuscript is in the Dartmouth archives), Occom saw the publication of two of his works. The second is *A Choice Collection of Hymns and Spiritual Songs, Intended for the Edification of Sincere Christians, of All Denominations* (1774), which includes over one hundred hymns, mostly by such hymnodists as Isaac Watts and Charles Wesley; this book required several editions. The first of Occom's publications is *A Sermon, Preached at the Execution of Moses Paul, an Indian* . . . (1772). Enormously popular, the sermon went through many editions and is now regularly included, sometimes in abbreviated form, in anthologies of American literature. Although by the 1770s America had a tradition of execution sermons, Occom's was more popular than most of them; it is also probably the first sermon by an Indian to be published in English-speaking America. Execution sermons had a dual purpose: solace for the person about to be executed and instruction for the people gathered to witness the event. The prisoner, Moses Paul, was a Christianized Mohegan convicted of having murdered, while inebriated, a prominent citizen of Waterbury, Connecticut. Paul requested that Occom deliver the sermon at his hanging. Occom focuses, among other topics, on the evil effects of immoderate drinking on Paul and Indians generally, women as well as men. The intensity of the preacher's prose probably helps account for its popularity.

Occom encouraged Indian neutrality during the American Revolution. Subsequently, he preached to Indians in New Stockbridge, New York, where he died in 1792. All his known writings—prose, letters, petitions, sermons, hymns, and journals—were published as *The Collected Writings of Samson Occom, Mohegan* (2006), edited by Joanna Brooks.

TOPICS FOR DISCUSSION AND RESEARCH

1. Occom is one of many authors benefiting from the expanding canon of American literature. Until relatively recently, he was generally unknown; now, he is included in most if not all anthologies of American literature. Scholarly articles have been and continue to be written about him. He published little of what might be called literature: a sermon and a brief autobiography published posthumously. Either individually or together, do these works constitute significant literature? If so, on what basis? Or are they of interest primarily for cultural reasons, for what they reveal about an Indian who "succeeded" in white culture and what they indicate about his perceptions of Indian and white cultures? Or might they be deemed important largely because Occom, an educated Indian who wrote in English, is a curiosity? Or for all these reasons? One can begin answering these questions by comparing his execution sermon with others in the genre, such as those by Increase Mather and Cotton Mather, and by comparing his autobiography with that of Benjamin Franklin, as well as with Jonathan Edwards's "Personal Narrative."

2. In eighteenth-century America, white people were usually literate but darker people—Indians and blacks—typically were not, though some darker people became literate and, as a result, were able to pursue professions within white society. One such person was Occom, who, in his autobiography, emphasizes the importance of reading, going so far as to explain how he taught it to Indians. Students interested in the subject of literacy would benefit from comparing Occom's comments about it with those in *The Interesting Narrative of the Life of Olaudah Equiano, or Gustavus Vassa, the African* (1789) and with a nineteenth-century text such as *Narrative of the Life of Frederick Douglass* (1845). Analysis of these accounts might consider what the narratives imply about the values of the two cultures, what the newly literate person gains from literacy, what if anything this person lost in becoming literate, and the processes by which literacy is acquired. These and other considerations of a single narrative such as Occom's can be worthwhile, but comparative study would be even more beneficial.

3. The most famous autobiography of an eighteenth-century American, that of Benjamin Franklin, is notable partly because of its emphasis on self-fashioning, the ability of the individual to create himself. Occom's narrative concludes by implying that race keeps him from creating himself: he believes he has been treated badly because he is "a poor Indian" and that he cannot "help that God has made me So; I did not make myself so." Does the rest of the narrative support a reading that sees identity as a given rather than something that can be shaped by the individual? On this topic, comparing Occom's narrative with Franklin's autobiography would prove illuminating. Other points of comparison with Franklin might deal with how the two men describe their dealings with other people, especially in the context of business relationships. Consider, for example, Franklin's discussion of his ill treatment by Governor Keith and Occom's account of his neglect by the Boston commissioners. Hilary E. Wyss's arguments about native efforts at self-assertion would be useful when analyzing Occom's narrative along these lines.

4. Occom's narrative begins as a standard spiritual narrative. The latter part of the autobiography focuses on financial dealings within the context of Occom's missionary and ministerial duties. Students would benefit from analyzing the plots of the narrative, taking this shift in focus into account. If readers examine Occom's spiritual growth through the narrative, where might they locate the conflict, climax, and resolution? How does this plot differ from that of the author's financial fortunes? Of Occom's professional success? In what ways are Occom's plots similar to Franklin's? How do the plots of the two autobiographies differ?

5. Significant differences in attitude can be observed between the speaker in Occom's autobiography and in the sermon Occom delivered at the hanging of Moses Paul. In the two works, how does his treatment of Indian-white relations differ? How dissimilar are his attitudes toward white clergy? How does he portray his ministry to other Indians? The sermon was composed for people to hear and, ultimately, read; the narrative is a private document. How is Occom's perception of audience reflected in the speakers of these two works?

6. Although Occom differentiated himself from other Mohegans by becoming literate, converting to Christianity, and having a missionary career, he maintained aspects of Mohegan life. What rhetorical function does Occom's description of Indian living conditions serve in his narrative? A useful point of comparison is Equiano's description of Ibo ways of life in the opening chapter of his narrative. Students interested in this topic should consult Katy L. Chiles's article about race in Occom's and Phillis Wheatley's writings. If we accept Chiles's argument that Occom saw race as malleable, does that change the way we understand his depiction of Indian habits and behavior?

RESOURCES

Biography

Harold Blodgett, *Samson Occom* (Hanover, N.H.: Dartmouth College, 1935).
A still-valuable biography of Occom; despite the dullness of his diary, "occasionally, as in the all too brief autobiographical sketch of his boyhood days, prepared while he was thinking of writing his life, Occom is genuinely interesting. . . ."

W. DeLoss Love, *Samson Occom and the Christian Indians of New England* (Boston: Pilgrim Press, 1899).
Details Occom's life within the context of Indian culture.

Bernd Peyer, "Samson Occom: Mohegan Missionary and Writer of the 18th Century," *American Indian Quarterly,* 6, no. 3/4 (Autumn–Winter 1982): 208–217.
A brief biography of Occom.

Criticism

Katy L. Chiles, "Becoming Colored in Occom and Wheatley's Early America," *PMLA: Publications of the Modern Language Association of America,* 123 (2008): 1398–1417.
Argues that Occom and Wheatley viewed race as being produced by environment and therefore subject to change over time.

Keely McCarthy, "Conversion, Identity, and the Indian Missionary," *Early American Literature,* 36, no. 3 (2001): 353–370.
Argues that in his autobiography Occom "rejects dominant British-American notions that there were necessary links between race and culture and between culture and religion."

Dana D. Nelson, "'(I Speak Like a Fool but I Am Constrained)': Samson Occom's *Short Narrative* and Economies of the Racial Self," in *Early Native American Writing: New Critical Essays,* edited by Helen Jaskoski (Cambridge, England: Cambridge University Press, 1996), pp. 42–65.
Suggests that Occom's autobiography "is literally *about* finding a multiculturalist vision of America."

Samson Occom, *The Collected Writings of Samson Occom, Mohegan: Leadership and Literature in Eighteenth-Century Native America*, edited by Joanna Brooks (New York: Oxford University Press, 2006).
Reproduces all known writings by Occom, including ministerial works (sermons and hymns) and personal papers (letters and diaries), as well as petitions.

Hilary E. Wyss, *Writing Indians: Literacy, Christianity, and Native Community in Early America* (Amherst: University of Massachusetts Press, 2000).
Argues that writing in English was an essential component of Indians' negotiations with the white establishment and that early writing in English by Indians should be viewed as bicultural.

William Penn (1644–1718)

Despite living only briefly in America, the peripatetic and often-jailed William Penn is one of the most significant late-seventeenth-century Americans. He was born in London on 14 October 1644 to William Penn and Margaret Jasper Vanderschuren Penn, who had married the previous year. His father was a naval officer, later an admiral, who spent little time at home; his mother had been widowed before marrying his father. The couple had three children, two boys and a girl. Although technically Anglican, the family was not particularly religious.

Penn apparently had little early formal education, though he attended, for less than a year, the Chigwell Free Grammar School near the family's home in Wanstead. The Penns moved to Ireland in 1656 so Penn's father could collect payment due for rentals on land granted him by Oliver Cromwell. There, in an event that would have life-altering repercussions, young Penn met Thomas Loe, a Quaker evangelist from Oxford. In 1660 Penn matriculated at Christ Church, Oxford, where he wrote a poem that was published; he was dismissed the following year for nonconformism. Back in England after a period in France, he studied law at Lincoln's Inn, London, in 1665 but did not complete a semester. Around this time, he became friendly with Charles II and the duke of York, who became James II. Probably in 1667, after living in Ireland, Penn reunited with Thomas Loe and converted to Quakerism, a risky move in a country that restricted all religions except Anglicanism, the state church. A friend of George Fox, the founder of Quakerism, Penn soon became one of the most important Quakers. As a result of attending meetings of and preaching for a forbidden group, he was frequently jailed; he was also imprisoned in the Tower of London for having written *The Sandy Foundation Shaken* (1669), which questions the concept of the Trinity. While in the Tower, he made notes for and conceivably composed *No Cross, No Crown* (1669), in which he argues, essentially, for the equality of all mankind, for the supremacy of no one over anyone else, while criticizing the Church of England. Penn rewrote this work in 1682. In 1670 he was arrested for public preaching. The judge would not permit Penn to defend himself and instructed the jury to find him guilty. They found him innocent. After the judge jailed Penn and the jurors, they pressed and won their case against unlawful imprisonment, thereby establishing the independence of juries, a concept that became important in American jurisprudence. Also in 1670 Penn published *The Great Case of Liberty of Conscience*, a tract making a case for religious freedom. In 1672 he married Gulielma Maria Springett; of their six or seven children, three survived into adulthood.

During the next few years, Penn wrote in defense of Quakerism and engaged in disputes within the Society of Friends over the issue of governance. Then, an issue arose that involved him with America. Penn arbitrated a disagreement among Quakers over the ownership of land in what is now the state of New Jersey. As a result, he and others in England oversaw the management of the colony. At this time, Penn continued writing in defense of Quakerism and freedom of conscience, including *A Treatise of Oaths Containing Several Weighty Reasons Why the People Call'd Quakers Refuse to Swear* (1675) and *The Continued Cry of the Oppressed for Justice* (part 1, 1675; part 2, 1676). He is the probable author of *The Description of West New Jersey* (1676), which encouraged settlement of this area. Thereby encouraged, and viewing West New Jersey as a haven where they could live peacefully and worship unmolested, many Quakers sailed for America.

In 1681 British Parliament granted Penn a charter for and named him proprietor of an enormous area that is now the state of Pennsylvania (the word means "Penn's woods"). Penn viewed the area as a home for Quakers as well as a place of business opportunity. Before sailing to America in 1682, he wrote about Pennsylvania in *Some Account of the Province of Pennsilvania in America* (1681) and *A Brief Account of the Province of Pennsilvania in America* (1681), which are largely promotional tracts. Then, he wrote the constitution of Pennsylvania that was published as *The Frame of the Government of the Province of Pennsilvania in America* (1682). This document specifies that all citizens are free as long as they obey the law, which they help create. It incorporates certain Quaker beliefs, such as religious toleration and freedom of conscience. He returned to England in 1684 to tend to issues relating to the Pennsylvania-Delaware border. He lost the Pennsylvania charter in 1692 because he could not persuade Pennsylvanians to help England in its war with France. His *Essay Towards the Present and Future Peace of Europe* was published in 1693. In it Penn proposes a parliament of nations and suggests disarmament as the means by which peace can be attained and sustained. Penn was again awarded the Pennsylvania charter in 1694, when he was in financial distress; that same year, his wife died. In 1696, he married Hannah Callowhill, with whom he had seven children. The next year, Penn proposed an annual meeting of all the American colonies to discuss defense and trade, issues of common interest. Two years later, he sailed for Pennsylvania for the second and last time, but returned to England in early 1702 to protect his Pennsylvania interests. In order to alleviate his onerous debt that resulted from having been defrauded, among other reasons, he tried selling his proprietorship to the Crown. Unsuccessful, he was confined to a debtors' prison in 1708. He suffered two strokes in 1712 and died in Ruscombe, England, on 30 July 1718.

Penn wrote voluminously, with well over a hundred publications, mostly pamphlets. His influence on Pennsylvania and America is profound, primarily in the area of ideas, concepts. Believing, as Quakers do, that mankind possesses Inner Light, he thought of all people as equal. As a result, they are all able to participate in government; they are expected to obey laws because they helped create them. His egalitarianism extended to the Indians, whom he treated fairly.

TOPICS FOR DISCUSSION AND RESEARCH

1. Penn spent only a few years in America. On what basis is he considered not only an American, but an American icon? Does the fact that a state bears his name matter? Or is this just an incidental issue? Is it significant that he was the first proprietor of Pennsylvania and as such was largely responsible for its conceptual underpinnings and early success? How important is his drafting of the Pennsylvania constitution? Does it matter that Penn stipulates in it that juries will be independent, an idea that became central to the American system of laws? In the context of subsequent American democracy, how significant are Penn's strong beliefs in religious freedom and the equality of all mankind? In proposing annual meetings for colonies to discuss defense and trade, did Penn anticipate the nature of the United States, a collection of states that are represented by members of congress who discuss issues of common interest? For information about Penn and the government of Pennsylvania, see Mary Maples Dunn's *William Penn* and Joseph E. Illick's *William Penn the Politician*.

2. Although Penn composed a few poems, he generally wrote religious and political tracts, not belles lettres. On what basis is he considered a literary figure? Some Puritan ministers (the Mathers) and historians (William Bradford) also wrote primarily in a non-belletristic manner and are widely considered literary. How similar or dissimilar from them is Penn in this regard? Could "literary" be construed so as to include ideas, however expressed, that help shape or define a culture? Reading selected passages from these authors would aid in answering these questions.

3. How prescient are the views Penn expresses in *Essay Towards the Present and Future Peace of Europe*? Might his call for a European parliament be seen as a distant precursor of the League of Nations, the United Nations, and the European Union? Do his recommendations for disarmament presage contemporary discussion about this very issue, including within the context of nuclear proliferation? How do these ideas reflect his Quaker beliefs? Information for answering these questions may be found in Mary K. Geiter's *William Penn* and Harry Emerson Wildes's *William Penn*.

4. The Quaker Penn was involved with America—New Jersey, then Pennsylvania —when the Puritans still largely dominated New England, especially Massachusetts. How does Quakerism differ from Puritanism? One group considers people innately good; one, innately evil. What accounts for these differences? How did the Quaker view influence Penn's conception of Pennsylvania? The two groups have different conception of government. What are they? How do the Quakers and Puritans differ in their attitudes toward Indians? Toward women? In answering these questions, students would benefit from

consulting Melvin B. Endy Jr.'s *William Penn and Early Quakerism*, John A. Moretta's *William Penn and the Quaker Legacy*, and Gary B. Nash's *Quakers and Politics*.

RESOURCES

Biography

Mary K. Geiter, *William Penn* (Harlow, England: Longman, 2000).
A biography that evaluates much of the subject's success in the context of Penn's membership in the ruling class, a position that "influenced his outlook as much if not more than did his religion."

Joseph E. Illick, *William Penn the Politician: His Relations with the English Government* (Ithaca: Cornell University Press, 1965).
A biography that serves as a corrective to biographies that focus on Penn mainly within the context of religion.

John A. Moretta, *William Penn and the Quaker Legacy* (New York: Pearson Longman, 2007).
While acknowledging Penn's religious beliefs, this biography focuses on Penn as a man of action, of political influence, and of other qualities that many studies slight.

Harry Emerson Wildes, *William Penn* (New York & London: Macmillan/Collier Macmillan, 1974).
A full-scale, detailed biography that attempts to humanize Penn.

Criticism

Edwin B. Bronner, *William Penn's "Holy Experiment": The Founding of Pennsylvania, 1681–1701* (New York: Temple University, 1962).
This study of the first two decades of the Pennsylvania colony focuses on "the struggle for politico-economic-religious self-realization by the dominant element of society, the English-speaking people."

Mary Maples Dunn, *William Penn: Politics and Conscience* (Princeton: Princeton University Press, 1967).
Corrects scholarly oversight by examining Penn as politician and political thinker.

Melvin B. Endy Jr., *William Penn and Early Quakerism* (Princeton: Princeton University Press, 1973).
A serious, detailed examination of Penn's religious thought.

Gary B. Nash, *Quakers and Politics: Pennsylvania, 1681–1726* (Princeton: Princeton University Press, 1968).
Examines the Quakers' struggles with political realities for almost half a century following the issuance of the Pennsylvania charter.

William Penn and the Founding of Pennsylvania, 1680–1684, a Documentary History, edited by Jean R. Soderlund (Philadelphia: University of Pennsylvania Press/Historical Society of Pennsylvania, 1983).

Reproduces documents crucial to the founding of Pennsylvania, from Penn's 1680 petition to Charles II to Penn's 1684 farewell letter to the people of Pennsylvania.

The World of William Penn, edited by Richard S. Dunn and Mary Maples Dunn (Philadelphia: University of Pennsylvania Press, 1986).
Five essays by various hands on each of four general topics: "William Penn Reconsidered," "Penn's Britain," "Penn's America," and "Meeting House and Counting House."

Mary Rowlandson
The Soveraignty & Goodness of God, Together, with the Faithfulness of His Promises Displayed
(Cambridge, Mass.: Printed by Samuel Green, 1682)

Mary White Rowlandson was born in Somerset County, England, to John White and Joan West White around the year 1637, the fifth of eight children. In America, the family settled first in Wenham, Massachusetts, then in Lancaster, where, probably in 1656, Mary White married the local minister, Joseph Rowlandson. The couple had four children, though the first died at age three. During King Philip's War, while Joseph Rowlandson was in Boston, Mary Rowlandson and her three children were captured during an Indian attack on Lancaster. About a week later, the youngest Rowlandson child, Sarah, died in her injured mother's arms. After Mary Rowlandson and her surviving two children were freed, the reunited family settled, in 1677, in Wethersfield, Connecticut, where Joseph Rowlandson ministered to the local church. He died the following year. In 1679 Mary Rowlandson married Captain Samuel Talcott (Harvard class of 1658), with whom she apparently had no children; his first wife had died in 1678. Samuel Talcott died in Wethersfield in 1691. Mary White Rowlandson Talcott died there on 5 January 1711, aged approximately seventy-three, survived by her son, Joseph Rowlandson Jr., and presumably by her daughter, Mary.

Rowlandson's importance stems from her authorship of the first female captivity narrative, *The Soveraignty & Goodness of God, Together, with the Faithfulness of His Promises Displayed* (1682), which recounts Rowlandson's twenty removes (changes of location) during an almost three-month captivity by Indians. Indeed, it is the first published prose narrative by an American woman. Internal evidence indicates that Rowlandson wrote it in 1677 and 1678. The book was popular to the degree that it required at least sixteen American editions to 1800, plus one English edition titled *A True History of the Captivity & Restoration of Mrs. Mary Rowlandson, a Minister's Wife in New England* (1682). No complete copy of the first edition survives (four pages of a copy of the first edition exist), and the second edition is represented only by a single copy.

The narrative is important on several levels: it testifies to one woman's fortitude and religious faith during a period of severe crisis; it provides a firsthand account of a white person's life with Indians who killed many whites, including some of Rowlandson's family, but who nonetheless are occasionally thoughtful and even kind to their captive; it raises issues of gender, race, and cultural values; it challenges readers to address possibly unanswerable questions about narration, editing, and publishing; and more. In sum, it is one of the most important seventeenth-century American texts.

TOPICS FOR DISCUSSION AND RESEARCH

1. Rowlandson states that before King Philip's War, she preferred death to capture by Indians. In *The Name of War,* Jill Lepore suggests that while Rowlandson wrote her narrative mainly to illustrate God's goodness in permitting her to survive and return to white society, she also composed it to expiate guilt caused by permitting herself to be taken captive (she had a choice), for not having the power of her convictions. What evidence does Lepore use to support this claim? How convincing is it? If it is convincing, how does it affect the reading of Rowlandson's narrative and a consideration of the author herself? Does it indicate her moral weakness? Does it humanize her? Within the context of these questions, how significant is Rowlandson's statement that the author's sister also preferred death to captivity and, unlike Rowlandson, was killed by Indians? Other scholars offer additional possible reasons for Rowlandson's having written the narrative. In "Puritan Orthodoxy and the 'Survivor Syndrome' in Mary Rowlandson's Indian Captivity Narrative," for example, Kathryn Zabelle Derounian argues that Rowlandson wrote it in order to overcome survivor syndrome, while Mitchell Robert Breitwieser believes that she composed it within the context of grief occasioned by the death of her daughter. Read these arguments and ask how convincing they are.

2. Lepore notes that Rowlandson's narrative was popular partly because the author's descriptive strategies—her use of images—make it compelling. What examples does she give? Students would benefit from identifying additional images that enhance the text. Had Rowlandson written less vividly, how weakened would the narrative be? Are the events gripping enough to make the narrative engaging even without such deft use of images? In other words, how artful is Rowlandson's narrative?

3. Some early editions of Rowlandson's narrative include works by others: a preface probably written by Increase Mather (though possibly by Gershom Bulkeley) and a concluding sermon by Joseph Rowlandson, the author's husband; the sermon is introduced by B.W., who is probably Benjamin Woodbridge. Students might reasonably ask why such additional material was deemed necessary, especially since the dramatic nature of Rowlandson's work would alone attract readers. Might publishers have thought that a woman's narrative needed endorsement by members of the religious establishment, namely ministers, all male? If so, why? What is the nature of these men's comments, which are all reproduced in *The Sovereignty and Goodness of God, Together with*

the Faithfulness of His Promises Displayed, Being a Narrative of the Captivity and Restoration of Mrs. Mary Rowlandson and Related Documents, edited by Neal Salisbury, who addresses this issue and collateral issues on pages 44–48? What is the likelihood that one or more of these men assisted in the composition of the narrative? Anne Bradstreet's *The Tenth Muse* (1650) is also introduced by writings by men. How similar are the probable reasons for including men's writing in these two books by seventeenth-century women?

4. Under the leadership of Paul Lauter, numerous scholars addressed the issue of the American literary canon and decided to expand it significantly in an anthology for college students, one that emphasizes diversity. Their efforts resulted in *The Heath Anthology of American Literature* (1990), which includes most of Rowlandson's narrative. Among the episodes it omits is that of Goodwife Joslin, which Rowlandson introduces at the end of the third remove and details at the beginning of the fourth. Rowlandson tells of advising fellow captive Joslin—nine months pregnant and accompanied by a two-year-old child—to resist the temptation to escape her captors. Later, after being separated from Joslin, Rowlandson learns that the Indians stripped her naked, danced around her, hit her head, and burned mother and child to death. Students would benefit from speculating on why the editors of *The Heath Anthology of American Literature* elected to omit the Joslin episode, a dramatic, memorable scene that captures the attention of even the most casual reader. Might they have thought that advising Joslin to accept her uncertain fate taints Rowlandson, making her complicit in the deaths of Joslin and her child? Might they have believed that in supporting her recommendation by quoting the last verse of Psalm 27 *("Wait on the Lord, Be of good courage, and he shall strengthen thine heart, wait I say on the Lord")* Rowlandson indicates that God forsakes his believers and condones and even causes evil? With reason, Rowlandson often depicts Indian cruelty. For editors of an anthology of diverse American literature, including that by Indians, might the barbarism and sadism depicted in the Joslin scene present the Indians in too cruel a manner? Might the editors have thought that because Rowlandson heard about the Joslins' deaths and did not observe them, the information is unreliable and therefore should not be included? What other reasons might the editors have had for omitting this scene? In the introduction to the selections from Rowlandson's narrative in the anthology, Paula Uruburu states that Rowlandson's work "is important for its literary, social, theological, anthropological, and psychological documenting of life in early America." Does the Joslin episode contribute to our understanding of any of these aspects of early American life? If so, which? How? Mitchell Robert Breitwieser discusses Joslin on pages 111–112 of his book.

RESOURCES

Biography
David L. Greene, "New Light on Mary Rowlandson," *Early American Literature,* 20 (Spring 1985): 24–38.
The most detailed, authoritative account of Rowlandson's life.

Criticism

Mitchell Robert Breitwieser, *American Puritanism and the Defense of Mourning: Religion, Grief, and Ethnology in Mary White Rowlandson's Captivity Narrative* (Madison: University of Wisconsin Press, 1990).
Argues that Rowlandson sublimates her real emotions in deference to seventeenth-century Puritan values while attempting to retain grief at the death of her daughter and refusing to characterize her captors as totally evil.

Michelle Burnham, *Captivity and Sentiment: Cultural Exchange in American Literature, 1682–1861* (Hanover: Dartmouth College/University Press of New England, 1999).
"Finds that what is at stake in the fate of [female captives, including Rowlandson] is nothing less than the reproduction of the nation."

Kathryn Zabelle Derounian, "Puritan Orthodoxy and the 'Survivor Syndrome' in Mary Rowlandson's Indian Captivity Narrative," *Early American Literature*, 22 (Spring 1987): 82–93.
Argues that the psychological commentary in the narrative stems from Rowlandson's suffering from survivor syndrome.

Derounian, "The Publication, Promotion, and Distribution of Mary Rowlandson's Indian Captivity Narrative in the Seventeenth Century," *Early American Literature*, 23, no. 3 (1988): 239–261.
Discusses various aspects of Rowlandson's book, including its seventeenth-century editions, its place in the Anglo-American book trade, how it was promoted, and the nature of its readership.

Kathryn Zabelle Derounian-Stodola, Introduction, *Women's Indian Captivity Narratives*, edited by Derounian-Stodola (New York: Penguin, 1998).
Asserts that Rowlandson reveals herself as "victim, survivor, Puritan model, [and] author."

Derounian-Stodola and James Arthur Levernier, *The Indian Captivity Narrative, 1550–1900* (New York: Twayne, 1993).
Explores the background, aesthetics, and influence of arguably the most significant example of the captivity narrative form.

Rebecca Blevins Faery, *Cartographies of Desire: Captivity, Race, and Sex in the Shaping of an American Nation* (Norman: University of Oklahoma Press, 1999).
Suggests that Rowlandson's narrative is "an important site for producing and articulating ideologies of race [which] helps to explain the reappearance of her text at various pivotal moments in American history."

The Heath Anthology of American Literature, edited by Paul Lauter (Lexington, Mass.: D. C. Heath, 1990), 2 volumes.
This anthology, which dramatically expands the canon of American literature, includes excerpts from Rowlandson's narrative, but omits one of the most vivid scenes.

Jill Lepore, *The Name of War: King Philip's War and the Origins of American Identity* (New York: Knopf, 1998).
Argues that Rowlandson wrote her narrative "to redeem herself, to deliver herself from the demons of memory and to reconcile herself with her first, fateful choice: choosing captivity over death."

Neal Salisbury, Introduction, *The Sovereignty and Goodness of God, Together with the Faithfulness of His Promises Displayed, Being a Narrative of the Captivity and Restoration of Mrs. Mary Rowlandson and Related Documents,* by Mary Rowlandson, edited by Salisbury (Boston: Bedford Books 1997).
Places Rowlandson's narrative in historical, social, and literary context.

Richard Slotkin, *Regeneration through Violence: The Mythology of the American Frontier, 1600–1860* (Middletown: Wesleyan University Press, 1973).
Suggests that Rowlandson's narrative is an archetype, "the initiator of a genre of narrative within American culture, the primary model of which all subsequent captivities are diminished copies, or types."

Slotkin and James K. Folsom, "Mary Rowlandson: Captive Witness," in *So Dreadfull a Judgment: Puritan Responses to King Philip's War, 1676–1677,* edited by Slotkin and Folsom (Hanover: Wesleyan University Press/University Press of New England, 1978).
Posits that Rowlandson's narrative is "to be taken not only as the creation of a Puritan myth, but as the starting point of a cultural myth affecting America as a whole."

Teresa A. Toulouse, *The Captive's Position: Female Narrative, Male Identity, and Royal Authority in Colonial New England* (Philadelphia: University of Pennsylvania Press, 2007).
Examines "how and why religious narratives of *women*'s captivity [including Rowlandson's] came so powerfully to represent a distinctive identity position for powerful second- and third-generation colonial *men*."

Samuel Sewall (1652–1730)

One of the most interesting figures in colonial America, Samuel Sewall was born on 28 March 1652 to Henry Sewall and Jane Dummer Sewall in Bishop Stoke, Hants, Hampshire, England. His father, a merchant, spent considerable time in New England. In 1661 the family departed for America, not for religious reasons but rather for business ones, to join Sewall's father, who was living in Roxbury, Massachusetts. The date Mrs. Sewall and her five children left home was, coincidentally, the day of Charles II's coronation. The Roxbury minister, Thomas Parker, taught Sewall, preparing him for admission to Harvard, at which he matriculated in 1667 and where his roommate and bedfellow was Edward Taylor, later a minister and important poet. Following graduation with the class of 1671,

Sewall served his college as tutor and received a master's degree in 1674. In 1676, Simon Bradstreet, widower of poet Anne Bradstreet and future governor of the colony, married Sewall and Hanna Hull, daughter of John Hull, a wealthy man who was then treasurer of the colony. The couple had fourteen children. Two years after her death in 1717, he married Abigail Tilley, who died in 1720; two years after her death, he married Mary Gibbs. To readers of his diary, however, his most memorable interaction with a woman was with Katharine Winthrop following the death of his second wife. In the diary, he details his endearing and sometimes humorous but unsuccessful courtship of her when he was in his late sixties. Sewall died in Boston on the first day of 1730.

Trained at Harvard for the ministry, in 1674 Sewall was offered a position at the church in Woodbridge, New Jersey, which he declined. Although he was religious (his master's thesis was about original sin), he became not a minister but a businessman, instructed in trade by his father-in-law. He was made a Boston constable in 1679 and a few years later was appointed to the General Court, succeeding John Foster. By virtue of this second position, he became manager of the Massachusetts printing press. This meant that in addition to selecting the printer, he also chose the books to be published and sold them. Following John Hull's death in 1683, Sewall devoted himself to business: purchasing goods and selling them, importing and exporting, land transactions, and banking. The Massachusetts charter was revoked in 1684. To protect his property holdings that this action jeopardized, in 1688 he sailed to England to urge, with Increase Mather, restoration of the charter. They failed.

The new charter of 1691, which made Massachusetts a royal colony, affected Sewall's life dramatically. It empowered the royal governor, the first being Sir William Phips, to make appointments to special courts. Phips named Sewall and others, including John Hathorne (great-great-grandfather of Nathaniel Hawthorne), to serve as councilors of a Special Court of Oyer and Terminer. This body was asked to deal with people accused of witchcraft. In Salem, nineteen people—fourteen women and five men—were ultimately judged to be witches and hanged; one man was convicted and pressed to death. Sewall alone of the judges repented of his involvement with the trials: on 14 January 1697 he stood before the members of the Old South Church as its minister, Samuel Willard, read a statement Sewall composed, one expressing his remorse and requesting forgiveness.

In December 1692, Sewall was made a Superior Court judge, a position he held for a quarter-century before becoming its Chief Justice, a position he resigned in 1727. His first publication, a small book, was published in 1697 as *Phaenomena Quaedam Apocalyptica ad Aspectum Novi Orbis Configurata. Or, Some Few Lines towards a Description of the New Heaven, As It Makes to Those Who Stand upon the New Earth*. In it, Sewall argues that, among other things, New England will become the New Jerusalem. His next work, *The Selling of Joseph, a Memorial* (1700), is probably the earliest published American statement against slavery. He continues the theme of his first publication in his third, *Proposals Touching the Accomplishment of Prophecies, Humbly Offered* (1713). As he was sympathetic toward slaves, so too was he toward Indians, as may be discerned in *A Memorial Relating to the Kennebeck Indians* (1721). In 1724 he wrote "*Talitha Cumi,* or An Invitation to Women to Look after their Inheritance in the Heavenly Mansions," an essay arguing for the equality of the sexes in the sense that men and women retain their sex in heaven (parts of this last title were published in 1871–1873, but the entire essay was not published until 2007, in Eve LaPlante's *Salem Witch Judge*). His most famous and lasting work is his diary, which covers the years 1674–1729, though there is a gap from mid 1677 to early 1685, apparently because the manuscript for this period has not been located. He also wrote poems.

TOPICS FOR DISCUSSION AND RESEARCH

1. The Salem witchcraft trials were part of a long tradition of witchcraft, one that began before the Christian era, though witches were originally considered benign. The Salem frenzy began in 1692 with the aberrant, seemingly inexplicable behavior of a few girls. When they identified the shapes of people who had afflicted them, these people were arrested and tried as witches, as people allied with the devil. Despite the advice of Cotton Mather not to convict the accused solely on the basis of spectral evidence—evidence that was difficult if not impossible to disprove—the judges disregarded his counsel. Sewall and the other judges were intelligent men dealing with a serious issue. As a result of their decisions, twenty people were executed. On what basis might the judges have believed in the concept of witchcraft? Why might they have accepted spectral evidence, especially when people's lives were at risk? Sewall is praised for asking forgiveness for his participation in the trials. Assuming that the other judges ultimately thought the proceedings unwise, if not unfair and even tragic, does their refusal to disavow their actions reflect poorly on them? Why might they have elected not to emulate Sewall in this regard? All thorough histories of the witchcraft trials discuss their context. For information about Sewall's participation in them and later regret for his involvement, consult Richard Francis, *Judge Sewall's Apology*.

2. American slavery was not limited to the southern states; it was permitted in the North until late in the eighteenth century, after the Revolutionary War. Although *The Selling of Joseph, a Memorial* is probably the initial published American work arguing against slavery, Sewall was not the first American to think slavery evil and wish it gone or even the first to write about it in such terms. The Germantown Friends (Pennsylvania Quakers) did so in 1688. Sewall's essay is brief and available in the biography by Eve LaPlante. What is the nature of Sewall's argument? What are his objections to slavery? Does he consider its elimination a religious issue? A humane one? Both? How does his position reflect on him as a thinker and as a human being? How might his attitude toward slavery be similar to his request for forgiveness for his involvement in the witchcraft trials? For information about Sewall's attitude toward slavery, see LaPlante's *Salem Witch Judge*.

3. Sewall's diary is uniformly praised for the facts it includes about Sewall's life and times, for the image of Sewall that emerges from it, and so forth. Yet, in *American Diary Literature*, Steven E. Kagle argues that it is unimpressive as literature, by

which he means that it lacks "the quality and unity of style, subject, and structure." One might beneficially apply these criteria to random passages to see if Kagle is correct. If he is, are there other criteria by which the diary might qualify as significant literature? If not, why has it been so popular, as judged by selections from it being included in seemingly every anthology of American literature? The diary is not an autobiography. How do the two genres differ?

4. Sewall's courtship of Katharine Winthrop is one of the most memorable episodes in the diary, primarily because it reveals Sewall as a normal human being, as when he asks her to remove her glove so he can hold a woman's hand rather than a dead goat. During the courtship, Sewall gave her gifts. What were some of them? What do they indicate about him? About her? Often, he recorded the amount he paid for a gift. Why is this significant? The diary selections dealing with Winthrop are frequently anthologized. They are also available in most editions of Sewall's diary, including the most authoritative one, that edited by M. Halsey Thomas, who annotates the text helpfully.

RESOURCES

Biography

Eve LaPlante, *Salem Witch Judge: The Life and Repentance of Samuel Sewall* (New York: HarperOne, 2007).
A contemporary biography by a descendant of Sewall; includes the texts of *Phaenomena Quaedam Apocalyptica ad Aspectum Novi Orbis Configurata. Or, Some Few Lines towards a Description of the New Heaven, As It Makes to Those Who Stand upon the New Earth; The Selling of Joseph;* and *"Talitha Cumi,* or An Invitation to Women to Look after their Inheritance in the Heavenly Mansions."

T. B. Strandness, *Samuel Sewall: A Puritan Portrait* (East Lansing: Michigan State University Press, 1967).
In order to rescue Sewall from the realm of myth, this biography is as factual as possible, as evidenced by its frequent citations from Sewall's diary and other primary documents.

Ola Elizabeth Winslow, *Samuel Sewall of Boston* (New York: Macmillan, 1964).
A reliable, readable biography.

Mel Yazawa, Introduction, *The Diary and Life of Samuel Sewall,* edited by Yazawa (Boston: Bedford Books, 1998).
A comprehensive introduction to Sewall's life and the diary.

Criticism

Richard Francis, *Judge Sewall's Apology: The Salem Witch Trials and the Forming of an American Conscience* (New York: Fourth Estate, 2005).
Argues that Sewall's apology for his involvement in the Salem witchcraft trials represents "one of the birth pangs of the modern world" because the diarist learned that the "trials represented a last-ditch attempt to continue to see the

world as a simple allegorical struggle between the forces of good and evil, God and Satan."

Judith S. Graham, *Puritan Family Life: The Diary of Samuel Sewall* (Boston: Northeastern University Press, 2000).
Focuses on Sewall's diary to provide a picture of family life during the third generation of New Englanders.

Steven E. Kagle, *American Diary Literature, 1620–1799* (Boston: Twayne, 1979).
In this survey of early American diaries, the author acknowledges the importance of Sewall's diary as a historical document but argues against its significance as literature.

Samuel Sewall, *The Diary of Samuel Sewall, 1674–1729*, 2 volumes, edited by M. Halsey Thomas (New York: Farrar, Straus & Giroux, 1973).
Thomas discusses issues relating to the diary; this edition is the authoritative text of Sewall's diary.

John Smith (1580–1631)

The life of John Smith reads like a novel. He was born on 9 January 1580 in Willoughby-by-Alford, Lincolnshire, England, to George Smith, a farmer, and Alice Rickard Smith. Schooled in the towns of Alford and Louth, he was apprenticed to a merchant at King's Lynn, Norfolk, Lincolnshire at age fifteen. At age sixteen or seventeen, he left his apprenticeship to go to the Continent, where he fought with English troops in support of Dutch independence. A few years later, after being thrown overboard in the Mediterranean while en route to Italy and rescued, he visited various countries, including Egypt and Greece. Finally in Italy in 1601, he joined forces involved in fighting the Turks, who had invaded Hungary and Austria. During this period, he successfully dueled and decapitated three of his Turkish adversaries. Captured after being wounded at a battle at Rotenthurn, he was enslaved in Constantinople. After killing the brother of his female master, he fled first to Russia and then Poland before returning to central Europe. He went to Morocco as a mercenary. In 1605 he was back in England, from which he sailed for America in December of the next year as part of an enterprise sponsored by the Virginia Company of London. In March 1607, his ship landed at an island that became known as Martinique; the next month, he and others arrived at a place they named Cape Henry in Chesapeake Bay, where his experiences in what is now the United States began.

Almost immediately, his party was attacked by Indians, though no one was killed. Smith was named a member of the governing council. The Englishmen established a community and named it Jamestown after the king of England, James I. During one of his trips among the Indians to procure provisions, Smith was captured by some of them under the leadership of Opechancanough. Taken to his captor's older brother, chief Powhatan, Smith was presumably sentenced to death. The saving of his life by Pocahontas—Powhatan's daughter who was possibly as young as eleven years old—is one of the most enduring images in all of American history. It is also the earliest of our mythic images, antedating by over a decade the landing of the Pilgrims at Plymouth.

Smith's account of events in Virginia was published in London as *A True Relation of Such Occurrences and Accidents of Noate as Hath Hapned in Virginia since the First Planting of That Collony* (1608), the same year he was elected president of the governing council. In this position, he encouraged his group to greater industry in order to avoid starvation. After being badly burned while on a boat, Smith returned to England in 1609. Little is known about him during the next five years, other than that in London was published his *A Map of Virginia. With a Description of the Countrey, the Commodities, People, Government and Religion* (1612).

Smith sailed to America in 1614, but returned to England later that year after exploring the northeast coast of what is now the United States, an area he named New England. During another voyage to America the next year, he was captured by French pirates. While in their hands, he wrote a manuscript that he took with him when he escaped his capturers during a storm; rescued from an island, he was taken to La Rochelle, France, from which he returned to England, where, in 1616, the manuscript was published as *A Description of New England; or, the Observations and Discoveries of Captain John Smith*. Also in London in 1616, Smith met Pocahontas, the woman who saved him from death. She was married to John Rolfe, who had brought fine-quality tobacco seeds to Virginia, thereby providing the basis for Virginia's later economy. During the next few years, Smith attempted to return to America, without success.

In 1620 the Pilgrims rejected Smith's offer to assist them on their voyage to America on the *Mayflower*. This same year Smith's *New Englands Trials. Declaring the Successe of 26. Ships Employed Thither within These Six Years* was published in London; two years later it was published in revised form. In 1624 appeared his *The Generall Historie of Virginia, New-England, and the Summer Isles*, which includes accounts of American exploration by earlier writers. *An Accidence or the Path-way to Experience. Necessary for All Young Sea-men* was published in 1626; enlarged, it was published the next year as *A Sea Grammar, With the Plaine Exposition of Smiths Accidence*. In 1630 he published his autobiography, *The True Travels, Adventures, and Observations of Captaine John Smith, in Europe, Asia, Affrica, and America, from Anno Domini 1593. to 1629*. Although Smith hoped to write a history of the sea, his last publication was *Advertisements for the Unexperienced Planters of New-England, or Any Where. Or, the Path-way to Experience to Erect a Plantation* (1631). At age fifty-one, he died in London on 21 June 1631, having never married.

TOPICS FOR DISCUSSION AND RESEARCH

1. Smith is a man of mythic proportions. His reputation rests primarily on his accounts of his activities, accounts doubtless sometimes exaggerated. Fundamentally, one might question—as many have done—whether Smith should be believed. The story of his being saved by Pocahontas, for example, raised questions, especially in the nineteenth century. In his initial account of his ordeal

with Powhatan, in *A True Relation*, he does not mention her rescuing him. Although he tells of his captivity in *A Map of Virginia*, again he does not relate the event, as he also fails to do in the first edition of *New Englands Trials*. He details it in the enlarged version of this last book. Some readers therefore wondered why, given the dramatic nature of the event—her willingness to sacrifice herself for him—he failed to record her action at the first opportunity, and the second, and the third. This logic is faulty, as J. A. Leo Lemay has argued in the fullest, most convincing examination of the topic. He concludes his study by stating, "It actually happened." Other scholars have shown that Smith's accounts of his life are at least rooted in reality. Students might beneficially examine Lemay's argument and evidence in the context of earlier, skeptical writers, such as Moses Coit Tyler and J. Franklin Jameson.

2. Smith was born in England and spent little time in America. Students might, therefore, wonder why he is considered an American author. Does his relatively brief residence there or the fact that he wrote about the country, including when a resident of North America, qualify him for such a designation? Does his naming of New England bear on this issue?

3. Assuming that Smith is an American, might he be seen as the first American author and therefore as the father of American literature? In what ways does his persona anticipate such disparate self-aggrandizing figures as Benjamin Franklin, Walt Whitman, and Ernest Hemingway? What similarities might aspects of his life share with James Fenimore Cooper's Natty Bumppo, as well as other fictional characters of frontier literature? How does he depict the wilderness? The Indians? In demonstrating courage, shrewdness, and confidence in the future, might Smith be considered the first American hero? What later American heroes, real or fictional, share these traits? In order to answer some of these questions, one should consult Lewis Leary's "The Adventures of Captain John Smith as Heroic Legend."

4. Smith and the Puritans seem opposite in many ways: he was a man of the world but they were relatively insular; religion was apparently of little importance to him while it dominated their lives; he helped establish Jamestown and they ultimately established Boston; his town did not flourish but theirs did. They shared, nonetheless, a dedication to hard work that helped them survive in hostile environments. Compare this attitude to that of Thomas Morton, gadfly of the Puritans. What might a comparison of Smith and the Puritans with Morton indicate about their seriousness, their desire to succeed? Reading representative passages from the works of Smith, Morton, and William Bradford will help answer this question.

RESOURCES

Biography

Philip L. Barbour, *The Three Worlds of Captain John Smith* (Boston: Houghton Mifflin; Cambridge: Riverside Press, 1964).

A dispassionate biography that includes "hints and clues that have long been lurking in insignificant sidelights, in documents which do not mention Smith directly, in the place-names strewn on his maps, honoring those from whom he had, or hoped to have, this, that or the other favor."

Dorothy Hoobler and Thomas Hoobler, *Captain John Smith: Jamestown and the Birth of the American Dream* (Hoboken N.J.: John Wiley, 2006).
By drawing on letters and diaries by residents of Jamestown and England, as well as Smith's writings, the authors create a biography of Smith during his residence in Jamestown, as well as a picture of the colony itself.

Bradford Smith, *Captain John Smith, His Life and Legend* (Philadelphia: Lippincott, 1953).
The best early biography of Smith; it is enhanced by Laura Polanyi Striker's appendix, "Captain John Smith's Hungary and Transylvania."

Alden T. Vaughan, *American Genesis: Captain John Smith and the Founding of Virginia* (Boston: Little, Brown, 1975).
As much a history of early Virginia as a biography of Smith, Vaughan's study offers generally reliable commentary on both.

Criticism

Everett Emerson, *Captain John Smith,* revised edition (New York: Twayne, 1993).
Surveys Smith's life and analyzes the adventurer's writings.

Kevin J. Hayes, *Captain John Smith: A Reference Guide* (Boston: G. K. Hall, 1991).
Evaluates all known writings about Smith through 1988.

J. Franklin Jameson, *The History of Historical Writings in America* (Boston: Houghton Mifflin, 1891).
Questions Smith's objectivity and believes that the Pocahontas episode did not happen.

Lewis Leary, "The Adventures of Captain John Smith as Heroic Legend," in *Essays in Early Virginia Literature Honoring Richard Beale Davis,* edited by J. A. Leo Lemay (New York: Burt Franklin, 1977).
Discusses Smith's persona as anticipating the personae of later American writers.

J. A. Leo Lemay, *Did Pocahontas Save Captain John Smith?* (Athens: University of Georgia Press, 1992).
The fullest, most convincing examination of Pocahontas's saving of Smith. Lemay identifies doubters' biases and concludes that the event actually occurred.

David Read, *New World, Known World: Shaping Knowledge in Early Anglo-American Writing* (Columbia: University of Missouri Press, 2005).
Argues that Smith—like William Bradford, Thomas Morton, and Roger Williams—renders "an organized account of a newly experienced colonial world that will make that world distinct from the one—'Old' or just generically familiar —that previously formed the ground of knowledge."

Moses Coit Tyler, *A History of American Literature, 1607–1765* (New York: Putnam, 1878).
Praises Smith but disbelieves that Pocahontas saved him.

Solomon Stoddard (1643–1729)

One of the most important ministers of his time, Solomon Stoddard was born in Boston on 27 September 1643 to Anthony and Mary Downing Stoddard. He was one of his father's fifteen sons; his mother, a niece of John Winthrop, died when he was three. Stoddard attended elementary school in Boston and grammar school in Cambridge. Less than a month shy of his fifteenth birthday, in 1658 he matriculated at Harvard College and was graduated with the class of 1662 that included Simon Bradstreet (son of the poet Anne Bradstreet and her husband, Simon) as well as the poet Benjamin Tompson. Three years later, he received a master's degree from the same institution. In 1666 he was named a fellow of the college, and became its first librarian the next year. He did not last long as librarian because, in the capacity of chaplain and apparently because of illness, he moved to Barbados for approximately two years with its former governor, Daniel Searle (or Serle). Back in Massachusetts, in 1670 he married the widow Esther Warham Mather, with whom he had fourteen children. Two years later, he succeeded her first husband, Eleazar Mather (son of Richard Mather and brother of Increase Mather), as minister of the Northampton church, which he served for the remainder of his life.

Stoddard was a fairly prolific author in a publishing career that spanned more than a third of a century (1687–1724), beginning with the radical *The Safety of Appearing at the Day of Judgment, in the Righteousness of Christ.* Stoddard presented "Nine Arguments against Examinations Concerning a Work of Grace before Admission to the Lord's Supper" at the Reforming Synod of 1679–1680, which discussed ways of improving piety in New England. Against Congregational orthodoxy, he emphasizes the importance of an inner religious experience rather than outward, material success in gauging an individual's spiritual condition. This work was not published until 1976. *Sermon on Paul's Epistle to the Galatians,* delivered in 1690, was not published until 1974. In it, Stoddard states so boldly that the Lord's Supper is a converting ordinance—and that he would treat it as such—that he incurred the wrath of Increase Mather, Cotton Mather, and Edward Taylor, a bitterness that would continue for many years. In *The Doctrine of Instituted Churches Explained and Proved from the Word of God* (1700), Stoddard argues against the Congregational form of church government, in which individual churches are entities unto themselves, ordaining their ministers, determining their members (ordination and membership were not transferable from one church to another), and so forth. Believing that God, not a church, unites mankind, Stoddard proposes a national church, with ordained ministers eligible to preach in any church and with doctrines applying to all churches, though he proposes permitting individual churches to select their own officers.

In *The Inexcusableness of Neglecting the Worship of God. Under a Pretence of Being in an Unconverted Condition* (1708), Stoddard argues for a national church, admits to the failure of treating communion as a converting ordinance (too few people were converted), and proposes a kind of evangelicalism. *The Efficacy of the Fear of Hell to Restrain Men from Sin* (1713) consists of eight sermons, some of which inspired the Northampton religious awakening of late 1712. These are evangelical sermons, and as such they helped set the stage for the Great Awakening, inspired in the 1730s by Jonathan Edwards, Stoddard's grandson, preaching from the same Northampton pulpit. Stoddard continued calling for evangelicalism in later sermons, including those in *A Guide to Christ. Or the Way of Directing Souls That Are under Conversion* (1714)—the book that marks the end of hostilities with Increase Mather, who wrote a prefatory epistle for it—as well as in his last work published during his lifetime, *The Defects of Preachers Reproved* (1724).

Stoddard died in 1729 at age eighty-five; his wife outlived him by seven years. In addition to Edwards, Stoddard's progeny include great-grandson Timothy Dwight, an important poet and president of Yale College, and great-great-grandson Aaron Burr, vice president of the United States.

TOPICS FOR DISCUSSION AND RESEARCH

1. Stoddard became embroiled in controversy soon after affiliating with the Northampton church. The issue concerned which people were entitled to receive communion. It was considered an ordinance reserved to church members who provided evidence of saving grace (assurance of salvation). After initially limiting the Lord's Supper to such people, Stoddard began thinking of the sacrament as a converting ordinance, one that leads to salvation. In 1677, he started offering communion to all adults wishing to partake of it as long as they agreed to the articles of faith and behaved well. Stoddard's view and action rocked the Congregational establishment. Increase Mather and Cotton Mather went so far as to attempt to stop Stoddard's first publication, *The Safety of Appearing at the Day of Judgment, in the Righteousness of Christ,* a sermon delivered in 1685 but not published until two years later. Edward Taylor also criticized it, and Increase Mather and Samuel Willard refused to write prefaces for this publication in which Stoddard challenges the Congregational interpretation of communion but also considers emotion more important than the mind in the conversion process, a notion anathema to Congregationalists. Ultimately, all Congregational churches embraced Stoddard's interpretation of the nature of the Lord's Supper. Students could beneficially place this controversy in cultural and political context. How might Stoddard's liberal, even radical ideas have paralleled or possibly been influenced by events occurring in New England at the time? Stoddard and Edward Taylor corresponded about the nature of the Lord's Supper. Though they strongly disagreed about it, their letters were civil. What does this indicate about them? What does it say about the nature of the times? For information about these and collateral issues, consult Thomas M. Davis's introduction to *Edward Taylor vs. Solomon Stoddard.* Additionally, E. Brooks Holifield addresses some of these topics in *The Covenant Sealed.*

2. Face to face in 1679, Stoddard and Increase Mather debated their beliefs about the Lord's Supper and church membership at a synod where members considered ways of reforming their society that was in upheaval because, they believed, of God's displeasure. Church membership was the most contentious issue. Despite the members reaching a consensus, the issue festered until the debate was renewed publicly in 1700 with the publication of Increase Mather's *Order of the Gospel, Professed and Practised by the Churches of Christ in New England*, Stoddard's *The Doctrine of Instituted Churches Explained and Proved from the Word of God*, Mather's anti-Stoddard introduction to John Quick's *The Young Mans Claim unto the Sacrament of the Lords-Supper*, and *The Gospel Order Revived, Being an Answer to a Book Lately Set Forth by the Reverend Mr. Increase Mather . . . Entituled, The Order of the Gospel*, which criticizes both Mather and Stoddard. The last title, "By sundry Ministers of the Gospel in New-England," was probably written by Benjamin Colman, Simon Bradstreet, and Timothy Woodbridge. Students would benefit from reading all or parts of these works, considering the arguments, and determining which side makes the more compelling case. For direction, consult Paul R. Lucas's *Valley of Discord*.

3. As expressed in *The Inexcusableness of Neglecting the Worship of God. Under a Pretence of Being in an Unconverted Condition* and elsewhere, Stoddard emphasized the importance of emotion in religious conversion. Earlier Puritan ministers had attempted to sway listeners by appealing to their mind, their reason. Yet, thought Stoddard, while the mind is one part of a human being, emotion is another, so why not also appeal to emotion? He did, both in theory and practice. In fact, within this context he valued emotion more than intellect. As a result, he established the basis for the evangelical movement that continues to the present day. Jonathan Edwards embraced this attitude, one result of which is "Sinners in the Hands of an Angry God" (1741), surely one of the most famous and frightening sermons ever delivered. One might fruitfully examine the men's views by reading *The Inexcusableness of Neglecting the Worship of God* and Edwards's sermon. Students might also compare Stoddard's sermon with almost any seventeenth-century American Puritan sermon in order to understand the revolutionary nature of Stoddard's emphasizing of emotion in the conversion process. In *The Shattered Synthesis*, James W. Jones provides a good introduction to Stoddard and his thought.

4. What difference does it make that Stoddard, unlike almost all American authors writing before him, was born in America? Might this reality have affected his self-perception? His thinking? His attitude toward his native country? Might his place of birth have colored others' impressions of him, and therefore of his work, including preaching and writing?

RESOURCES

Criticism

Ralph J. Coffman, *Solomon Stoddard* (Boston: Twayne, 1978).

Details Stoddard's life, provides reliable readings of Stoddard's writings, and convincingly analyzes religious issues.

Thomas M. Davis, Introduction, *Edward Taylor vs. Solomon Stoddard: The Nature of the Lord's Supper*, edited by Davis and Virginia L. Davis (Boston: Twayne, 1981).
Provides the context for and details about the correspondence between Stoddard and Edward Taylor concerning the Lord's Supper; the book includes all known letters on this topic the two men wrote to each other.

Keith J. Hardman, *The Spiritual Awakeners: American Revivalists from Solomon Stoddard to D. L. Moody* (Chicago: Moody Press, 1983).
Considers Stoddard as evangelical and places his ideas and career in context.

E. Brooks Holifield, *The Covenant Sealed: The Development of Puritan Sacramental Theology in Old and New England, 1570–1720* (New Haven: Yale University Press, 1974).
Discusses Stoddard within the context of his attitude toward the Lord's Supper.

James W. Jones, *The Shattered Synthesis: New England Puritanism before the Great Awakening* (New Haven: Yale University Press, 1973).
Examines Stoddard's life and thought within the context of the Puritan schism between the head and the heart, rationality and emotion, objectivity and subjectivity.

Paul R. Lucas, *Valley of Discord: Church and Society along the Connecticut River, 1636–1725* (Hanover, N.H.: University Press of New England, 1976).
Investigates the evolution of seventeenth-century Congregationalism by focusing on the Connecticut Valley, where Stoddard was the major late-century figure.

Edward Taylor (1642–1729)

In 1642, Edward Taylor was born in England, probably in Sketchley, Leicestershire, into a family about which little is known, other than that it was Puritan, that his father William Taylor was a farmer, that his mother Margaret died during his teenaged years, and that he had several siblings. He grew up during the English Civil War. Chafing under the Act of Uniformity, which dictated adherence to the Book of Common Prayer, Taylor sailed for America in late April 1668, arriving in Boston in early July. He and Samuel Sewall were bedfellows at Harvard, which Taylor entered with advanced standing and from which he was graduated in 1671. After moving to Westfield, recently established on the frontier approximately a hundred miles west of Boston and vulnerable to Indian attack, he married Elizabeth Fitch in 1674, served as physician, and in 1679 became minister of the church. His wife died in 1689; Taylor then married Ruth Wyllys in 1692. With his two wives, Taylor fathered fourteen children, five of whom died in infancy. He died in Westfield in 1729.

For various reasons, Congregational ministers sometimes withheld the sacrament of the Lord's Supper from their flocks. Such was the case with Taylor in 1712 or 1713, when he denied it to all members of his church after some of them challenged his right to discipline them. This episode indicates the seriousness with which Taylor viewed the sacrament, an attitude he held consistently from before the time of his ordination. In fact, the Lord's Supper was at the heart of the major theological dispute of his life: one with Solomon Stoddard, minister at Northampton. The issue concerned the qualifications of people to receive communion. The conservative Taylor followed the Half-Way Covenant of 1662 in reserving it for church members demonstrating evidence of saving grace; after doing similarly, in the 1670s the liberal Stoddard began considering the sacrament as a converting ordinance, one leading to saving grace. In time, Stoddard offered communion to all adults wishing to partake of it, as long as they agreed to the articles of faith and behaved well. Taylor first disputed Stoddard's thinking in his Foundation Day sermon of 1679, with Stoddard in attendance. The debate continued for many years and ultimately involved others, including Increase Mather and Cotton Mather, both arguing Taylor's position. In 1694, Taylor countered Stoddard in a series of eight sermons. Ultimately, most Congregational churches, including Taylor's at Westfield, embraced Stoddard's interpretation of the nature of the Lord's Supper.

Despite his involvement in the important doctrinal issue of communion, Taylor is most significant as a poet, though he was not known as one during his lifetime, when only part of one poem, "Upon Wedlock, and Death of Children," was published—in London, in a 1689 book by Cotton Mather. His major achievement is *Preparatory Meditations,* unpublished until the twentieth century, two series totaling over two hundred meditative poems composed every other month, on average, from 1682 to 1725. They are preparatory in the sense that Taylor composed them to prepare himself for administering the Lord's Supper. They deal with man's sinful nature, God's majesty, and the possibility of living eternally in heaven. The speaker of the poems seems to be Taylor himself. Whether he is confident of his own salvation is open to question.

In these poems, Taylor was indebted stylistically to, among other writers, such English metaphysical poets as John Donne and George Herbert. Taylor especially embraced their use of extended metaphors, as in Meditation 8, first series, where Christ is presented as "Soule Bread" offered to ravenous mortals. Taylor occasionally favored ordinary images, such as flowers, wine, candles, quills, and birds; often, he used more exotic images, such as diamonds, *canta pantos* (an Aristotelian law), and "George Nevill's Feast at Yorks." He also employed typology, using something from the Old Testament (Adam, for example) to prefigure something in the New Testament (Christ), a technique he addresses in the first poem of the second series of *Preparatory Meditations:*

> The glory of the world slickt up in types
>   In all Choise things chosen to typify
> ....
> The glory of all Types doeth meet in thee [Christ],
>   Thy glory doth their glory quite excell

Among Taylor's other writings is *Gods Determinations Touching His Elect,* a series of poems justifying God's ways to man, most of whom are damned. Dramatically, the poems depict the battle between Satan and Christ for the souls of mortals. "The Preface," the initial poem in the series, recounts the creation and mankind's fall; the last, "The Joy of Church Fellowship Rightly Attended," presents the elect in a coach singing sweetly "as they to Glory ride therein."

Of Taylor's other poems, "Huswifery" and "Upon a Spider Catching a Fly"—each containing an extended metaphor—are among the most famous because they are frequently anthologized. Some of his sermons have been published, as has his diary, his *Metrical History of Christianity,* and other works.

TOPICS FOR DISCUSSION AND RESEARCH

1. Edward Taylor's poems were not known until the 1930s. Then, Thomas H. Johnson discovered them at Yale University—which Taylor's grandson, Ezra Stiles, had served as president—and published some of them. Almost immediately, Taylor was viewed as the major seventeenth- and early-eighteenth-century American poet, a judgment that has proved lasting. Critics quickly observed his indebtedness to the metaphysical tradition of such poets as Donne and Herbert, a view that generally lessened in importance as time passed. The critics meant that in addition to composing extended metaphors, Taylor wrote meditative poems characterized by metrical irregularity (like Herbert), unconventional diction (like Donne), and sexual imagery (like Herbert and Donne), among other things. How well, if at all, Taylor knew these poets is open to question. As Barbara Kiefer Lewalski argues, their similarities could result from writing in a similar religious (Protestant) context. Consult her study for information about Taylor and the metaphysicals.
2. Critics have debated Taylor's American-ness. On the frontier, removed from Boston literary culture, he wrote in a manner reminiscent of, if not derived from, European poets. Still, scholars have identified elements in Taylor's verse that anticipate such writers as Jonathan Edwards, Ralph Waldo Emerson, Walt Whitman, and Emily Dickinson, though Taylor could not have influenced them directly because they could not have known his work. In time, the entire question of Taylor's American-ness devolved into an issue of definition: what is American? Who or what was Taylor? For information about Taylor's similarity to later American authors, consult Albert Gelpi, *The Tenth Muse.*
3. Whether Taylor was a mystic—a person coming as close as possible to a spiritual relationship with the creator, through Christ—has been debated. Norman S. Grabo details the mystical process and asserts boldly that "the mystical process is the subject of Taylor's poetry." While not denying mystical elements in Taylor's verse, Donald T. Stanford believes that Grabo goes too far in identifying Taylor as a mystic. Other scholars second Stanford's opinion. In time, Grabo moderated his view. Read each author's evidence and consider its effectiveness. Which poems support the depiction of Taylor as mystic?
4. A question arising from Taylor's meditations is whether the poet considers himself among the elect. By focusing on the poems and believing that Puri-

tans considered certainty of election impossible, such a critic as William J. Scheick concludes that Taylor is not confident of his salvation. Noting the hopeful nature of the poems, however, Lewalski thinks, tentatively, that he did. This positive view is supported by the texts that governed Puritan belief: John Calvin's *Institutes of the Christian Religion* (1536), *The Canons of the Synod of Dort* (1618–1619), and *The Westminster Confession of Faith* (1646). How, then, should one interpret the concluding line of such a poem as the eighth preparatory meditation, first series? To mankind, God has sent Christ in the form of a loaf of bread. The poem ends with bread in a human's mouth, crying to the person, "Eate, eate me, Soul, and thou shalt never dy," though the person does not consume it. Does this soul gain salvation? Read Scheick and Lewalski for arguments about Taylor's stance on awareness of election and apply them to the eighth meditation.

5. Critics have debated Taylor's quality as a poet. Is he sophisticated? Primitive? Are such characteristics as his sometimes jarring rhymes and irregular meter accidental, thereby lessening his poetic value? Or did Taylor aim for imperfection in order to reflect the fallen nature of mankind, thereby demonstrating his deftness at fusing manner and matter? The question has not been answered—and probably cannot be answered—definitively. For examples of Taylor's care with his writing, though, consult Donald Junkins's "Edward Taylor's Revisions."

RESOURCES

Criticism

Thomas M. Davis, *A Reading of Edward Taylor* (Newark: University of Delaware Press; London: Associated University Presses, 1992).
A balanced study in the sense that Davis acknowledges Taylor's poetic deficiencies while arguing that they do not ultimately undercut his accomplishment.

Albert Gelpi, *The Tenth Muse: The Psyche of the American Poet* (Cambridge, Mass.: Harvard University Press, 1975).
Argues that Taylor's "liveliness and originality . . . reside not in prosody but in the qualities of language, diction, and imagery" and presents Taylor as anticipating future American poets.

Norman S. Grabo, *Edward Taylor* (Boston: Twayne, 1988), revised edition.
A revision of a 1961 book, the first to evaluate Taylor's literary accomplishment.

Jeffrey A. Hammond, *Edward Taylor: Fifty Years of Scholarship and Criticism* (Columbia, S. C.: Camden House, 1993).
An authoritative discussion of all significant Taylor scholarship into the early 1990s.

Donald Junkins, "Edward Taylor's Revisions," *American Literature*, 37 (1965): 135–152.
After examining the revisions to the poems, concludes that Taylor was a careful poetic craftsman.

Barbara Kiefer Lewalski, *Protestant Poetics and the Seventeenth-Century Religious Lyric* (Princeton: Princeton University Press, 1979).
Broad in scope, Lewalski's study argues that a consensus about Protestant doctrine and life unites such poets as Donne, Herbert, Henry Vaughan, Thomas Traherne, and Taylor, be they Puritan or Anglican.

William J. Scheick, *The Will and the Word: The Poetry of Edward Taylor* (Athens: University of Georgia Press, 1984).
Following Grabo, this is the second book-length study of Taylor's work.

Donald E. Stanford, *Edward Taylor* (Minneapolis: University of Minnesota Press, 1965).
Though only a pamphlet, this study surveys Taylor's life and offers solid readings of the poet's work.

The Tayloring Shop: Essays on the Poetry of Edward Taylor, in Honor of Thomas M. and Virginia L. Davis, edited by Michael Schuldiner (Newark: University of Delaware Press; London: Associated University Presses, 1997).
A collection of six Taylor essays by various authors.

Benjamin Tompson (1642–1714)

One of the significant seventeenth-century American poets primarily because of one book, Benjamin Tompson was born in Braintree, Massachusetts, on 14 July 1642, the youngest of five children of William Tompson and Abigail Tompson. While his father, a noted minister, was performing missionary duties among Indians and Anglicans in Virginia and elsewhere, Abigail Tompson died. As a result, the Tompson children were placed with other families. The neighboring family of Thomas Blanchard, a farmer, adopted six-month-old Benjamin. William Tompson apparently never reclaimed any of his children, despite returning to Braintree in 1644 and remarrying two years later.

In his will, Blanchard addressed the importance of Tompson's education. Sharing his values, his widow honored his wishes: Tompson was a member of the Harvard class of 1662. His classmates included young men with significant ties to contemporaneous and later American literature, including Simon Bradstreet, son of poet Anne Bradstreet and her husband, Simon, as well as Solomon Stoddard, who became an important minister and the grandfather of Jonathan Edwards. Despite the critical theological issues of the day—this year is significant as the date of the Half-Way Covenant, which addressed the issue of Congregational church membership, and the publication date of Michael Wigglesworth's *The Day of Doom,* a frightening poem intended to encourage religious behavior by what the poet perceived as backsliders—Tompson did not enter the profession of his father, but rather became a teacher who also practiced medicine, studied mathematics, and wrote verse. Because William Tompson died shortly after his son's graduation from Harvard, however, Benjamin Tompson delayed establishing himself in a profession so he could assist family members, including his half sister and his father's second wife.

In 1667 Tompson married Susanna Kirkland, with whom he had eight children. This same year, he succeeded Robert Woodmansey as master of the Boston Latin School, where he taught young Cotton Mather. Tompson held this position until 1670, when he was succeeded by Ezekiel Cheever, who became the most respected American educator of the seventeenth century. Why Tompson was replaced is not known, though he was offered a position as Cheever's assistant, which he declined in favor of succeeding Cheever as schoolmaster in Charlestown, Massachusetts. He remained a teacher there until 1674, when he was replaced by Samuel Phipps. The reason for his apparent dismissal is again unknown. He remained in Charlestown, possibly practicing medicine, until 1678, when he returned to Braintree where, the following year, he became master of the local school, a position he held for two decades until being replaced by Nathaniel Eells. During this period, in 1693, Susanna died; five years later he married the widow Prudence Payson and, a few years later, became the schoolmaster at Roxbury. After serving again as schoolmaster at Braintree (1704–1710), Tompson returned to Roxbury, where he died in April 1714.

In 1658, Tompson wrote what is apparently the first of his twenty-nine known poems. He was most active as a poet from 1666 until 1683 and again from 1695 until 1713. While the author was living in Charlestown, Tompson's major work, *New Englands Crisis. Or a Brief Narrative of New Englands Lamentable Estate at Present, Compar'd with the Former (but Few) Years of Prosperity,* was printed by John Foster and published in Boston in 1676. When the first two parts of the poem were published later this same year in London as *Sad and Deplorable News from New England, New Englands Crisis* became the first book of verse initially published in America to be republished in England. Revised and enlarged, it was again published in London, this time as *New-Englands Tears for Her Present Miseries,* also in 1676.

New Englands Crisis treats King Philip's War (1675–1676), so named because of attacks on English settlements by Indians under the leadership of Metacomet, known to the settlers as King Philip. The immediate cause of the war was the apparent murder of John Sassamon, a Harvard-educated Indian who alerted the colonists to pending attacks by Indians frustrated by the encroachment of Europeans on their land and possibly because a paucity of goods made them unable to trade satisfactorily with the settlers. When three Wampanoags were tried and hanged for Sassamon's murder, Indians, believing that the trial violated their sovereignty, began attacking colonists' settlements. In the end, the number of people killed made this the bloodiest war, based on the number of casualties as a percentage of the population, in American history.

Puritans believed that occurrences in life—natural or caused by man—reflect God's wishes. As a result, they attempted to interpret events, hoping to understand God's will. Although Tompson does not emphasize this tendency, he knew that many of his readers doubtless understood the war as God's disapproval of their irreligious behavior. As a result, they were probably interested in the poet's account of hostilities that threatened the European presence in New England, an account that favors the colonists but that also criticizes them while sympathizing, to a limited degree, with the Indians. Once known, *New Englands Crisis* almost certainly attracted readers because of its lively style, humor, and reportorial quality, the last of which speaks to Tompson's imagination and sense of drama, because he did not participate in the war other than by treating people who had been wounded in it.

Tompson's other verses are mostly elegies that trace what Peter White, in *Benjamin Tompson, Colonial Bard,* terms the "civil and spiritual progress" of the deceased. His subjects include John Woodmansey and Ezekiel Cheever, his predecessor and successor, respectively, as master of the Boston Latin School ("The Grammarians Funeral"); Connecticut governor John Winthrop Jr. ("A Funeral Tribute"); Connecticut governor (and son of John Winthrop Jr.) Fitz-John Winthrop ("The Illustrious Fitz-John Winthrop Esquire"); Massachusetts Bay governor John Leverett ("New-Englands Grand Eclips"); minister and Harvard overseer Samuel Whiting ("Upon the Very Reverend Samuel Whiting"); and others, including several family members. He also wrote prefatory poems for William Hubbard's 1677 *A Narrative of the Troubles with the Indians in New-England* ("Upon the Elaborate Survey of New-Englands Passions from the Natives") and Cotton Mather's 1702 *Magnalia Christi Americana* ("Celeberrimi Cottoni Matheri, Celebratio"), two important histories. Additionally, in 1699 he wrote a poem welcoming the new governor, Lord Bellamont ("To Lord Bellamont When Entering Governour of the Massachusetts").

TOPICS FOR DISCUSSION AND RESEARCH

1. Few seventeenth-century American books went through three editions in one year. *New Englands Crisis* did, in 1676, and students should consider why this happened. Why might English readers in particular have been interested in the book, as two English editions indicate that they were? One also might wish to compare the American edition with the second English edition *(New-Englands Tears for Her Present Miseries)*. Why might Tompson have decided to revise and expand the original text? What is the nature of the new material, and what does it add substantively to the poem? In answering these questions, students would benefit from consulting Samuel A. Green's essay about Tompson. Both poems are reproduced in Peter White's edition of Tompson's verse, as are all the poems mentioned here.

2. From the beginning of English presence in America, settlers were fascinated and often threatened by the Indians. Such early authors as John Smith, William Bradford, and Edward Johnson focus on them, as does Tompson in *New Englands Crisis*. Writing during King Philip's War, Tompson could not have known its resolution, though he was aware of its devastating effects. The most notable lines in the long poem are a speech by King Philip himself. In an effort to inspire his followers to attack the settlers, he laments that earlier Indians sold land to the English, who want more of it, and notes that the settlers apply their laws, such as ones concerning drunkenness and sex, leniently to their own people but harshly to Indians. Tompson implies that these and other

concerns are legitimate, and in doing so mildly criticizes the settlers. Yet, he introduces the speech by characterizing King Philip unflatteringly, including calling him a "greasy *Lout.*" After the speech, Tompson terms the Indians "A ragged regiment, a naked swarm, / Whome hopes of booty doth with courage arm." Students might consider why, given the seriousness of the war, Tompson grants the Indians even minimal understanding and implies criticism of his own people, whose cause he obviously favors. Is it for dramatic effect? To keep from presenting one people as all bad and the other as all good, when doing so would strain credulity? For some other reason or reasons? For information about Tompson within the context of King Philip's War, consult Jill Lepore's *The Name of War.*

3. In *The Name of War,* Jill Lepore quotes the first six lines of King Philip's speech to illustrate that "the war created a world full of distortions, fictions, and confusion. . . . The crucial rivalry was . . . between the differing views of the war held by English colonists and Indians." In stressing that Tompson had no way of knowing if King Philip addressed his men in the manner the poet presents, Lepore places Tompson in the history of English-speaking American authors from the seventeenth century into the nineteenth, who fabricated Indians' thoughts and words. Students could benefit from charting this tendency and asking why writers fabricated Indians' words and motives rather than limiting their narratives to known facts, even in poetry, as in the case of Tompson. Consult Lepore for direction.

4. Most of Tompson's poems are elegies. Many were written for public presentation, though some were intended only for the family of the deceased. The majority of the public ones were published; the private ones were not until Peter White collected Tompson's verse in 1980. One might beneficially consider the differences between Tompson's public and private elegies: Is he more consoling in one type than in another? Does he praise the dead immoderately? Is he restrained? Do his focus and the nature of his images differ? Are the subjects, the deceased, of different social standing, and if so does Tompson treat them differently, according to class?

RESOURCES

Criticism

Neil T. Eckstein, "The Pastoral and the Primitive in Benjamin Tompson's 'Address to Lord Bellamont,'" *Early American Literature,* 8 (February 1973): 111–116.

Argues that Tompson uses rustic elements within the Virgilian tradition of the classical pastoral.

Edwin S. Fussell, "Benjamin Tompson, Public Poet," *New England Quarterly,* 26 (December 1953): 494–511.

Suggests that Tompson is transitional from the earlier "line of wit" to the "neo-classical assumptions of his day" and terms Tompson "the most social and realistic of the American seventeenth-century poets."

Samuel A. Green, untitled essay, *Proceedings of the Massachusetts Historical Society,* second series, 10 (1895): 263–285.
This first serious study of Tompson identifies him as the author of certain poems, places him in historical context, and compares *New Englands Crisis* and *New-Englands Tears.*

Howard Judson Hall, Introduction, *Benjamin Tompson, 1642–1714, First Native-Born Poet of America: His Poems,* edited by Hall (Boston: Houghton Mifflin, 1924).
The first, though incomplete, collection of Tompson's verse; Hall considers the poems artless. This work is superseded by Peter White's edition of Tompson's work.

Jill Lepore, *The Name of War: King Philip's War and the Origins of American Identity* (New York: Knopf, 1998).
Tompson figures in the argument, about war, that "wounds and words—the injuries and their interpretation—cannot be separated, that acts of war generate acts of narration, and that both types of acts are often joined in a common purpose: defining the geographical, political, cultural, and sometimes racial and national boundaries between people."

Peter White, *Benjamin Tompson, Colonial Bard: A Critical Edition* (University Park: Pennsylvania State University Press, 1980).
Collects all of Tompson's known poems and includes chapters on Tompson as colonial bard, on his poetic achievement, and on the historic Tompson, in addition to a chapter on William Tompson, the poet's father.

John Trumbull (1750–1831)

The fourth of eight children of John Trumbull and Sarah Whitman Trumbull, the poet John Trumbull was born on 24 April 1750 in Westbury, Connecticut, which is now Waterbury. His father was a minister; his mother, a granddaughter of Solomon Stoddard and a cousin of Jonathan Edwards. Young Trumbull was schooled at home, mainly by his parents, but especially by his mother. At age seven he passed the entrance examination at Yale College, though he did not matriculate there until 1763, at age thirteen. After being graduated with the class of 1767 (he delivered the commencement address), he remained at Yale, receiving a master's degree in 1770; following two years of studying law, he again affiliated with Yale, serving as tutor in 1772 and 1773. Aspiring to professional authorship, he wrote poems in the neoclassical mode as well as Addisonian essays during his Yale years, going so far as to compose, with Timothy Dwight, a series of ten essays titled "The Meddler" that were published in *The Boston Chronicle* in 1769 and 1770. These essays comment wittily on things social and political. Following this series, the two teenagers undertook another: all thirty-eight numbers of "The Correspondent" were published in *The Connecticut Journal, and the New-Haven*

Post-Boy from 1770 to 1773. These essays are generally less Addisonian and more local in subject matter than those in "The Meddler"; for example, for this series Trumbull composed essays about slavery, quacks, and ministers.

Trumbull is best known for, and his reputation rests on, two poems, *The Progress of Dulness* and *M'Fingal*. The former, which he began composing at age twenty-one, was published in three parts: the first, in 1772; the second and third, in 1773. Each part focuses on one character: the first, on Tom Brainless; the second, on Dick Hairbrain; the third, on Harriet Simper. The names alone indicate the nature of the poem, which is satiric, principally about education but secondarily about the clergy. Trumbull's goal is reform, both of colleges that demand little of students and of unmotivated students, like Brainless, who, in turn, do not benefit from whatever opportunities are available to them. As a result of these two realities, when a young man completes his schooling and enters life—as a minister, in the case of Brainless—he offers society little. Brainless's sermons are predictably dull, "And [he] does no good, and little harm." In the second part of *The Progress of Dulness,* Trumbull focuses on Dick Hairbrain as an example of a young man whom education disserves and who rejects whatever education offers. He is a fop, a dandy, wishing for his appearance and apparent sophistication to impress the world. Ultimately, his life is unsatisfactory. He desires, among other things, to captivate the ladies, the coquettes. One such woman is the subject of the third and final part of the poem. Harriet Simper typifies women who suffer from inadequate education; like Hairbrain, she values externals, such as dressing well and being gracious. Ultimately, after being rejected by Hairbrain, she marries a minister similar to Brainless and leads a life of dullness.

Upon completing *The Progress of Dulness* in 1773, Trumbull moved from New Haven to Boston, where he studied law with John Adams. This was a difficult time in Boston in particular as colonists were becoming increasingly dissatisfied with English rule, a discontent that led to the outbreak of hostilities at Lexington and Concord, Massachusetts, in 1775. Though he was sympathetic to the colonial cause, Trumbull did not support it ardently. As tensions increased, in 1774 he returned to New Haven to practice law. At the suggestion of friends who wanted to rally support for the Whigs' cause, he soon began writing what became the first canto of *M'Fingal,* which was published in 1776. In time, he expanded the poem to four cantos, which were published together in 1782 bearing the subtitle, "a modern epic poem." *M'Fingal* is a satire, mainly on the British but also, in a minor way, on the Patriots (Whigs). M'Fingal, himself, is a blustery Scottish Tory living outside Boston who, in the course of debating political issues with the dignified but pompous colonist Honorius in the first two cantos ("The Town Meeting A.M." and "The Town Meeting P.M."), makes a fool of himself while attempting to realign what he perceives as the cowardly colonists with the Crown. He argues, for example, that the Patriots will be defeated and that the king will reward the Tories and their supporters with land and titles of nobility, arguments Honorious rebuts and, implicitly, ridicules. In the third canto ("The Liberty Pole"), the heart of the poem, the Whigs capture M'Fingal and one of his associates, a constable, and position the constable on a liberty pole. Probably the most memorable scene in the entire poem occurs near the end of this canto when M'Fingal, tarred and feathered, and the constable are driven through town in a cart and then stuck to the liberty pole. (The artist Elkanah Tisdale captured these scenes memorably in illustrations for the 1795 New York edition of the poem.) In the fourth canto ("The Vision"), M'Fingal sees, in a vision, ultimate Patriot victory over British forces. Fearing this reality as the Whigs approach him threateningly, he flees to Boston.

In this poem, Trumbull succeeds in supporting the Patriot cause by ridiculing M'Fingal, the Tory representative, and lauding the Whigs. Ever a man of moderation, even in troubled times that generated high passions, he also disliked excess, which he observed in some of the Patriots' actions: he criticizes the Whigs not only for breaking the law but also for establishing their own inadequate laws. At the same time, Trumbull credits M'Fingal with a few accurate observations, as when commenting on the incompetence of some American (Whig) politicians. Viewed centuries after the American Revolution and from a literary, not a political, perspective, Trumbull's minor criticisms of the Whigs and slight crediting of M'Fingal enhance the poem by making the adversaries somewhat human and believable, and not merely unbelievable extremes of goodness and evil.

Trumbull's literary career largely concluded with the publication of the complete *M'Fingal* in 1782. Although he thereafter composed a few modest poems, his most significant subsequent literary effort was to *The Anarchiad* in 1786 and 1787, though his contributions cannot be determined with certainty; in these newspaper essays in favor of a strong central government he collaborated with David Humphreys, Joel Barlow, and Lemuel Hopkins. These men, along with Timothy Dwight and others, were part of an unofficial group known as the Connecticut Wits. *The Poetical Works of John Trumbull, LL.D.* was published in 1820 in two volumes.

Trumbull became treasurer of Yale in 1776, the year he married Sarah Hubbard; they had seven children, four of whom survived childhood. He held various political positions (he was a Federalist), became a judge, and received an honorary degree from his alma mater in 1818. After spending decades in Hartford, Connecticut, in 1825 he began living with his daughter in Detroit, where he died on 11 May 1831, at age eighty-one.

TOPICS FOR DISCUSSION AND RESEARCH

1. Trumbull introduces each section of *The Progress of Dulness* with a preface. Anticipating reader confusion over the meaning of the first part, for example, he explains his intention: *"The author was prompted to write by a hope that it might be of use to point out, in a clear, concise, and striking manner, those general errors, that hinder the advantages of education, and the growth of piety."* In truth, reading the poem independent of the preface reveals his intention clearly. If this is the case, then why might Trumbull have written the preface? Did he do so in order to reassure readers who might object to his depictions of colleges, students, and clergy, even though these depictions are a means to the end of urging reform? (And according to the preface to the Dick Hairbrain section,

this is how many readers responded to the first part, though in making this claim Trumbull might be ironic, or satiric.) Did Trumbull, still young, lack confidence in his ability to show, not tell? One may find help in answering these questions in Edwin T. Bowden's preface to Trumbull's satiric poems, as well as in Victor E. Gimmestad's *John Trumbull*.

2. How successful is satire if its author feels compelled to explain it, for whatever reason, as is the case with Trumbull in *The Progress of Dulness*? Cannot satire be effective, even most effective, when discomfort results from uncertainty about the author's intention, as, for example, in Jonathan Swift's "A Modest Proposal," a satiric masterpiece? For information about satire, consult such books as J. A. Cuddon, *A Dictionary of Literary Terms and Literary Theory* and Mary Ellen Snodgrass, *Encyclopedia of Satirical Literature*.

3. In the third part of *The Progress of Dulness*, Trumbull partly blames the reading of novels and plays for Harriet Simper's perverted values. Assuming that he is serious, not ironic or satiric, what does this attitude toward fiction indicate about the author himself? Because the first American novel was not published until 1789, Americans read English novels. Which of them did many Americans read? What aspects of these books might Trumbull have considered dangerous for young women, such as his Simper? Despite the popularity of novels and plays, they were often criticized; Massachusetts went so far as to ban theatrical performances. Why might parts of American society of the time have been suspicious of fiction and plays? A good overview of drama in early America, such as that by Michael T. Gilmore in "Literature of the Revolutionary and Early National Periods," will help provide answers to such questions.

4. Although Trumbull refers to *M'Fingal* as "a modern epic poem," it may more rightly be called a mock epic. What is a mock epic? How does it differ from an epic? Among other mock epics is one with which students might be familiar, Alexander Pope's *The Rape of the Lock*. What are other mock epics, and what are their characteristics? Which of these characteristics are also present in *M'Fingal*? Edwin T. Bowden addresses aspects of these questions in his preface to *The Progress of Dulness* and *M'Fingal*. For information about mock epics generally, as well as about satire, consult the books by J. A. Cuddon and Mary Ellen Snodgrass.

5. Leon Howard writes that Trumbull envisioned *M'Fingal* "as a running commentary on events." One would benefit from identifying contemporary events in the poem and comparing their depiction with what is known about them historically. How accurately does the poem depict the events? Does the degree of accuracy depend on which character depicts the events?

RESOURCES

Biography

Alexander Cowie, *John Trumbull, Connecticut Wit* (Chapel Hill: University of North Carolina Press, 1936).
The only full-scale biography of Trumbull.

Criticism

Edwin T. Bowden, Preface, *The Satiric Poems of John Trumbull:* The Progress of Dulness *and* M'Fingal (Austin: University of Texas Press, 1962).
Provides an overview of Trumbull's life and discusses the poet's two major creations.

J. A. Cuddon, *A Dictionary of Literary Terms and Literary Theory,* fourth edition (London: Blackwell, 1998).
A reliable dictionary of literary terms and literary theory.

Michael T. Gilmore, "Literature of the Revolutionary and Early National Periods," *The Cambridge History of American Literature, vol. 1, 1570–1820* (Cambridge, England: Cambridge University Press, 1994).
Surveys aspects of late-eighteenth- and early-nineteenth-century literature, including a good evaluation of drama.

Victor E. Gimmestad, *John Trumbull* (New York: Twayne, 1974).
A solid analysis of Trumbull's literary career, with convincing readings of the poet's works.

Leon Howard, *The Connecticut Wits* (Chicago: University of Chicago Press, 1943).
Examines Trumbull's literary career and the poet in the context of Joel Barlow, Timothy Dwight, and David Humphreys, who are, with others, known as the Connecticut Wits.

Louis Parrington, Introduction, *The Connecticut Wits,* edited by Parrington (1926; New York: Crowell, 1969).
Establishes the context in which the Connecticut Wits wrote, surveys their writings, and characters them as "the literary old guard of eighteenth century Toryism."

Mary Ellen Snodgrass, *Encyclopedia of Satirical Literature* (Santa Barbara: ABC-CLIO, 1996).
A comprehensive encyclopedia of satire.

Nathaniel Ward (circa 1578–1652)

Nathaniel Ward is important to the history of seventeenth-century American literature because of the book for which he is best known, *The Simple Cobler of Aggawam in America* (1647), the first American satire. He also contributed significantly to American jurisprudence. Born in Haverhill, Suffolk, England, around 1578, he was the son of John Ward, a Puritan minister, and a woman about whom nothing appears to be known. At Emmanuel College, Cambridge, Ward studied law, receiving a master's degree in 1603. Approximately a dozen years later in Heidelberg, the eminent Calvinist David Patreus inspired him to become a minister. Following his 1618 ordination, Ward ministered to Englishmen in Elbing, Prussia, until 1624; then, in England, from 1626 to 1628 he served as curate of St. James's in Picadilly, and next, from 1628 to 1633, as rector of Stondon-Massey in Essex. In 1631, his wife, Elizabeth, died. During the Stondon-Massey ministry, Ward, a nonconformist who refused to follow Anglican rituals, was forced to quit preaching by William Laud who was, in 1633, made archbishop of Canterbury and became notorious as enforcer of religious uniformity. Wifeless and apparently unemployed, Ward decided to immigrate to America, possibly because he knew, from his Cambridge days, people already there or who would become part of the Massachusetts Bay Colony; additionally, in America, he would be free to minister according to his own Calvinist principles. He sailed in 1634, settling in Agawam—residence of Simon Bradstreet and his wife, the poet Anne Bradstreet—which later that year was renamed Ipswich.

Life at Ipswich was so difficult that Ward became seriously ill; possibly as a result, in 1636 he resigned his position as co-pastor of the local church. Thomas Parker was the other minister. Five years later, drawing on his legal training, he was probably the leading force behind and the major author of *The Body of Liberties*, the first code of laws in New England, one that protected commoners from the unfettered rule of magistrates. It was intended as a guide for the General Court.

Granted land in Haverhill, Massachusetts Bay, in recognition of his work on *The Body of Liberties*, Ward moved there, where he again became ill. He then settled in Boston, where, in 1645, he wrote *The Simple Cobler of Aggawam in America*. He moved to London in 1647, where he soon preached a sermon before Parliament that Stephen Bowtell published in 1649 as *A Sermon Preached before the Honourable House of Commons at Their Late Monethly Fast*.

Ward's most important year as author was 1647. Ward probably wrote *A Word to Mr. Peters, and Two Words for the Parliament and Kingdom*, published that year in London. Also in 1647, Bowtell published both *A Religious Retreat Sounded to a Religious Army*, which addresses issues relating to the English army, and four editions of *The Simple Cobler of Aggawam in America*, which bears the pseudonym Theodore de la Guard as author. Within the context of American literature, Bowtell is important not only for publishing works by Ward, including his most famous and important composition, but also for publishing, possibly at Ward's urging, *The Tenth Muse Lately Sprung up in America* (1650), by Ward's former Ipswich neighbor, Anne Bradstreet. To this book, Ward contributed an introductory poem in which he characterizes Bradstreet as "a right *Du Bartas* Girle." He means that she was indebted to and was the equal of the French poet Guillaume Du Bartas. In this poem, he also warns male poets about a threat to their standing by such an accomplished woman as Bradstreet. Possibly in 1648, Ward became minister in Shenfield, Essex, a position he held until his death there in 1652.

Understanding *The Simple Cobler of Aggawam in America* requires knowledge of religious controversies of the time in England. Basically, the narrator argues against tolerating religious extremism, be it Roman Catholics or radical Protestants, because it helps fragment society, as evidenced in part by the English Civil War; he believes that only the true religion, that of Protestant Elizabethan England, can help heal the social fragmentation of his native country. Most commentary on Ward's work examines it within this context. Robert D. Arner and William J. Scheick are the most important of the few scholars to have approached Ward's book as art.

Most evaluators characterize Ward's work as satire. Arner best explains the basis for so considering it. He reads *The Simple Cobler of Aggawam in America* as a three-fold satire on "the dangers of religious toleration, the excesses of women's fashions, and the political, ecclesiastical, and civil strife in England." He also distinguishes between rural, unlearned Theodore de la Guard and the worldly, educated Ward and argues that war, architectural, astrological, and health and sickness imagery help unify Ward's rambling work.

With any piece of literature, a reader must understand the nature of the narrator, speaker, or voice that is relating it. As does Arner, so, too, does Scheick examine the nature of the narrator in *The Simple Cobler of Aggawam in America*. While acknowledging that there is a seeming disparity between the knowledge the narrator possesses and that which a frontier cobbler might be expected to have, Scheick argues that there is reason to believe the narrator's awareness of realities outside his profession. The narrator, a widower for almost a dozen years, is in a position, from experience, to know about noncobbler issues to which he refers, including "marriage, adultery, prostitution, and parturition." These issues provide him with significant "structuring metaphors" and make him "more consistent and realistic." Therein, Scheick argues, lies the art of *The Simple Cobler of Aggawam in America*.

Ward's satire also possesses humor, especially in its depiction of female fashion and men's hair, though Ward also puns and creates neologisms. Even though the narrator is desperate for a wife, he is offended by women's dressing ostentatiously in the manner of the queen or of French women. He states, "I truly confesse it is beyond the ken of my understanding to conceive, how those women should have any true grace, or valuable virtue, that have so little wit, as to disfigure themselves with such exotick garbes, as not only dismantles their native lovely luster, but transclouts them into gantbar-geese, ill-shapen-shotten-shell-fish, Egyptian Hyeroglyphicks, or at the best into French flurts of the pastery, which a proper English woman should scorne with her heels. . . ." To the narrator, that is, such attire suggests falsity, immodesty, and, by extension, prostitution; as a result, it violates social decorum, balance, and order, qualities he values in his discussion of religion. Similarly, the narrator dislikes men's long hair because it compromises his desired social normalcy.

In writing *The Simple Cobler of Aggawam in America*, the first American satire, Ward secured himself a permanent place in the history of American letters.

TOPICS FOR DISCUSSION AND RESEARCH

1. Although the precise details of Ward's involvement in *The Body of Liberties* (1641) is not known, he was probably its instigator and major author. Students would benefit from reading this document, as well as commen-

tary about it, and asking why people at the time thought such codification of laws was necessary. Did the magistrates abuse their power? Were they dismissive of commoners and their needs? This document influenced the writing of the Massachusetts constitution. Students would also benefit from comparing *The Body of Liberties* and the Bill of Rights to the United States Constitution, noting how many provisions in the former also appear in the latter. One is equal justice. What are others? Within this context, how significant is Ward to the liberties granted to citizens of the United States, a country that did not exist until almost a century and a half after *The Body of Liberties* was published? For help in answering these questions, consult Frederick S. Allis's *Nathaniel Ward: Constitutional Draftsman.*

2. That *The Simple Cobler of Aggawam in America* required four London editions in 1647 indicates its popularity. Why might it have been so popular? What aspects of the work possibly appealed to English readers? One might consider the conclusion of P. M. Zall: the popularity resulted from Ward's "conservative stand against religious toleration." Why would Ward, who contributed significantly to *The Body of Liberties,* wish to limit or prohibit some religious expression in England? Ward made additions to each of the three editions published after the first edition, which indicates his concern about the text, about saying all he wanted to say, about getting it right. For example, to the second edition he added some new text and marginal notes. Students would benefit from consulting Zall's discussion of the textual changes, reading Ward's work with these changes in mind, and determining the effect of these alterations.

3. One would benefit from applying Arner's and Scheick's observations about metaphors to a reading of Ward's work, charting architectural and marriage metaphors, for example, to see how effectively Ward uses them. Are the metaphors appropriate, given the nature of the narrator and his subject? Do they in fact unify Ward's text, as these two critics claim? How significant are the marriage metaphors in bolstering the narrator's depiction of Charles I, the person most criticized in this satire? What were the historical ramifications, for example, of Charles's marriage to Henrietta Maria of France?

4. Ward was neither the first nor the last person to complain about contemporary fashions. One might beneficially learn about the normal attire of the time by reading appropriate sections in cultural histories of mid-seventeenth-century London. What would the typical woman have worn in public? What examples does the narrator give of women dressing ostentatiously? Why might he object to ostentation? How similar is this attitude to one about the same issue in *The Contrast,* an eighteenth-century play by Royall Tyler?

RESOURCES

Criticism
Frederick S. Allis Jr., *Nathaniel Ward: Constitutional Draftsman* (Ipswich: Ipswich Historical Society, 1984).
Considers Ward's importance as the main author of *The Body of Liberties.*

Robert D. Arner, "*The Simple Cobler of Aggawam:* Nathaniel Ward and the Rhetoric of Satire," *Early American Literature,* 5, no. 3 (1971): 3–16.
Observes that *The Simple Cobler of Aggawam in America* is a three-part satire unified by several different metaphors.

Jean F. Beranger, "Voices of Humor in Nathaniel Ward," *Studies in American Humor II,* 2 (1975): 96–104.
Discusses Ward's different uses of humor in *The Simple Cobler of Aggawam in America.*

Patricia L. Bradley, "The Unifying Pauline Sub-Text of Nathaniel Ward's *The Simple Cobler of Aggawam,*" *Early American Literature,* 34, no. 1 (1999): 32–47.
Maintains that the major subtext of Ward's work "is the Apostle Paul's first epistle to the Corinthian church," which is a "model of epistolary disorder."

William J. Scheick, "The Widower Narrator in Nathaniel Ward's *The Simple Cobler of Aggawam in America,*" *New England Quarterly,* 47, no. 1 (March 1974): 87–96.
Argues that the narrator, a widower for almost twelve years, uses metaphors of marriage, sex, and birth as structuring devices in Ward's satire.

P. M. Zall, Introduction, *The Simple Cobler of Aggawam in America* (Lincoln: University of Nebraska Press, 1969).
In introducing the only modern edition of Ward's work, Zall places the satire in historical perspective while touching on its artistry, such as Ward's use of language and humor.

Mercy Otis Warren (1728–1814)

Descended from a *Mayflower* passenger, Mercy Otis Warren was one of the most significant American women of the American Revolution and after. A friend of such important people as John and Abigail Adams, Warren was a woman of accomplishment, primarily as dramatist, poet, and historian. Born in Barnstable, Massachusetts, on 25 September 1728, Mercy Otis was the third of thirteen children of James and Mary Allyne Otis. Most of her siblings died young. The oldest child, James Jr., became an early Patriot and is supposed to have said "taxation without liberty is tyranny," which resonated with pre-Revolution Americans. At a time when girls were seldom educated, Mercy Otis was tutored along with her older brothers. In 1754, at age twenty-six, she married James Warren, another early Patriot. Together they had five children, all sons, born between 1757 and 1766. By the time the Warren family was nearing completion, Americans were reacting against British rule, as in their response to the Stamp Act of 1765. Seven years later, Warren began commenting publicly on political realities in *The Adulateur,* a play that appeared anonymously in

Isaiah Thomas's anti-British newspaper *The Massachusetts Spy* (1772); the next year, it was published in pamphlet form with material added by an unknown author. Also in 1773, her play *The Defeat* was published in the *The Boston Gazette*. In 1775, when armed conflict between the colonists and the Crown began at Lexington and Concord, her play *The Group* was published. The next and last plays definitely known to be by her—*The Sack of Rome* and *The Ladies of Castile*—appeared in 1790 in *Poems, Dramatic and Miscellaneous*, a book that bears Warren's name as author and that is dedicated to George Washington. In addition to writing plays, Warren also composed poems, a history, and many letters, though within a literary context she is best known as the author of her first three plays, closet dramas. She has been identified as the author of plays other than those mentioned here—*The Blockheads* (1776), *The Motley Assembly* (1779), and *Sans Souci* (1785)—though the evidence for attribution is less than totally convincing; of them, the first seems most likely hers.

Warren was a Whig, a Patriot whose political beliefs are obvious in her early plays. Because she wrote about unresolved contemporary issues—those between Whigs and Tories and between America and England—she could not address the ultimate conclusion of these issues that came to a head in the American Revolution. Therefore, when wishing to resolve issues in a play, she had to focus on small matters, not the large picture. *The Adulateur* presents conflict between an oppressive government led by Rapatio (based on Governor Thomas Hutchinson) and Patriots under the leadership of Brutus (James Otis, the author's brother). One faction is bad; the other, good. They are irreconcilable. At the end of the play, the Patriots are in trouble, but it ends without resolution as Brutus speaks noble, hopeful words. Although *The Defeat* continues the action of *The Adulateur* and uses some of the same characters, this short, fragmentary play is the least satisfactory of Warren's early dramatic productions. In it, Rapatio is about to be hanged, which indicates a preliminary victory by the Patriots. Warren's most popular play is *The Group*, which went through at least three separate editions in 1775; it was inspired by the recent decision of the Crown to appoint, without consulting the colonists, the mandamus councilors, the major advisers to the governor of Massachusetts. The play focuses on the discussions of the Tories and offers some hope for the Whigs by having Brutus's successor, Sylla (Thomas Gage), at least acknowledge the justness of the Patriots' cause. It also deals with issues relating to women. In addition to being anti-Whig, the Tories are also anti-woman, or are at least indifferent to women's needs and desires. The character Simple prefers his political cause to his wife's contentment, going so far as to offer to lodge British troops in their house; if she objects, she and their children can find lodging elsewhere. The character Hateall admits that he married his wife only for her dowry. Such sentiments imply Warren's belief that women must be treated respectfully and her further belief that this has a chance of happening when Tories no longer infest the land. Warren's two later plays—both complete, five-act tragedies obviously technically superior to their predecessors—are less compelling than the earlier ones because they lack passion, which the plays of the 1770s possess. In Warren's dramas, emotion trumps formalism.

In addition to the two plays, *Poems, Dramatic and Miscellaneous* includes eighteen poems, her only ones published in book form, though she wrote other verse. These poems, most of which appeared in newspapers in the 1770s, are largely in the neoclassical mode and deal primarily with politics, religion, and morality. The political poems reinforce themes in her plays and provide examples of Warren's wit ("The Squabble of the Sea Nymphs" is a mock epic about the Boston Tea Party; "To the Hon. J. Winthrop, Esq." satirizes women more interested in comfort than freedom), while the poems on religious and moral themes reveal a side of Warren not obvious in the plays. She argues, for example, against deism and excessive reliance on reason ("To Torrismond"), suggests that a good life leads to eternal reward ("To a Young Lady"), and believes that God blesses America because its values are simple and pure ("To a Patriotic Gentleman").

Though of little literary interest, Warren's most ambitious effort was *The History of the Rise, Progress and Termination of the American Revolution*, published in three volumes (1805). One result of this publication was the alienation of John Adams, who objected to Warren's depiction of him, though Abigail Adams and Warren remained friendly. Warren and the former president reconciled in 1813. She died a year later, on 14 October 1814, at age eighty-six.

TOPICS FOR DISCUSSION AND RESEARCH

1. Theresa Freda Nicolay suggests that Warren "expands the subjects available to women writers by moving from acceptable female genres, such as the epistolary and the poetic, to satirical drama . . . and, finally, the male province of history"; as a result she "moved female authorship further into traditionally male cosmopolitan territory, extending society's notions of what women could acceptably write about and moving female authorship from belletristic to historical letters." Students would benefit from investigating the accuracy of this statement. Who were other American women authors of Warren's time and before? What is the general nature of their writings? Are there examples of women writing in genres other than letters and poetry? If Nicolay's assertion is correct, when did American women authors begin following Warren's example by writing satires and histories, and who were these authors? In other words, what was the nature of Warren's influence? For help in answering these questions, read Nicolay's 1995 essay about Warren.

2. Mary Beth Norton makes a related argument. Smarting from Warren's depiction of him in *The History of the Rise, Progress and Termination of the American Revolution*, John Adams declared that history is not the province of women, thereby belittling her and diminishing her historical study. Citing this statement and similar sentiments by men, Norton argues that Warren, and intellectual women like her, had to overcome sexual bias in order to be taken seriously when writing in genres considered solely men's. Students would benefit from reading Norton's argument, pondering it, and asking how convincing it is.

3. Warren's early and late plays are different in many ways, including their degrees of emotion: the plays of the 1770s reflect the author's passionate feelings

about political events of the time; the post-Revolution plays are cooler, more detached. Jeffrey H. Richards observes that one of these later plays, *The Ladies of Castile*, "displays the author's skills in structure and language to better effect than any of her earlier plays." Commenting on the other play, *The Sack of Rome*, he suggests that its strength derives from Warren's not making its meaning obvious. Students would benefit from reading the plays, as well as Richards's analysis of them. After doing so, they should consider whether the critic's reasons for commending the plays are enough to elevate them to the realm of significance, however defined. Structure and the appropriate use of language are generally desirable, but they alone seem largely irrelevant unless they serve to convey meaning. What is the meaning of *The Ladies of Castile*? Is the meaning important? Is conveying a significant message inelegantly (the early plays) less desirable than expressing an inferior message artfully (the late ones)? Consider Richards's comment about the meaning of *The Sack of Rome* not being obvious and apply it to the early plays. How obvious are their meanings? If they are obvious, does this lessen their quality? Although these are aesthetic questions with no obvious, provable answers, Warren's plays invite readers to ask them.

4. Warren's early plays are allegorical. Readers in the 1770s could have identified the people and events about which Warren writes. Far removed from that decade, many modern readers are unfamiliar with these people and events. Is awareness of them necessary for enjoying the plays? Why?

RESOURCES

Biography
Katharine Anthony, *First Lady of the Revolution: The Life of Mercy Otis Warren* (Garden City, N.Y.: Doubleday, 1958).
The second full-scale biography of Warren.

Alice Brown, *Mercy Warren* (New York: Scribners, 1896).
The first full-scale biography of Warren.

Nancy Rubin Stuart, *The Muse of the Revolution: The Secret Pen of Mercy Otis Warren and the Founding of a Nation* (Boston: Beacon, 2008).
A modern biography that draws extensively on Warren's correspondence.

Criticism
Kate Davies, *Catharine Macaulay and Mercy Otis Warren: The Revolutionary Atlantic and the Politics of Gender* (Oxford: Oxford University Press, 2005).
Examines the lives and friendship of Catharine Macaulay and Warren, arguing that they "saw themselves, as women and as writers, at the intellectual heart of Atlantic political culture."

Benjamin Franklin V, Introduction, *The Plays and Poems of Mercy Otis Warren*, compiled by Franklin (Delmar, N.Y.: Scholars' Facsimiles and Reprints, 1980).
Comments on Warren's belletristic writings, especially her plays.

Jean Fritz, *Cast for a Revolution: Some American Friends and Enemies, 1728–1814* (Boston: Houghton Mifflin, 1972).
Posits that Warren was important in her own right but also was at or near the center of revolutionary activity because of her associations with such men as her brother, husband, and John Adams.

Theresa Freda Nicolay, *Gender Roles, Literary Authority, and Three American Women Writers: Anne Dudley Bradstreet, Mercy Otis Warren, Margaret Fuller Ossoli* (New York: Peter Lang, 1995).
Observes that Warren wrote in genres previously unavailable to—or uninvestigated by—American women.

Mary Beth Norton, *Liberty's Daughters: The Revolutionary Experience of American Women, 1750–1800* (1980; Ithaca: Cornell University Press, 1996), pp. 121–123.
Examines the ramifications of "the discomfort caused by the ambiguity inherent in her [Warren's] status as an intellectual woman."

Jeffrey H. Richards, *Mercy Otis Warren* (New York: Twayne; London: Prentice Hall, 1995).
A reliable examination of Warren's life and works.

Phillis Wheatley (circa 1753–1784)

Phillis Wheatley is, with Samson Occom, one of the least-likely authors in American history. Born in western Africa around 1753, she was transported to Boston in 1761 aboard a slave ship. Purchased by the Wheatleys, John and Susanna, she assumed the family name, as well as that of the ship that brought her to America, the *Phillis*. Taught mainly by Susanna Wheatley and her daughter, Mary, the young girl learned so quickly and well—she soon read widely, including in the Bible and the classics—that she became better educated than most whites, both women and men. The earliest known writing of Phillis Wheatley is a 1765 letter, now lost, to Occom, an Indian minister who soon helped found Dartmouth College. Her first publication was a poem in *The Newport Mercury* (1767). She became famous when, three years later at approximately age seventeen, her *An Elegiac Poem, on the Death of That Celebrated Divine, and Eminent Servant of Jesus Christ, the Reverend and Learned George Whitefield* was published in Boston; it was published in London the next year. Because in 1770 he preached four times at the Old South Church in Boston, where Wheatley was baptized the following year by Samuel Cooper, she probably heard Whitefield preach and possibly knew this man who, in the 1740s, was largely responsible for inspiring the religious fervor that characterized the Great Awakening. After having written numerous poems, at the urging and with the assistance of Susanna Wheatley, Phillis Wheatley tried unsuccessfully in 1772 to interest Boston publishers in her work. The next year, she accompanied the Wheatleys' son, Nathaniel, to London, where the bookseller Archibald Bell published her *Poems on Various Subjects, Religious and Moral*, dedicated to the Countess of Huntingdon, her English patron. In order to tend to Susanna Wheatley, who was ill, Phillis Wheatley left England for Boston before the book was published. Around this time, probably because of her literary accomplishments and the attention her book attracted, Wheatley was manumitted, though she continued living in the Wheatley home, even following Susanna Wheatley's death in 1774.

In 1775, Wheatley wrote the poem "To His Excellency General Washington," which she sent to George Washington, along with a letter, from Providence, Rhode Island. Though involved with military matters as commander in chief of the Continental Army, he responded to her gesture, thanking her warmly, praising her talent, and inviting her to visit him, which she did the following year when he was headquartered in Cambridge.

The next decade of Wheatley's life was largely unsettled and was one of decline. The Wheatleys were removed from her by the death of John Wheatley and Mary Wheatley in 1778; Nathaniel Wheatley resided in London, where he remained, dying there in 1783. She married John Peters in 1778 and assumed his surname. Little is known about her husband other than that he was a free black man who worked at various jobs, apparently largely unsuccessfully. In 1779 and again in 1784 she proposed a new book of her poems, though the project did not come to fruition. Her circumstances were dire in 1784. By then, her first two children had died, and she was seriously ill. Late in the year, on 5 December, she died, at approximately age thirty-one. Her third and last child died on the same day; mother and child are buried together in an unmarked grave. *The Boston Magazine* of December 1784 includes a memorial to her, "Elegy on the Death of a Late Celebrated Poetess," by an author using the pseudonym Horatio. Her book of poems was published for the first time in America by Joseph Crukshank in Philadelphia in 1786. Her widower presumably sold her manuscripts and books in order to pay his debts. In the nineteenth century, abolitionists used her poems to demonstrate that blacks are intellectually capable.

TOPICS FOR DISCUSSION AND RESEARCH

1. Wheatley is often derided for writing in imitation of such great English poets as John Dryden and Alexander Pope, masters of neoclassical verse. Yet, these and other poets inspired so many American writers that neoclassicism became the dominant American poetic mode for most of the eighteenth century. Students would benefit from identifying the characteristics of neoclassical verse, which may be found in reputable dictionaries of literary terms. Once the characteristics are understood, identify examples of them in Wheatley's poems. Did she master neoclassical techniques? If so, does her failure to approach the sophistication of a Dryden or Pope diminish her value? If not, what is her value as a poet? On what artistic bases may her verse be appreciated?

2. Wheatley has been criticized for failing adequately to protest slavery, the institution responsible for taking her from homeland and family. Although slavery is not a major issue in her verse, she does address it, especially in the third stanza of "To the Right Honourable William, Earl of Dartmouth, His Majesty's Principal Secretary of State for North-America, &c." (1772). After lamenting the pain her abduction must have caused her parents, she concludes, "And can I then but pray / Others may never feel tyrannic sway?" What does her modest (and infrequent) overt criticism of slavery indicate about her? Although there is no definitive answer to this question, one might consider possibilities: that while she regrets the grief her abduction must have caused her parents, she, herself, does not feel particularly disadvantaged because, while technically enslaved, she is owned by people who treat her well, give her advantages (learning paramount among them), and encourage her literary undertakings? Or might she feel deeply, possibly subconsciously, that her situation is profoundly unjust, as hinted at in the stanza in the poem to Lord Dartmouth, but that she could not risk losing her relatively benign personal and social situation by writing about racial injustice directly? Or something else? For thoughts about this issue, consult John C. Shields's *Phillis Wheatley's Poetics of Liberation*.

3. In *Poems on Various Subjects* appear the names of eighteen of "the most respectable Characters in *Boston*," all of whom attest that Wheatley, a black female slave, is indeed the author of this book of poems. These men include the Massachusetts governor, Thomas Hutchinson, as well as John Hancock, Charles Chauncy, Mather Byles, and her master, John Wheatley. What does the statement indicate about their perceptions of the white public, the audience for Wheatley's poems? Does it merely indicate that they think the public would disbelieve that she wrote the poems because no American slave had previously published a book of any description? Or do the men believe that the public would think such a person incapable of writing a book, especially of verse, because of her perceived racial inferiority? The men conclude their comments with this sentence: "She has been examined by some of the best Judges, and is thought qualified to write" the poems. Does this statement help answer these questions?

4. Vincent Carretta and A. L. Nielsen both comment on "To the University of Cambridge, in New-England," which Wheatley wrote at around age fifteen. Carretta observes that in this poem "Wheatley appropriates the persona of authority or power normally associated with men and social superiors"; further, he points out the irony of a person of Wheatley's youth, race, sex, and situation presenting the speaker of her poem as a wise instructor of the privileged Harvard students, advising them to take advantage of the opportunities they are afforded and to avoid sin. Nielsen observes that in addition to exploiting readers' biases in this poem, Wheatley contrasts her speaker's knowledge with the students' probable perception of her. One would benefit from reading this short poem and considering it with these critics' comments in mind. What is the speaker's real stance? Her real motivation? Is her role as the students' adviser genuine? Ironic? Is she jealous of the students' oppor-

tunities, which she is denied on several grounds? Is she subversive, implying that she is at least as intellectually competent and morally good as the students she addresses? Is she merely attempting to be helpful?

5. Wheatley's "On Being Brought from Africa to America" expresses the speaker's gratitude for having been taken from pagan Africa to Christian America; the poem concludes with the couplet "Remember, *Christians, Negros,* black as *Cain,* / May be refin'd, and join th' angelic train," by which she means that anyone may qualify for admission to heaven. Russell Reising concludes his examination of Wheatley with this comment about the poem: "The 'angelic train' Wheatley describes in her poetry, then, can be (and has been) read as a one-way trip to oblivion and racial accommodation, but it might also be read as a prophetic anticipation of the Underground Railroad." Consider this and other Wheatley poems and ask if her speaker is being accommodative of Western, Christian, white culture or is actually protesting her presence in it. Reising provides guidance for considering this question.

RESOURCES

Criticism

Vincent Carretta, Introduction, *Complete Writings,* by Phillis Wheatley (New York: Penguin, 2001).
Surveys Wheatley's life, work, and times.

Henry Louis Gates Jr., *The Trials of Phillis Wheatley: America's First Black Poet and Her Encounters with the Founding Fathers* (New York: Basic Civitas Books, 2003).
This brief book, based on the author's Thomas Jefferson Lecture in the Humanities, comments on Wheatley's relationships (sometimes epistolary) with founding fathers Benjamin Franklin, John Hancock, George Washington, and especially Thomas Jefferson.

Julian D. Mason Jr., Introduction, *The Poems of Phillis Wheatley* (Chapel Hill: University of North Carolina Press, 1966; revised, 1989).
Takes recent scholarship into account when surveying Wheatley's life and works; examines the criticism of Wheatley's writings.

A. L. Nielsen, "Patterns of Subversion in the Works of Phillis Wheatley and Jupiter Hammon," *Western Journal of Black Studies,* 6, no. 4 (Winter 1982): 212–219.
Argues that Wheatley rejects "white imputations of inferiority and subtly [pleads] for emancipation."

Russell Reising, *Loose Ends: Closure and Crisis in the American Social Text* (Durham: Duke University Press, 1996), pp. 73–115.
Examines "the socio-ideological issues that infuse and disrupt" Wheatley's works.

M. A. Richmond, *Bid the Vassal Soar: Interpretive Essays on the Life and Poetry of Phillis Wheatley (ca. 1753–1784) and George Moses Horton (ca. 1797–1883)* (Washington, D.C.: Howard University Press, 1974), pp. 3–78.

While dismissing the quality of Wheatley's verse, this book argues that it is nonetheless important for what it indicates about the author, a slave, as well as about slavery itself.

John C. Shields, *Phillis Wheatley's Poetics of Liberation* (Knoxville: University of Tennessee Press, 2008).
Finding most previous commentary about Wheatley inadequate, this brash, provocative book attempts "to facilitate a fair and balanced reading of Phillis Wheatley's life and work by providing a more thorough account than has heretofore been attempted of the backgrounds and contexts out of which her oeuvre evolved."

Frank Shuffelton, "On Her Own Footing: Phillis Wheatley in Freedom," in *Genius in Bondage: Literature of the Early Black Atlantic*, edited by Vincent Carretta and Philip Gould (Lexington: University Press of Kentucky, 2001), pp. 175–189.
Discusses how Wheatley benefited from opening "a connection to an imperial public sphere."

Michael Wigglesworth
The Day of Doom: or, a Description of the Great and Last Judgment. With a Short Discourse about Eternity
(Boston: Printed by Samuel Green, 1662)

Born on 18 October 1631, probably in Yorkshire, England, Michael Wigglesworth emigrated with his Puritan family in 1638, settling in New Haven in what became the state of Connecticut. Unsuited for the farming life of his father, Edward, Wigglesworth entered Harvard in 1647 to study medicine. Following a spiritual conversion, he prepared for the ministry. After completing his degree in 1651, Wigglesworth remained at Harvard for three years as a tutor, teaching, among others, Increase Mather, who became a lifelong friend. Invited to become the minister in Malden, Massachusetts, he moved there in 1654, though he was not ordained until 1657. He married his cousin Mary Reyner in 1654; she died in 1659. Wigglesworth served Malden as minister, teacher, and physician until, in the early 1660s, poor health caused him to cease many activities including preaching, though he did not resign his pastorate. In 1661 and 1662, while ill, he composed the poems that were published in *The Day of Doom*; in 1662 he wrote the poem "God's Controversy with New-England," though it was not published until the 1870s.

Attempting to regain his health, Wigglesworth went to Bermuda in 1663. Upon returning to Malden somewhat improved, he devoted himself to ministering to the physical ailments of the residents, as well as to tutoring youth for admission to Harvard. In 1670 he published poems under the title *Meat out of the Eater*. He created a scandal, in 1679, by marrying his maid, Martha Mudge. The

Malden church refused his 1680 offer to resign as minister. He became healthy enough in the mid 1680s to be offered the presidency of Harvard, which he declined. He delivered the 1685 artillery sermon in Cambridge and, the following year, the election sermon in Boston. (He preached another election sermon in 1696.) Around this time, he resumed his long-neglected pastorate in Malden. The year after the death of his wife, Martha, Wigglesworth married Sybil Sparhawk Avery, a widow. At the time of his death, on 4 July 1705, Wigglesworth was a well-regarded religious figure in New England.

Wigglesworth is one of three major colonial American poets. Unlike the other two, Anne Bradstreet and Edward Taylor, he intended his poems for publication. While some of Bradstreet's poems have often been praised and many of Taylor's have been lauded, Wigglesworth's have been derided as possessing more doctrine than art, an assessment that has moderated in recent years when, among other things, the poet's use of voice has been admired by Ronald A. Bosco. In Wigglesworth's major poem, the 1,792-line "The Day of Doom," the poet depicts a harsh, unrelenting Christ on Judgment Day, meting out justice in a doctrinally accurate manner.

The 446-line "God's Controversy with New-England" indicates that God inflicted various sufferings on the people of New England because of their backsliding. The poem, a jeremiad, reminds readers that they live in a land blessed by God and that His continued blessing and their own salvation may be secured by proper devotion to God. In this poem, Wigglesworth wants most to justify God's ways to man and inspire his readers to embrace Christ. He does this partly by focusing on natural phenomena. Not only did he compose "God's Controversy with New-England" when he perceived religious commitment in decline, but also at a time when nature was making life difficult for New Englanders. He notes that he wrote the poem "in the time of the great drought Anno 1662." To Wigglesworth, other Congregational ministers, and the general Puritan population, adverse natural phenomena were not accidental; rather, they were God's creations, reflecting divine displeasure with them and their society. In the poem, Wigglesworth implies the mildness of the drought when compared with the agony of eternal damnation that awaits an unrepentant people.

Wigglesworth's third and last major composition is *Meat out of the Eater* (1670), much longer than *The Day of Doom* and considerably less significant than "The Day of Doom" and "God's Controversy with New-England." In it, Wigglesworth argues, in meditations, the necessity of enduring human travail as preparation for uniting with Christ. In songs and meditations, he explains Christian riddles, or paradoxes, such as "Light in Darkness," "Strength in Weakness," and "Joy in Sorrow."

TOPICS FOR DISCUSSION AND RESEARCH

1. Wigglesworth's verse generally and "The Day of Doom" particularly have been maligned for possessing little if any art. In *American Poets* (1968), one of the major studies of the entirety of American verse, Hyatt Waggoner ignores

Wigglesworth. Yet, in *Seventeenth-Century American Poetry*, published the same year, Harrison T. Meserole ranks Wigglesworth with Bradstreet and Taylor as the major American poets of the century, going so far as to print the entirety of "The Day of Doom." In not only defending but praising Wigglesworth, Meserole notes the obvious: Wigglesworth wanted to inspire his readers to find salvation through Christ, and the poem "succeeds on its own terms." Appreciation of Wigglesworth reached its zenith in 1989, when Ronald A. Bosco published *The Poems of Michael Wigglesworth*. In the introduction to this volume, the editor places Wigglesworth in context and makes a solid case for him as poet, primarily by pointing out the various voices he assumes in "The Day of Doom." Students would benefit from reading a few poems by Bradstreet and Taylor in anthologies of American literature and comparing their artfulness with Wigglesworth's in "The Day of Doom." After asking if Waggoner was wise to omit Wigglesworth from his study of American verse, consider Meserole's judgment in ranking Wigglesworth with Bradstreet and Taylor. Which scholar's judgment seems more convincing? Also, read Bosco's analysis of Wigglesworth's poetic skill in "The Day of Doom." Is it compelling? Does it make the poem palatable to the inexperienced reader who might not share the religious views of Wigglesworth and many seventeenth-century American readers?

2. Bosco identifies a useful psychological approach to Wigglesworth's poems by observing that "the principal occasion for Wigglesworth's poetry, New England's apparent decline from the piety and ideals of the first Puritan settlers, coincided with his own physical and periodic psychological distress." As a result of this distress, Wigglesworth was incapable of preaching. Possibly feeling a need to offer alternative religious instruction, he might have composed "The Day of Doom" to convey what he perceived as the precarious state of his contemporaries' souls. While one cannot prove that he wrote this poem to compensate for his inability to preach, one might benefit from thinking through the implications of his writing such a harsh poem while ill. Read Bosco's introduction for guidance, and especially heed his comments about New England declension and the need at the time for powerful preaching.

3. *The Day of Doom* (the book that includes "The Day of Doom" as its major poem) became the first American best seller, with approximately one in every thirty-five New Englanders owning a copy. The 1,800-copy first edition sold out quickly; during Wigglesworth's lifetime, the book required three English editions and as many as five American ones. To what might the popularity of the book be attributed? To help answer this question, students should become familiar with the Half-Way Covenant of 1662 and the reasons for it.

4. In an effort to encourage a religious commitment similar to that of the Puritan fathers, Wigglesworth made "The Day of Doom" didactic and threatening, and effective, both emotionally and intellectually. After permitting the elect to enter heaven, Christ is strict, unbending, as He counters all the damned souls' arguments for salvation. When, for example, infants complain

of being denied heaven without having had the opportunity to transgress, Christ acknowledges their argument by placing them in "the easiest room of Hell." Throughout the poem, Wigglesworth lends authority to its various points by citing appropriate Bible verses in marginal glosses, such as Rom. 3:19 to validate Christ's treatment of children. As a result, readers can be assured that Wigglesworth's views are correct and therefore may be believed. Wigglesworth was far from the first author to use marginal glosses, however. So did the translators of the Geneva Bible, which was used by some early American Puritans. Students should gain a sense of the great number of marginal glosses in the Geneva Bible, which will probably surprise them. (It is available on-line; see below.) Then, read William W. E. Slights's "Margin-all Notes that spoile the Text" in order to understand the function and effect of such glosses. Finally, apply what you have learned about marginal glosses to "The Day of Doom." What does Wigglesworth's use of them indicate about the author's perception of the poem's audience? About the nature of the poem itself?

RESOURCES

Biography

Richard Crowder, *No Featherbed to Heaven: A Biography of Michael Wigglesworth, 1631–1705* (East Lansing: Michigan State University Press, 1962).
This first book-length study of Wigglesworth focuses on the poet's life but mentions his work only in passing.

John Langdon Sibley, *Biographical Sketches of Graduates of Harvard University*, Volume 1 (1642–1658) (Cambridge, Mass.: Charles William Sever, 1873), pp. 259–286.
A substantial biographical sketch based largely on Wigglesworth's diary.

Criticism

The Bible and Holy Scriptvres Conteyned in the Olde and Newe Testament (Geneva, Switzerland: Rovland Hall, 1560) <http://www.thedcl.org/bible/gb/> [accessed 9 June 2009].
A sixteenth-century Bible (best known as the Geneva Bible) with numerous marginal glosses.

Ronald A. Bosco, Introduction, *The Poems of Michael Wigglesworth* (Lanham, Md.: University Press of America, 1989).
Surveys criticism of Wigglesworth's poetry and offers new interpretations of it.

Jeffrey A. Hammond, *Sinful Self, Saintly Self: The Puritan Experience of Poetry* (Athens: University of Georgia Press, 1993).
Focuses on Wigglesworth, Bradstreet, and Taylor, arguing that Wigglesworth appealed to his contemporaries because his verses served "as catalysts and echoes of their own feelings."

Harrison T. Meserole, *Seventeenth-Century American Poetry* (Garden City, N.Y.:
    Doubleday, 1968); republished as *American Poetry of the Seventeenth Cen-
    tury* (University Park: Pennsylvania State University Press, 1985).
This major anthology of seventeenth-century verse establishes a hierarchy of
early American poets, identifying Wigglesworth, Bradstreet, and Taylor as the
major writers, others as minor writers, and yet others as representative writers.

William W. E. Slights, "'Marginall Notes that spoile the Text': Scriptural
    Annotation in the English Renaissance," *Huntington Library Quarterly*, 55
    (Spring 1992): 255–278.
Addresses the question of whether marginal glosses "fix or free
interpretation."

Roger Williams (circa 1603–1683)

Roger Williams was born in Smithfield, a suburb of London, probably in 1603.
Documentation of his birth was destroyed in the 1666 London fire. His father,
James Williams, was a tailor; his mother, Alice Pemberton Williams, was the
daughter of a tradesman. He had three siblings. Little is known about his early
years. As a result of the patronage of lawyer and Puritan Sir Edward Coke, Williams was enrolled at Charterhouse, a school for boys aged ten to fourteen, then at
Pembroke Hall, Cambridge University, from which he was graduated in 1627. He
began studying for a master's degree, but withdrew from Cambridge midway into
the three-year program. Possibly in early 1629, he became chaplain to Sir William
Masham, a gentleman connected to the Puritans. Later that year, Williams married Mary Barnard, a maid of Masham's stepdaughter, with whom he ultimately
had six children. By then a Puritan, he was in a tenuous religious position in
Anglican England. As a result, and because of a desire to minister to the American Indians, he and his wife sailed from England in December 1630 on the *Lyon*,
arriving in Boston two months later. There, his most serious troubles began.
   Soon after arriving in Boston, Williams was offered a position in the local
church, which he declined because he, a Separatist, would not affiliate with a
non-Separatist church. Separatists disavowed the Anglican Church and severed
their relationship with it; technically speaking, non-Separatists remained part of
the Church of England. He accepted a position as assistant to the minister of the
Salem church, but stayed only a few months before removing to the Separatist
community of Plymouth, where he served as assistant to the minister from 1631
to 1633. After creating a firestorm by writing that the Plymouth charter was
illegitimate because it claimed American land for a European monarch when he
had no right to it, Williams was no longer welcome in Plymouth. He returned
to Salem, where he again served as ministerial assistant until becoming minister
upon the death of his predecessor, Samuel Skelton. In 1635 the General Court
tried Williams for professing ideas that threatened the colony, such as denying its
right to the Indians' land and stating that the magistrates' authority was limited

to civil issues and did not extend to religion. Ordered to leave the colony, he fled south to Indian territory in January 1636. Four months later, he and a few others founded Providence, which became the capital of Rhode Island. He intended it as a refuge for people persecuted for reasons of conscience, like himself; he also insisted on a separation of church and state. In 1644, Williams succeeded in procuring a charter for the Providence Plantations. Despite what might be termed Williams's liberal attitudes, as evidenced by his accepting people of various faiths in Rhode Island, he was harshly critical of the Quakers, primarily because they valued Inner Light more than the Bible. In the 1650s, Williams served three years as president of Rhode Island. He died in early 1683.

Williams was most active as a writer from 1643 to 1652. Appreciation of the Indians and championing of their rights is reflected in his first publication, *A Key into the Language of America* (1643), written during the trip to England when he was seeking a charter for the Providence Plantations. This and all but one of his subsequent works were published in London. Of the several controversies in which Williams was involved, a published debate with the esteemed John Cotton was probably the most significant. Cotton wrote a letter, published in London in 1643, in which he explains why Williams was banished from Massachusetts Bay. Williams presents his view of the issues in *Mr. Cottons Letter Lately Printed, Examined and Answered* (1644). Then, he wrote *Queries of the Highest Consideration* (1644). Addressed to the Westminster Assembly of Divines, not Cotton—though Williams also intended it for Cotton and others in Massachusetts Bay—it presents Williams's views on, among other things, the separation of church and state, a topic at the heart of his most important publication, *The Bloudy Tenent, of Persecution, for Cause of Conscience, Discussed* (1644), written to criticize Cotton's intolerance on matters of conscience. Williams concluded his published debate with Cotton with *The Bloody Tenent Yet More Bloody* (1652), written during a later trip to England. It, too, deals with issues relating to church and state, as well as to matters of conscience. The most significant of the later writings is *George Fox Digg'd Out of His Burrowes* (1676), in which Williams discusses the Quakers.

TOPICS FOR DISCUSSION AND RESEARCH

1. Williams came into conflict with the main figures in Massachusetts Bay— John Cotton and John Winthrop paramount among them—over the nature of government. Cotton, Winthrop, and other non-Separatists believed that because their government was authorized by God, magistrates could rule about religious issues; the Separatist Williams believed that the government had authority only in civil matters, not religious ones. Especially in *The Bloudy Tenent, of Persecution, for Cause of Conscience, Discussed*, Williams argues that because people elect and thereby empower the magistrates, magistrate involvement in church matters implies that people, not God, control the church. Williams found such thinking ludicrous, blasphemous. His opinions—so threatening that he was banished from the colony—did not then prevail, though in time they did. They are reflected in the First Amendment to the

Constitution of the United States (1791). One might beneficially examine the decline of Winthrop's and Cotton's position and the elevation of Williams's. Because the proper relationship between government and religion continues to be disputed, one could examine current debates and legal cases about this issue by using Williams and his positions as starting points. For direction, consult Edwin S. Gaustad's *Liberty of Conscience*.

2. Williams removed to America mainly to convert the Indians. As a result of living with them, studying their customs, speaking their language, and generally observing and participating in their culture, in time he composed *A Key into the Language of America*. In it, he presents his views of the Narragansett Indians while noting that they are often more kind and humane than many Christians he has known, a reality that must have given him pause in his efforts to convert the Indians. The concluding stanza of a poem in this book makes his point: "*If Natures Sons both wild and tame, / Humane and Courteous be: / How ill becomes it Sonnes of God / To want Humanity?*" In mentioning Christians' inhumanity, he means Christians' treatment of the Indians, but also, probably, the actions against him by the religious establishment of Massachusetts Bay. Williams was concerned with the issue of land ownership. Because of the royal charters that gave their enterprise legitimacy and that permitted them to own land, English settlers in America viewed the land as theirs. In a decidedly minority view, Williams believed that it belonged to the Indians and that no one—not even the king of England—was authorized to grant it to anyone. The magistrates could not countenance such an opinion. How to perceive of and treat the Indians has been an issue since the beginning of English settlements in America. Think of them as the devil's minions and kill them? Picture them as noble savages and admire them? In charting the evolution of attitudes toward the Indians by settlers and their progeny, one might begin by considering the different ideas expressed by Williams and the white society in Massachusetts Bay. For information about Williams's relationship with and attitudes toward the Indians, consult John Garrett's *Roger Williams*.

3. After banishment from the colony, Williams, with four other men, established Providence as a haven for people persecuted for matters of conscience. It was different in concept from the Massachusetts Bay society of which he had been a part. The larger community was, essentially, a theocracy; in Providence church and state were separate entities. Providence was egalitarian in the sense that all settlers would have the same amount of land; all men could vote. Soon, Williams's ideal was compromised as people wanted more land than the allotted amount, though the community grew and ultimately flourished. One might compare the success of Williams's idealistic community with other such ventures, both real (the Amana Society in Iowa) and fictional (the Blithedale colonists in Nathaniel Hawthorne's *The Blithedale Romance*). For information about Providence, see Cyclone Covey, *The Gentle Radical*.

4. Williams was not accepting of all people who were persecuted for their beliefs. In particular, he considered the Quakers uncharitably, but for reason. Although he had several grievances against the group, he most objected to their enthusiasm (Inner Light) as a sign of salvation, their diminishment

of the importance of the Bible in religious affairs, and their considering of Christ more as an indwelling spirit than as an actual person. Williams had a raucous debate with several Quakers over these and other issues and published his positions in *George Fox Digg'd Out of His Burrowes*, to which Quakers responded in their own publication two years later. A question arises: how should one interpret Williams's seeming inconsistency in criticizing the Quakers while honoring other people and groups that had been persecuted for matters of conscience? For an understanding of Williams's position, consult Perry Miller's *Roger Williams*.

RESOURCES

Biography

Cyclone Covey, *The Gentle Radical: A Biography of Roger Williams* (New York: Macmillan; London: Collier-Macmillan, 1966).
A reliable biography of Williams.

Edwin S. Gaustad, *Liberty of Conscience: Roger Williams in America* (Grand Rapids, Mich.: William B. Eerdmans, 1991).
This biography discusses the issues with which Williams was involved and places them in historical context; it also addresses Williams's considerable legacy.

Ola Elizabeth Winslow, *Master Roger Williams, A Biography* (New York: Macmillan, 1957).
A biography that focuses on the facts of Williams's life and resists the temptation to make the minister a romantic, mythic figure.

Criticism

Henry Chupack, *Roger Williams* (New York: Twayne, 1969).
Surveys and analyzes Williams's life and work.

John Garrett, *Roger Williams: Witness beyond Christendom, 1603–1683* (New York: Macmillan; London: Collier-Macmillan, 1970).
An intellectual portrait of Williams that focuses on such topics as education, the gentry, mission, seekerism, politics, and theology.

Perry Miller, *Roger Williams: His Contribution to the American Tradition* (Indianapolis: Bobbs-Merrill, 1953).
After reproducing most of Williams's writing and commenting on it, Miller makes the case, in a brief epilogue, for Williams's significance in the American tradition: "he does remain the symbolic embodiment of that heroism which resists all those who, under whatever slogan, would force the conscience to things it cannot abide."

Edmund S. Morgan, *Roger Williams: The Church and the State* (New York: Harcourt, Brace & World, 1967).
Reconstructs "the course of [Williams's] thought and [exposes] the symmetry of the ideas that lay behind the polemics."

Irwin H. Polishook, *Roger Williams, John Cotton and Religious Freedom: A Contro-versy in New and Old England* (Englewood Cliffs, N.J.: Prentice-Hall, 1967). Examines the theological debate between Williams and John Cotton.

David Read, *New World, Known World: Shaping Knowledge in Early Anglo-American Writing* (Columbia: University of Missouri Press, 2005). Argues that Williams, like John Smith, William Bradford, and Thomas Morton, renders "an organized account of a newly experienced colonial world that will make that world distinct from the one—'Old' or just generically familiar—that previously formed the ground of knowledge."

John Winthrop (1588–1649)

On 22 January 1588, John Winthrop was born near Groton in Suffolk, England, to Adam Winthrop and Anne Browne Winthrop. His father was lord of the Groton manor, a position young Winthrop later assumed, and auditor of Trinity College, Cambridge University, where the son matriculated, though he did not complete his studies. In 1605, John Winthrop married Mary Forth, with whom he had six children, the first of whom, John Winthrop Jr., had a distinguished life in America. Soon after the 1615 death of his wife, he married Thomasine Clopton, who died a year later in childbirth. He had eight children with Margaret Tyndal, whom he married in 1618 and who followed him to America. The year after her death in 1647, he married Martha Rainsborough Coytmore. They had one child. Ultimately, Winthrop had sixteen children with his four wives.

During his first marriage, Winthrop had a religious awakening that aligned him with the Puritans. Although he was an attorney, not a cleric, religion informed his life. For political and religious reasons, in 1629 Winthrop and other Puritans agreed to remove to North America, under a charter from the Massachusetts Bay Company, where they would establish their own church, convert Indians, and so forth. Winthrop was elected governor of the group. The party sailed to America on the *Arbella*, in the vanguard of what became known as the great migration of Puritans to the New World, which lasted a decade. Among the passengers were Lady Arbella Johnson herself, as well as her friend Anne Bradstreet whose father, Thomas Dudley, and husband, Simon Bradstreet—also passengers—became major political figures in the Massachusetts Bay Colony. Puritans already inhabited part of what is now Massachusetts. Residing in Plymouth under the leadership of William Bradford, the Pilgrims (Separatists) believed the Church of England was so tainted that they withdrew from it. Although Winthrop and his group (non-Separatists, who landed at Salem) removed physically from the national church, they remained, technically, part of it. By the end of the century, Winthrop's larger group assimilated the earlier one.

Winthrop settled in Boston, where he was voted in and out of the gov-ernorship on several occasions, serving for the last time from 1646 until his death on 26 March 1649. He was involved in two of the major crises of early

American history, both in the 1630s. The first concerned Roger Williams; the second, Anne Hutchinson. The issues raised in these cases continue resonating in American life.

In addition to governing, Winthrop wrote. His major work is a journal, which he began aboard the *Arbella* and continued for the remainder of his life. It was published several times under different titles: *A Journal of the Transactions and Occurrences in the Settlement of Massachusetts and the Other New-England Colonies, from the Year 1630 to 1644* (1790), *The History of New England from 1630 to 1649* (1825–1826, and enlarged in 1853), and completely and definitively as *The Journal of John Winthrop, 1630–1649* (1996). Episodes from the journal are often anthologized. So is Winthrop's most famous composition, a sermon known as *A Modell of Christian Charity*, which argues, among other things, for sustaining a community because God ordains it. Although Winthrop wrote about the Hutchinson case in his journal, he also addressed it in *Antinomians and Familists Condemned by the Synod of Elders in New-England* (1644, republished the same year as *A Short Story of the Rise, Reign, and Ruin of the Antinomians, Familists & Libertines*). Additionally, Winthrop wrote miscellaneous pieces, including a pamphlet detailing the colony's decade-long and declining relationship with the Narragansett Indians (1645).

TOPICS FOR DISCUSSION AND RESEARCH

1. Although *A Modell of Christian Charity* is often identified as having been delivered aboard the *Arbella*, with American soil in sight, no definitive evidence indicates where or when Winthrop composed or delivered it. Regardless of venue, it seems clearly intended for the Puritans who would sail, or who were sailing, for America in 1630. It is important for detailing the nature of the society Winthrop envisions in America, as well as for an image he uses. In it, he argues that all citizens must work together for the common good and that God will endorse their mission for as long as they obey Him. Winthrop characterizes the group's undertaking with these words: "Wee must Consider that wee shall be as a Citty upon a Hill, the eyes of all people are upon us." The image is from Matt. 5:14. Winthrop could not have known the full significance of these words. While they refer to his group, they imply a sense of American exceptionalism that resonates to the present day: at least to Americans, the United States is *the* most important society, the one most admired, the one most emulated. Winthrop's statement is so significant and prescient that President Ronald Reagan quoted it in his farewell address in 1989. One might benefit from applying Winthrop's words to various periods in American history to chart the evolution, or ebb and flow, of Americans' impressions of their country. For a discussion of *A Modell of Christian Charity*, consult Francis J. Bremer's *John Winthrop*.

2. Winthrop corresponded with and wrote in his journal about Roger Williams, whose troubles in America began in 1631, when he refused to teach at the Boston church because it had not separated from the Church of England. Williams was a Separatist. In time, he objected to the requirement,

endorsed by Winthrop, that all residents of a town must attend its church, which was Congregational. Williams also believed that the magistrates were empowered by the people, while Winthrop thought them authorized by God. In other words, Williams believed in the separation of church and state, while Winthrop did not, thinking the two essentially one entity. This issue remains alive in American life. Students might wish to chart the evolution of this debate, beginning with Winthrop and Williams and including an examination of the First Amendment and Supreme Court cases dealing with it. Students would benefit from consulting Winthrop's own comments about Williams in *The Journal of John Winthrop;* for an analysis of the issue of church and state, consider the findings of Edmund S. Morgan in *Roger Williams.*

3. Winthrop was also involved with another gadfly, his neighbor Anne Hutchinson. As a result of his characterizing her as teaching antinomianism (which means against the law), this affair is known as the Antinomian Controversy of 1636–1638. Hutchinson, a follower of John Cotton, hosted meetings in her home to discuss Cotton's sermons. In time, she expressed her own views, criticizing Boston ministers, but not Cotton, for preaching a covenant of works, a belief that living a good life is evidence of salvation. She believed in a covenant of grace: that evidence of saving grace may be found only in the Holy Ghost, which resides within people who are of the elect. She thought that God cares not about human behavior because He has determined the souls that will reside in heaven; Winthrop and the Boston ministers believed that people whose souls are heaven-bound will necessarily comport themselves well in life. Hutchinson's insistence on her position—and she had many followers—caused factionalism in Boston, threatened the religious and political establishments, and violated the notion of Christian charity. As a result, she was tried for several reasons, but basically for upsetting the stability of Boston life. The court, with Winthrop as chief questioner, banished Hutchinson from the colony. One productive way of considering the Antinomian Controversy is from the perspective of women's roles in American life. Hutchinson was a lone woman standing up to the male establishment and suffering as a result. How significantly have things changed in this regard for women in contemporary America? For details about the Antinomian Controversy, see Emery Battis's *Saints and Sectaries;* for information about Anne Hutchinson's involvement in the crisis, see Eve LaPlante's *American Jezebel.*

4. In *Of Plymouth Plantation,* William Bradford is restrained in attributing earthly events to God's will. In "God's Controversy with New England," Michael Wigglesworth attributes a drought to God's displeasure with the Puritans in America. In his journal, Winthrop records seemingly trivial occurrences that anticipate Wigglesworth's interpretation of natural events. For example, he writes on 5 July 1632 of a mouse killing a snake in Watertown, which John Wilson of Boston interpreted as God sending his people (mouse) to defeat the devil (snake). Winthrop also writes, on 15 December 1640, about a book in his son's large library. Mice gnawed at a single book,

one containing the Book of Common Prayer, the book of Psalms, and the Greek New Testament. The animals ate through the Book of Common Prayer (disliked by the Puritans), but did not molest the other two parts of the book. Winthrop's meaning is obvious: God, acting through the mice, intends to show his displeasure with the Book of Common Prayer. Students might investigate how later American authors, especially some of the nineteenth century, respond to nature and natural phenomena. For a discussion of Winthrop's interpretation of natural events, see the introduction to *The Journal of John Winthrop*, edited by Richard S. Dunn, et al. For attitudes toward nature in the nineteenth century, read selected works by Ralph Waldo Emerson and Henry David Thoreau.

RESOURCES

Biography

Francis J. Bremer, *John Winthrop: America's Forgotten Founding Father* (Oxford: Oxford University Press, 2003).
Discusses Winthrop the man within the context of events of his time.

Eve LaPlante, *American Jezebel: The Uncommon Life of Anne Hutchinson, the Woman Who Defied the Puritans* (San Francisco: HarperCollins, 2004).
A biography of Hutchinson that addresses the issue of women's rights.

Criticism

Emery Battis, *Saints and Sectaries: Anne Hutchinson and the Antinomian Controversy in the Massachusetts Bay Colony* (Chapel Hill: University of North Carolina Press, 1962).
Argues that the Antinomian controversy resulted from societal discontent over religious issues.

Geoffrey Paul Carpenter, *A Secondary Annotated Bibliography of John Winthrop, 1588–1649* (New York: AMS Press, 1999).
Summarizes criticism about Winthrop through the twentieth century.

Richard S. Dunn, *Puritans and Yankees: The Winthrop Dynasty of New England, 1630–1717* (Princeton: Princeton University Press, 1962).
By focusing on three generations of Winthrops (John; John Jr.; Fitz; and Wait), argues that the family is the best guide to the development of New England.

Dunn, Introduction, *The Journal of John Winthrop, 1630–1649*, edited by Dunn et al. (Cambridge, Mass.: Belknap Press of Harvard University Press, 1996).
Discusses previous editions of the *Journal*, its genesis and composition, Winthrop as author-actor, and his providential interpretation of events.

Edmund S. Morgan, *The Puritan Dilemma: The Story of John Winthrop* (Boston: Little, Brown, 1958).

Discusses how Winthrop struggled with the dilemma of living in this world without being part of it.

Morgan, *Roger Williams: The Church and the State* (New York: Harcourt, Brace & World 1967).
Reconstructs "the course of [Williams's] thought and [exposes] the symmetry of the ideas that lay behind the polemics."

James G. Moseley, *John Winthrop's World: History as a Story; The Story as History* (Madison: University of Wisconsin Press, 1992).
Interprets Winthrop's world by focusing on Winthrop's *Journal.*

Lee Schweninger, *John Winthrop* (Boston: Twayne, 1990).
Discusses Winthrop's life and writings.

John Winthrop, *The Journal of John Winthrop, 1630–1649,* edited by Richard S. Dunn, et al. (Cambridge, Mass.: Belknap Press of Harvard University Press, 1996).
Reproduces the journal in which Winthrop details his observations, from the boarding of the *Arbella* in 1630 to his death.

John Woolman (1720–1772)

John Woolman was born on 19 October 1720 in Rancocas, Burlington County, New Jersey. One of thirteen children, he was the first son of Samuel Woolman, a weaver and farmer, and Elizabeth Burr Woolman. Because the Woolmans were Quakers, John Woolman attended a Quaker school. At the same time, he attended Meeting for Worship during which he and other Quakers quietly awaited God's inspiration while ministers spoke, sometimes rapturously. (To Quakers, the word "minister" generally meant one who speaks during Meeting for Worship after having been inspired; to them, a minister was not someone who presents a formal, prepared sermon while standing in a pulpit, separated from the congregation.) Not unlike young Jonathan Edwards, Woolman experienced a spiritual awakening during his youth. At age sixteen, he formed associations that apparently troubled him to the degree that he became ill. He resolved his issues and devoted himself to God. At age twenty, he left home for Mount Holly, New Jersey, where he served as a store clerk and began his ministry. A few years later, he became a shopkeeper and established his own tailoring business, a good profession for someone who believed that unnecessary possessions contribute to, if not cause, societal ills. Also at this time, he came to understand the evils of slavery, an institution he railed against to the degree that he is best known for this interest and is sometimes considered the father of American abolitionism. More-or-less concurrently, he began traveling (itinerant) ministries to encourage Quaker groups both near and far, an activity he would continue for the remainder of his life. Sometimes he walked to his destinations, even distant ones, alone. In 1749 he married Sarah Ellis, with whom he had two children, Mary and William, though the son died in infancy. Because he records little about the family in his journal and many travels kept him away from home, one might conclude that family meant less to him than what he perceived as his spiritual calling.

Woolman's first publication appeared in 1754. *Some Considerations on the Keeping of Negroes. Recommended to the Professors of Christianity of Every Denomination* is the first part of a two-part work; the second was published in 1762. Both were published in Philadelphia, with the second one printed by the firm of Benjamin Franklin and David Hall, though Franklin had ceased active involvement in the business in 1757. These publications were inspired by a trip to the American South, where Woolman observed the evils of slavery firsthand, though slaves were also kept in the North, even among some Quakers. And since Woolman knew and benefited from some of the slaveholding Quakers, he felt complicit in and tainted by the institution of slavery, even though he never owned a slave. He bases his argument against slavery on truth, by which he means the example of Christ, who is available to all people. And since He is, are not all people similar? Everyone is God's child, God's creation. If so, by what logic—by what truth?—are distinctions made among people, in the sense of a group or person being superior or inferior to another? Woolman took seriously the Golden Rule, which advises treating others as one wishes oneself treated. He further argues that mankind's natural state is unencumbered, free. Woolman uses these and other reasons to argue for the abolition of slavery.

In 1756, Woolman gave up his successful business so he could pursue virtuousness more earnestly than previously. The same year, he began writing his journal, which was initially published in 1774 and has never been out of print. In this spiritual autobiography, which he hoped would serve as a guide for others, he examines himself intently. This work impressed or influenced such nineteenth-century figures as William Ellery Channing, Ralph Waldo Emerson, Charles Lamb, Henry David Thoreau, and John Greenleaf Whittier, in addition to other notables then and later.

Woolman's *Considerations on Pure Wisdom and Human Policy; on Labour; on Schools; and on the Right Use of the Lord's Outward Gifts* (1758) contains essays about reform, both personal and social, though Woolman believes that the first reform should be of oneself. He wrote *A Plea for the Poor or a Word of Rembrance and Caution to the Rich* probably in the 1760s, though it was not published until 1793. Here, he argues, basically, that the poor suffer when the wealth of society is concentrated in the hands of a few people. He hopes that wealthy people will control their money lust in the name of a larger, common good. (In addition to calling for the abolition of slavery and urging the liberation of the poor, Woolman also championed the cause of the Indians.)

Woolman undertook a pilgrimage to England in 1772. True to form, aboard ship he stayed in steerage rather than a cabin because the cabin had unnecessary ornaments. That year, on 7 October, this American saint died of smallpox in York, England, where he reposes in a Quaker burial ground.

TOPICS FOR DISCUSSION AND RESEARCH

1. Quaker schools of Woolman's time focused on rudimentary education, not the intellectual probing that might prepare one for college. The Woolmans were rustics who tended to their farm, so not much formal education was required. Further, Quakers believed that the most important knowledge or awareness comes through a divine Inner Light. Contrast this attitude toward education to that of the Puritans. Why are they so different? Was education the means to an end for one group but not the other? Does preparation for correct understanding of the Bible bear on this issue? Did Woolman understand the Bible? What does his prose style indicate about the nature of his education? For a discussion of Woolman's and the Quakers' attitude toward education, consult Paul Rosenblatt's *John Woolman*. For information about the Puritans' views of education, see Samuel Eliot Morison's *The Intellectual Life of Colonial New England*.

2. Woolman believed that earthly possessions acquired or desired for their own sake impede one's quest for virtuousness, which, to him, is the goal of life. Benjamin Franklin, Woolman's contemporary, was also concerned about possessions ("success") and virtue. In what senses do the two men agree about these two issues? Disagree? Proclaiming a desire for virtuousness is easy; forswearing life's so-called comforts as a means of attaining virtue is another matter. Woolman demonstrated the power of his convictions by renouncing ordinary human comforts. In this context, what did he reject in order to eliminate distractions from his pursuit of earthly purity? Do such actions make him admirable? Foolish? On what bases could one argue one side or the other of this question? In general, American culture has embraced Franklin's views more than Woolman's. Yet, over time, elements in American society have adopted Woolman's, at least to a degree. What are some of these elements, and how successful were they in attaining and sustaining virtue? To understand the attitudes of these two eighteenth-century men, consult Woolman's *Journal* and Franklin's *Autobiography*.

3. American antislavery literature dates from Germantown Friends' Protest against Slavery (1688, though not published until much later), which went unheeded by Quakers who became the first—and for a time, only—American group favoring manumission. By the time Woolman wrote against slavery, others also had, including Samuel Sewall in 1700, though to little if any effect. In addition to making a reasoned, moral argument against the institution, Woolman writes about it plainly, calmly. He presents his views in an even tone, without berating slave owners. Given the depth of his conviction that slavery is evil, why did he write with such a mild tone? Did the fact that he was writing against the material interests of some friends possibly influence him? Is there an aspect of Quakerism that encourages a peaceful demeanor when confronting someone with whom one disagrees? Was he temperamentally unsuited to the inflammatory statement? Ultimately, how persuasive are his arguments? How successful were they? Might they be seen as antecedents of a long civil-rights movement that included riots in the 1960s, which were the antithesis of Woolman's calm reasoning? Might Woolman's approach anticipate that of Martin Luther King Jr., who, despite forceful speaking and writing, eschewed

violence? For a discussion of these issues, consult Thomas P. Slaughter's *The Beautiful Soul of John Woolman*.

4. Beginning around the time he gave up his businesses, Woolman increasingly denied himself ordinary conveniences, because the means to the end of convenience was tainted. For example, after considering a trip to the West Indies, he decided against it because he would have to travel on a ship that transported goods to and from there. He could not abide contributing to an enterprise that was connected with the slave trade, no matter how indirectly. Further, Woolman wore undyed clothing as a matter of principle: the coloring was superfluous. Additionally, the dyes came from the West Indies, where they were made by slave labor, which he did not want to encourage. How might one evaluate such asceticism? Is it admirable? If so, on what basis? Woolman was not the first person to hold such beliefs and act in such a manner. Who were some others who did so? Could one argue that in denouncing most things in life in the name of virtue, Woolman was essentially removing himself from life, where God's creatures, including Woolman, are meant to live? Information about Woolman's asceticism may be found in Slaughter's *The Beautiful Soul of John Woolman*.

RESOURCES

Biography

Henry J. Cadbury, *John Woolman in England: A Documentary Supplement* (London: Friends Historical Society, 1971).
Details Woolman's time in England by drawing on material not consulted by Woolman's biographers, including Woolman's travel notes and letters, journals by others, and additional documents.

Criticism

Edwin H. Cady, *John Woolman: The Mind of the Quaker Saint* (New York: Washington Square Press, 1966).
An evaluation of Woolman's thought in the context of the American tradition of radicalism.

Samuel Eliot Morison, *The Intellectual Life of Colonial New England* (New York: New York University Press, 1956).
The most detailed study of American Puritan intellectual life.

Phillips P. Moulton, Introduction, *The Journal and Major Essays of John Woolman* (New York: Oxford University Press, 1971).
In introducing the most reliable texts of Woolman's journal and essays, Moulton examines Woolman's life and work, with the discussion of slavery being especially thorough and convincing.

Paul Rosenblatt, *John Woolman* (New York: Twayne, 1969).
A solid examination of Woolman's life and work.

Daniel B. Shea, *Spiritual Autobiography in Early America* (Princeton: Princeton University Press, 1968).
Examines Woolman in the context of early American Quaker journals by John Churchman, Thomas Chalkley, David Ferris, and Elizabeth Ashbridge.

Thomas P. Slaughter, *The Beautiful Soul of John Woolman, Apostle of Abolition* (New York: Hill & Wang, 2008).
The most detailed, comprehensive, and convincing study of Woolman's life and thought.

Part IV
Annotated Bibliography

Allen, David Grayson, and David D. Hall, eds. *Seventeenth-Century New England.* Boston: Colonial Society of Massachusetts, 1984.
Ten essays by various scholars on issues relating to seventeenth-century New England, including "European Beginnings in the Northwest Atlantic," "The Puritan Portrait: Its Function in Old and New England," and "New England and a Wider World."

Amory, Hugh, and Hall, eds. *A History of the Book in America, Volume 1: The Colonial Book in the Atlantic World.* Cambridge, England: Cambridge University Press, 2000.
Essays by various scholars about books in colonial America.

Arch, Stephen Carl. *Authorizing the Past: The Rhetoric of History in Seventeenth-Century New England.* De Kalb: Northern Illinois University Press, 1994.
Details the gradual change in how New England historians viewed themselves, their locales, and their craft.

Baker, Jennifer J. *Securing the Commonwealth: Debt, Speculation, and Writing in the Making of Early America.* Baltimore: Johns Hopkins University Press, 2005.
Explains how literature reflects the early American belief in the advantages of using paper money.

Bellin, Joshua David. *The Demon of the Continent: Indians and the Shaping of American Literature.* Philadelphia: University of Pennsylvania Press, 2001.
Argues that the presence of Indians in America informs early American literature generally.

Bercovitch, Sacvan, ed. *The Cambridge History of American Literature, Volume I: 1590-1820.* Cambridge, England: Cambridge University Press, 1994.
Discusses five aspects of early American literature: "The Literature of Colonization," "New England Puritan Literature," "British-American Belles Lettres," "The American Enlightenment, 1750–1820," and "The Literature of the Revolutionary and Early National Periods."

Bonomi, Patricia U. *Under the Cope of Heaven: Religion, Society, and Politics in Colonial America.* New York: Oxford University Press, 1986.
Argues that religion remained important in eighteenth-century America and underlay the political fervor that led to the American Revolution.

Brown, Matthew P. *The Pilgrim and the Bee: Reading Rituals and Book Culture in Early New England.* Philadelphia: University of Pennsylvania Press, 2007.
Examines the reading practices of early Americans, considers the book as physical object, and argues for the value of book history as an area of study.

Brown, Richard D. *Knowledge Is Power: The Diffusion of Information in Early America, 1700–1865.* New York: Oxford University Press, 1989.
Investigates how information was disseminated in America from 1700 through the Civil War.

Clark, Charles E. *The Public Prints: The Newspaper in Anglo-American Culture, 1665–1740.* New York: Oxford University Press, 1994.
Discusses English newspapers before focusing on the development of newspapers in America.

Daly, Robert. *God's Altar: The World and the Flesh in Puritan Poetry.* Berkeley: University of California Press, 1978.
The first serious study of Puritan poetry.

Davis, Richard Beale. *Intellectual Life in the Colonial South, 1585-1763,* 3 volumes. Knoxville: University of Tennessee Press, 1978.
The major study of intellectual life in the colonial South.

Demos, John Putnam. *Entertaining Satan: Witchcraft and the Culture of Early New England.* New York: Oxford University Press, 1982.
In chapters on biography, psychology, sociology, and history, focuses not on the Salem witchcraft trials but rather on witchcraft generally, providing case studies of supposed witches and their accusers.

Elliott, Emory, ed. *American Colonial Writers, 1606–1734, Dictionary of Literary Biography,* volume 24. Detroit: Bruccoli Clark Layman/Gale, 1984.
Over ninety substantial essays on American authors active from 1606 to 1734, ranging, alphabetically, from James Alexander to John Peter Zenger.

Elliott, ed. *American Colonial Writers, 1735-1781, Dictionary of Literary Biography,* volume 31. Detroit: Bruccoli Clark Layman/Gale, 1984.
Over sixty substantial essays on American authors active from 1735 to 1781, ranging, alphabetically, from John Adams to John Joachim Zubly.

Elliott, et al., eds. *Columbia Literary History of the United States.* New York: Columbia University Press, 1988.
The first part of this five-part book deals with American literature to 1780, with essays written by some of the leading scholars of the period.

Hall, David D. *Worlds of Wonder, Days of Judgment: Popular Religious Belief in Early New England.* New York: Knopf, 1989.
Examines the religion of laymen and laywomen in early New England.

Harris, Sharon M., ed. *American Women Writers to 1800.* New York: Oxford University Press, 1996.
Hundreds of pages of selections from early American women writers, along with introductory essays about them.

Hayes, Kevin J., ed. *The Oxford Handbook of Early American Literature.* Oxford: Oxford University Press, 2008.
Twenty-six essays by various scholars, ranging from "The Literature of Exploration" to "The Place of Natural History in Early American Literature."

Kidd, Thomas S. *The Great Awakening: The Roots of Evangelical Christianity in Colonial America.* New Haven: Yale University Press, 2007.

Details the interconnectedness of various revivals and argues that the Great Awakening lasted for several decades.

Knight, Janice. *Orthodoxies in Massachusetts: Rereading American Puritanism.* Cambridge, Mass.: Harvard University Press, 1994.
Discusses two competing aspects of Puritanism: emotional and rational.

Lepore, Jill. *The Name of War: King Philip's War and the Origins of American Identity.* New York: Knopf, 1998.
Argues that writings about King Philip's War clarified the previously blurred distinctions between Indians and settlers and, as a result, hardened the feelings each group had toward the other.

Levernier, James A., and Douglas R. Wilmes, eds. *American Writers before 1800: A Biographical and Critical Dictionary,* 3 vols. Westport, Conn.: Greenwood Press, 1983.
Details the lives and works of almost eight hundred American authors active before 1800, ranging, alphabetically, from James Adair to John Joachim Zubly.

McWilliams, John. *New England's Crises and Cultural Memory: Literature, Politics, History, Religion, 1620–1860.* Cambridge, England: Cambridge University Press, 2004.
Focuses on varying responses to some early American crises, including King Philip's War and the Salem witchcraft trials.

Miller, Perry. *The New England Mind: The Seventeenth Century.* New York: Macmillan, 1939.
Miller. *The New England Mind: From Colony to Province.* Cambridge, Mass.: Harvard University Press, 1953.
Groundbreaking, lastingly influential studies of New England thought from the beginning to 1730.

Morgan, Edmund S. *Visible Saints: The History of a Puritan Idea.* New York: New York University Press, 1963.
Argues that the required demonstration of saving grace for church membership originated in the Massachusetts Bay Colony in the 1630s and was seriously challenged in 1677 by Solomon Stoddard.

Richter, Daniel K. *Facing East from Indian Country: A Native History of Early America.* Cambridge, Mass.: Harvard University Press, 2001.
Discusses the development of early America from the Indian point of view, looking eastward.

Scanlan, Thomas. *Colonial Writings and the New World, 1583–1671: Allegories of Desire.* Cambridge, England: Cambridge University Press, 1999.
Argues that colonial American literature reflects European influence and posits that the interpretive framework of the literature should be broadened.

Shields, David S. *Civil Tongues and Polite Letters in British America.* Chapel Hill: University of North Carolina Press, 1997.

Investigates the activities of the social elite from 1690 to 1760.

Shipton, Clifford K. *Biographical Sketches of Those Who Attended Harvard College,* volume 4 of *Sibley's Harvard Graduates.* Cambridge, Mass.: Harvard University Press, 1933.
Continues a series begun by John Langdon Sibley, treating members of the classes 1690-1700.

Shipton. *Biographical Sketches of Those Who Attended Harvard College,* 13 volumes, *Sibley's Harvard Graduates.* Boston: Massachusetts Historical Society, 1937–1975.
Continues a series begun by John Langdon Sibley, treating members of the classes 1701–1771.

Sibley, John Langdon. *Biographical Sketches of Graduates of Harvard University, in Cambridge, Massachusetts,* 3 volumes. Cambridge, Mass.: Charles William Sever, 1873–1885.
Provides detailed, invaluable biographical information about Harvard graduates from the class of 1642 through that of 1689.

Spengemann, William C. *A New World of Words: Redefining Early American Literature.* New Haven: Yale University Press, 1994.
Re-evaluates early American literature within the context of defining the words *early, American,* and *literature.*

Staloff, Darren. *The Making of an American Thinking Class: Intellectuals and Intelligentsia in Puritan Massachusetts.* New York: Oxford University Press, 1998.
Examines nonreligious aspects of New England life that empowered religion.

Warner, Michael. *The Letters of the Republic: Publication and the Public Sphere in Eighteenth-Century America.* Cambridge, Mass.: Harvard University Press, 1990.
Discusses the relationship between eighteenth-century American republican values and print culture.

Wilmeth, Don B., and Christopher Bigsby, eds. *The Cambridge History of American Theatre, Volume One: Beginnings to 1870.* Cambridge, England: Cambridge University Press, 1998.
Details the development of the American theater to 1870.

Wright, Conrad Edick, and Edward W. Hanson. *Biographical Sketches of Those Who Attended Harvard College,* volume 18 of *Sibley's Harvard Graduates.* Boston: Massachusetts Historical Society, 1999.
Continues a series begun by John Langdon Sibley and continued by Clifford K. Shipton; treats members of classes 1772–1774.

Youngs, J. William T., Jr. *God's Messengers: Religious Leadership in Colonial New England, 1700–1750.* Baltimore: Johns Hopkins University Press, 1976.
Examines how New England ministers active during the first half of the eighteenth century viewed themselves.

Part V
Glossary

Act of Uniformity (1662)   There were several Acts of Uniformity passed after the Protestant Reformation in an attempt to enforce uniform religion practice. Under Charles II, Parliament passed the Act of Uniformity in 1662 to quell religious dissent. The act required the use of the Book of Common Prayer in the Church of England and mandated that ministers be ordained by bishops. Nonconformist ministers could not obey these and other requirements; as a result, some 2,000 of them were ejected from the church.

Addisonian essay   The Addisonian essay—named for the creations of the English writer Joseph Addison—typically has a detached, learned speaker and a humane tone. Written in an elegant, balanced style, it often deals with morals, manners, and taste.

Anglican Church   *See* Church of England

Antinomian Controversy   The Antinomian Controversy of 1636–1638 concerned Anne Hutchinson, who believed that faith, not works, provides evidence of saving grace and that saving grace liberates one from obeying the Ten Commandments because the elect are already assured of salvation. These views, and her belief that the Holy Spirit resides in people who possess saving grace, threatened Puritan society to the degree that she was banished from Massachusetts Bay.

Arbella   The *Arbella* was the ship in the vanguard of the great migration of Puritans to America, which lasted for a decade beginning in 1630. Among its passengers were John Winthrop, Anne Bradstreet, Simon Bradstreet, Thomas Dudley, Richard Saltonstall, and Lady Arbella Johnson, for whom the ship was named.

Artillery sermon   When the Massachusetts Bay artillery company elected its officers each June, a minister delivered a sermon—a practice that began in the 1660s. Typically, the minister addressed issues relating to war, including its cause.

Battle of Bunker Hill   The Battle of Bunker Hill was fought in June 1775. After repeated charges, British troops took the hill but suffered heavy losses. This battle helped unite colonists in a desire for revolution and independence.

The Body of Liberties   Composed mainly by Nathaniel Ward, *The Body of Liberties* (1641) is the first code of laws in New England. A guide for the General Court, it protected commoners from the unfettered rule of magistrates.

Book of Common Prayer   The Book of Common Prayer is the prayer book of the Church of England. Because the Puritans objected to it on numerous grounds, it was outlawed during the Protectorate.

The Book of General Lavves and Libertyes   This document, which expanded *The Body of Liberties,* was adopted in 1648.

Broadside   A broadside is a single sheet of paper printed on one side.

Calvinism   Named for John Calvin, who formulated his ideas during the second third of the sixteenth century, Calvinism is based on the belief that God alone determines which humans will gain salvation and that humans are passive recipients of God's grace (predestination). The tenets of Calvinism were refined at the Synod of Dort in 1618 and 1619: total depravity, unconditional election, limited atonement, irresistible grace, and perseverance of the saints. The Puritans embraced Calvinism.

Cambridge Platform   Drafted by the Cambridge Synod in 1648 in response to critics of Congregationalism who wanted the church to adopt a more Presbyterian form, the Cambridge Platform detailed the tenets of the faith that governed until 1708.

Captivity Narrative   Captivity narratives, which gained popularity in the late seventeenth century, recount the experiences of settlers captured by Indians.

Church of England   Also known as the Anglican Church, the Church of England is important to colonial American history because many people objecting to its closeness to Roman Catholicism, its requirement of mandatory church attendance, and other stipulations were inspired to leave the country and settle in America.

Citty upon a Hill   In a sermon titled *A Modell of Christian Charity*, John Winthrop described America, a country he had not yet visited, as "a Citty upon a Hill." This phrase, which implies an American exceptionalism, has been quoted frequently, including by President Ronald Reagan in his 1989 farewell address.

Closet play (closet drama)   A closet play is intended to be read, not acted.

Coercive Acts   In 1774, George III and Lord Frederick North formulated the Coercive Acts, also known as the Intolerable Acts, against Massachusetts in response to the Boston Tea Party. These acts included the Boston Port Act, the Massachusetts Government Act, the Administration of Justice Act, the Quartering Act, and the Quebec Act. The onerousness of these acts helped unite the colonies and led to the First Continental Congress.

Commission for Regulating Plantations   In 1633, Charles I established the Commission for Regulating Plantations, headed by Archbishop William Laud, the Puritans' antagonist. The Commission made immigration to New England difficult and attempted unsuccessfully to revoke the 1629 charter of Massachusetts Bay.

Congregationalism   Congregationalism is the form of church government established by the Puritan settlers of Massachusetts Bay. Congregationalists freely came together as a church, which was self-governing; it was not under the jurisdiction of a synod, as was the Presbyterian church. Congregational churches selected their own ministers, and ordination was not transferable from one church to another. Congregationalism was given its name by John Cotton.

Council for New England   Led by Sir Ferdinando Gorges, the Council for New England (established in 1620) was a joint-stock company charged with populating and governing New England.

Covenant theology   The Puritans and others believed that God established with mankind, through Adam, a covenant of works. If Adam worked (behaved) as God instructed, he and all people would secure eternal life; if he disobeyed, he and all people would suffer death. After Adam violated this covenant, God offered the covenant of grace not to all humanity but rather to the people He had selected for salvation. If these people put their faith in the son of God, Jesus Christ, who died for their sins, they would have life everlasting.

Currency Act   The Currency Act of 1764 forbade English colonies in America to issue money.

Declaration of Indulgence   James II signed the Declaration of Indulgence in 1687. It removed penalties for failing to attend the Church of England and receive its communion, permitted people to worship outside the Anglican Church, and eliminated religious requirements for military and civil promotion. This declaration benefited the dissenters in Massachusetts Bay.

Declaratory Act   The Declaratory Act, passed by Parliament in 1766, subordinated American colonies to both the Crown and Parliament.

Deism   Deism is a rational approach to religion that acknowledges God but that posits that He rules in accordance with natural laws.

Divine right of kings   The divine right of kings is the belief that certain sovereigns rule by the grace of God and are answerable only to God. A result of this concept is the obedience of the sovereign's subjects: resisting the ruler would be resisting God.

Election sermon   Each election day in colonial Boston, beginning in 1634, a minister delivered a sermon to the newly elected political leaders—governor, lieutenant governor, and others—and the general populace. Typically, it dealt with the responsibilities of governmental officials, as well as with such topics common to regular sermons as mankind's sinfulness and the need for repentance. Being asked to deliver an election sermon was considered a high honor. The most famous election sermon in American literature is Arthur Dimmesdale's in Nathaniel Hawthorne's *The Scarlet Letter* (1850).

English Civil War   The English Civil War, generally considered to have lasted from 1642 to 1649 (though the terminal date is not always agreed upon), was a conflict between the forces of the Crown and those of Parliament, won by Parliament. The king during the conflict was Charles I, who was executed in 1649. Charles was succeeded by the Commonwealth (1649–1653) and then by the Protectorate of the Cromwells (1653–1660).

Enlightenment   The Enlightenment, the long eighteenth century (approximately 1650–1800), was a period that, among other things, valued reason and progress, believed that mankind is perfectible, and devalued religion. Such beliefs helped inspire the American and French Revolutions.

French and Indian War   The French and Indian War involved the French and English fighting over control of North American territory. The conflict, with England victorious, concluded with the Treaty of Paris in 1763. Because of expenses incurred, England needed revenue, which it attempted to procure by taxing the colonists. American objections to the taxes helped generate a desire for political independence.

General Court of Massachusetts Bay   Authorized by Charles I, the General Court was the legislative and judicial body of Massachusetts Bay.

Governor's Council of Virginia   The Governor's Council of Virginia consisted of six members, chosen by the governor, who served in the House of Burgesses; one member served as lieutenant governor.

Great Awakening   The Great Awakening was a period of revivalism, primarily in the 1740s, that was spearheaded by the English preacher George Whitefield; the philosopher-theologian behind the movement was Jonathan Edwards. The Great Awakening marks the beginning of evangelicalism in America. The ministers promoting revivalism were known as New Lights; their opponents, such as Charles Chauncy, as Old Lights.

Great Migration   The great migration of Puritans from England to America began in 1630 and lasted for approximately a decade. These people, originally under the leadership of John Winthrop, fled their native country because of unhappiness with the Church of England, which they thought too Catholic, too impure.

Half-Way Covenant   The Half-Way Covenant was a 1662 document that addressed the issue of membership in the Congregational Church. It stated that children of unregenerate church members could be baptized and subject to church discipline but could not receive the Lord's Supper or vote. Therefore, they became halfway members of the church.

House of Burgesses   The House of Burgesses was the legislative body of Virginia. Established in 1619, it was the first popularly elected legislature in British North America.

Hudibrastic verse   Verse considered Hudibrastic is written in a manner similar to Samuel Butler's *Hudibras* (1663, 1664, 1678), a mock-heroic poem in iambic tetrameter, often with feminine rhymes.

Independents   The Independents were radical English Puritans who removed Charles I from power and decapitated him. Unlike the English Presbyterians, the Independents wanted Parliament to have little if any control over religion.

Inner Light   Inner Light is the Quaker concept that divine love dwells within people and therefore unites them.

Inns of Court   The Inns of Court were the center of English legal activities where, in London, lawyers practiced their profession and often lodged, and where such students as William Byrd and John Dickinson studied to become lawyers.

Intolerable Acts   *See* Coercive Acts

Jeremiad   The seventeenth-century American Puritans used the term *jeremiad* to characterize a work that laments declining religiosity, which they believed resulted in unpleasant events (such as warfare) that signified God's displeasure. The term derives from the biblical Jeremiah.

Justification   Justification is the term used to indicate a state of salvation: a justified person has been preordained to grace.

King Philip's War   King Philip's War (1675–1676) resulted from colonists' execution of three Wampanoag Indians for the murder of John Sassamon, an educated Indian who provided valuable information to the settlers. Thinking their sovereignty compromised if not abrogated, the Wampanoags, under

Metacomet (King Philip), attacked colonists' settlements. This was and remains the deadliest war in American history, when considered as the percentage of the population killed.

London Company   Comprised of merchants from London, the London Company (also known as the Virginia Company of London) gained authorization, in 1606, to colonize the southern part of what was known as Virginia. As a result, it established Jamestown in 1607.

Long Parliament   The Long Parliament was called by Charles I in 1640. It is known as the Long Parliament because Parliament stipulated that it could be dissolved only with its consent, which it granted in 1660.

Lord's Supper   Lord's Supper is synonymous with Holy Communion, a sacrament.

Lords of Trade and Plantation   In 1675, Charles II established the Lords of Trade and Plantation—comprising twenty-one men—to strengthen administrative relations between the Crown and colonial governments. In 1684 this body revoked the Massachusetts Bay charter of 1629.

Loyalists   *See* Tories

Massachusetts Bay Company   A group of English Puritans, the Massachusetts Bay Company was established in 1628; the next year, it secured a charter for land controlled by its predecessor, the New England Company. Because the charter failed to specify where the Company should hold its annual meetings, the Company established the government in New England and made the colony, Massachusetts Bay, self-governing. The Company ceased to exist in 1684, when the charter of 1629 was annulled.

Massachusetts Government Act   One of the Coercive Acts, the Massachusetts Government Act of 1774, enacted by Parliament, banned town meetings, annulled the 1691 charter, and provided for other governmental reforms that inspired colonists to act in order to preserve their rights.

Mayflower   The *Mayflower* was the ship on which the Pilgrims sailed, in 1620, from Plymouth, England, to Plymouth, in what is now the state of Massachusetts. In addition to the crew, there were 102 passengers, approximately half of whom were Puritans known as Pilgrims.

Mayflower Compact   As the Pilgrims were anchored off Cape Cod before setting foot on American soil, they addressed the issue of governance. They formulated their ideas in the Mayflower Compact, which bound them to create laws for the common good and allowed for majority rule.

Meeting for Worship   Meeting for Worship is the occasion when Quakers gather in the hope of experiencing God's spirit.

Merry Mount   In 1624, Thomas Morton and others established Mount Wollaston, which Morton renamed Merry Mount; it is part of what is now Quincy, Massachusetts. The Puritans cut down the community's maypole and forced Morton to return to England.

Neoclassical verse   The neoclassical era extended from approximately 1660 to approximately 1798. Neoclassical writers often allude to classical literature and mythology. Frequently written in heroic couplets, neoclassical verse is usually satiric, philosophical, and artful.

New England Company   The New England Company existed in 1628 and 1629. John Endecott and others settled in Naumkeag (Salem), to which the Company held the patent.

New England Confederation   Assembled in 1643 primarily for purposes of defense, the New England Confederation included the colonies of Plymouth, Massachusetts Bay, Connecticut, and New Haven. It oversaw the colonists' actions during King Philip's War. When the Massachusetts charter was revoked in 1684, the Confederation was dissolved.

New England Restraining Act   The New England Restraining Act of 1775 mandated that New England colonies limit their trade to England and the British West Indies.

Nonconformists   Nonconformists were British subjects who refused to conform to the requirements of the Church of England.

Non-Separatists   Non-Separatists were the English Puritans who objected to aspects of the Church of England but who wished to reform it rather than reject it. Unsuccessful, they fled to North America; while separating physically from the Church, they remained, technically, members of it. The influx of these people to North America began in 1630 under the leadership of John Winthrop. For a decade, so many other Puritans followed this group that this period is known as the great migration. These people settled mostly in Boston. The non-Separatist population was so great that it soon dwarfed that of Plymouth. With the charter of 1691, the two groups became one as the smaller was incorporated into the larger. Their form of church government was Congregational.

Patriots   *See* Whigs

Pequot War   In retaliation for the killing of some settlers, other settlers fought the Pequot Indians in the Pequot War (1637). The Pequots were all but annihilated.

Pilgrims   *See* Separatists

Plain style   Plain style is a manner of writing that avoids ostentation. Simple, straightforward, and clear, it also was evident in other arts, such as architecture. William Bradford wrote in a plain style; Cotton Mather did not.

Plymouth Company   Comprising merchants from Plymouth, England, the Plymouth Company gained authorization, in 1606, to colonize the northern part of what was known as Virginia. Under the Company's charter of 1620, the Pilgrims settled the Plymouth Colony in what is now the state of Massachusetts.

Presbyterians   Unlike Independents, English Presbyterians wanted Parliament to control religion. Though sharing many beliefs with the Congregationalists, they differed on the issue of church government: each Congregational church was independent; Presbyterian churches were answerable to a synod.

Protectorate   The Protectorate refers to the period when the Puritan Oliver Cromwell (1653–1658) and his son Richard Cromwell (1658–1659) ruled England.

Protestant Reformation   The Protestant Reformation was a series of major religious challenges to the Roman Catholic Church. The word *protestant* means "protest." Begun by Martin Luther in 1517—but also involving Ulrich Zwingli, John Calvin, and others—the movement reacted against what was perceived as false Catholic doctrines, such as simony.

Providence Plantations Providence, Portsmouth, Newport, and Warwick, Rhode Island, were the four colonies that received a charter (1644) as the Incorporation of Providence Plantations in the Narragansett Bay in New England, or Providence Plantations, for short.

Puritans Because they were nonconformists, the Puritans were unwelcome in England. As a result, they settled New England, initially in 1620 (the *Mayflower* group known as the Pilgrims) but especially with the great migration beginning in 1630 (the group led by John Winthrop). Religiously, they were largely followers of John Calvin.

Quakers (Society of Friends) Founded by George Fox in the mid seventeenth century, the Quakers believed in Inner Light, rejected the swearing of oaths, refused to show signs of respect to supposed superiors, and were pacifists. Persecuted in Massachusetts Bay, they settled in Rhode Island until finding a home in Pennsylvania, a Quaker colony founded by William Penn.

Quartering Act The Quartering Act of 1774 required the quartering of British troops in the American colonies whenever the troops were needed to restore order.

Reforming synod Increase Mather invited Congregational ministers to meet in a reforming synod (1679–1680) to address what he and others believed was God's judgment against their society, as evidenced by King Philip's War, a smallpox epidemic, fires, shipwrecks, and other calamities. The goal of the synod was to identify the shortcomings that incurred God's wrath; general Godlessness was the major one.

Regeneration Regeneration is the conversion to holiness, a spiritual renewal, which results from examining oneself, among other means.

Royal Society Founded in 1660 in London, the Royal Society supported (and supports) scientific inquiry. William Byrd, Benjamin Franklin, and Cotton Mather are among the colonial American members of the Society.

Sacrament A sacrament is a visible sign of grace. Protestants have two sacraments, baptism and the Lord's Supper.

Saint A saint is a person consecrated by God, as is explained in 1 Cor. 1:2: "them that are sanctified in Jesus Christ, called to be saints."

Salem witchcraft trials When, in 1692, girls in Salem Village (now Danvers), Massachusetts, behaved aberrantly, they accused some women of bewitching them. Other accusations were made, and trials were held in Salem Town (the current Salem). Ultimately, of the twenty-nine people convicted of witchcraft, twenty were executed, nineteen by hanging and one by being pressed to death.

Sanctification Sanctification, to Calvinists, means that God has purged people of sins; as a result, they lead holy lives.

Separatists Separatists were a group of Puritans—known as Pilgrims—who objected to forced attendance at Church of England services, to the Church's similarity to Roman Catholicism, to its hierarchical form of church government, and to other aspects of the state church. Persecuted at home, they fled to Holland. In 1620 they sailed to North America on the *Mayflower*. They established the Plymouth Colony, whose most important person was William Bradford, who frequently served as governor and who wrote their history, *Of Plymouth Plantation*. With the charter of 1691, they became one with the non-Separatists who had settled mostly in Boston.

Society of Friends   *See* Quakers

Spectral (or spectre) evidence   Spectral evidence, when used in the context of the Salem witchcraft trials, means that witnesses testified to having dreamed the presence of the accused witch's spirit when the accused was physically elsewhere.

Stamp Act   Enacted by Parliament in 1765, the Stamp Act was the first direct tax that England imposed on its American colonies. The act authorized tax on numerous printed items. Colonists struck back by refusing to import goods from England; this caused English merchants to appeal to Parliament to repeal the act, which it did the following year.

Sugar Act   Also known as the American Revenue Act, the Sugar Act of 1764 was the initial Parliamentary act intended to pay down debt by taxing the American colonists. The colonists objected.

Synod of Dort   The Synod of Dort met in Dordrecht, Netherlands, in 1618 and 1619 to resolve issues relating to Calvinism, perhaps most importantly the issue of predestination. The synod defined the basic tenets of Calvinism.

Tea Act   Parliament passed the Tea Act of 1773 in order to give the East India Company a monopoly on tea exported to America. This resulted in the Company selling tea for less than could colonial merchants.

Tories (Loyalists)   The Americans who supported British rule before and during the American Revolution are known as Tories, or Loyalists. Among the most notable of them are William Franklin (son of Benjamin Franklin), Thomas Hutchinson, Mather Byles, and Benedict Arnold.

Townshend Acts   Parliament passed the Townshend Acts in 1767. They imposed a tax on certain goods imported to America, including tea, angering the colonists.

Virginia Company of London   *See* London Company

Westminster Assembly of Divines   The Westminster Assembly of Divines met during the English Civil War to reform the Church of England. It prepared the Westminster Confession of Faith, the creed of the reformed church, and two catechisms.

Whigs (Patriots)   The Americans who supported rebelling against British rule before and during the American Revolution are known as Whigs, or Patriots. Among the most notable of them are George Washington, Benjamin Franklin, John Adams, Samuel Adams, John Dickinson, Alexander Hamilton, and Thomas Paine.

Writs of Assistance   The Writs of Assistance of 1751 granted search warrants to customs officials. In objecting to the constitutionality of the Writs a decade later, James Otis arguably initiated revolutionary sentiment in America.

Index